DATE DUE		
OCT 16 '85			

WRITING: *Experience and Expression*

David Dillon

Southern Methodist University

D. C. HEATH AND COMPANY

Lexington, Massachusetts Toronto London

Published simultaneously in Canada.

Printed in the United States of America.

International Standard Book Number: 0–669–96693–2

Library of Congress Catalog Card Number: 75–32471

Acknowledgments

JAMES AGEE: from *Collected Short Prose of James Agee*. Copyright © 1968, 1969 by the James Agee Trust. Reprinted by permission of Houghton Mifflin Company.

MAX BEERBOHM: from *And Even Now*. Copyright 1921 by E. P. Dutton & Co.; renewal 1949 by Max Beerbohm. Reprinted by permission of the publishers, E.P. Dutton & Co., Inc., and William Heinemann & Sons, Ltd.

HARRY BEHN: from *More Cricket Songs: Japanese Haiku*. Translated and copyright © 1971 by Harry Behn. Reprinted by permission of Harcourt Brace Jovanovich, Inc.

MEYER BERGER: from *The New York Times*. Copyright © 1949 by the New York Times Company. Reprinted by permission.

ELIZABETH BOWEN: from *Collected Impressions*. Copyright 1950 by Alfred A. Knopf, Inc. Reprinted by permission of the publisher, and by permission of Curtis Brown Ltd.

JACOB BRONOWSKI: from *The Common Sense of Science*. Copyright 1953 by Harvard University Press. Reprinted by permission of Harvard University Press, and Heinemann Educational Books Ltd.

FRANK CONROY: from *Stop-Time*. Copyright © 1965, 1966, 1967 by Frank Conroy. Reprinted by permission of The Viking Press, Inc.

E. E. CUMMINGS: from *Six Nonlectures*. Copyright © 1953 by E. E. Cummings. Reprinted by permission of Harvard University Press.

JAMES DICKEY: from *Deliverance*. Copyright © 1970 by James Dickey. Reprinted by permission of Houghton Mifflin Company.

EMILY DICKINSON: from Thomas H. Johnson, Editor, *The Letters of Emily Dickinson*, Cambridge, Mass.: The Belknap Press of Harvard University Press. Copyright © 1958 by The President and Fellows of Harvard College. Reprinted by permission of the publishers.

JOHN DOS PASSOS: from *USA*. Copyright by Elizabeth H. Dos Passos. Reprinted by permission.

KENNETH FEARING: from *New and Selected Poems* by Kenneth Fearing. Copyright 1956 by Kenneth Fearing. Reprinted by permission of Indiana University Press, Bloomington.

F. SCOTT FITZGERALD: from *The Crack Up*. Copyright 1945 by New Directions Publishing Corporation. Reprinted by permission of New Directions Publishing Corporation.

To My Mother and My Father
Who Taught Me to Love Books

Author's Note

I wish to acknowledge the help of the following people in the preparation of this book: Susie Stump and Bobsy Thompson, who used an earlier version of the manuscript in their classes and sent back some fine writing and helpful criticisms; my colleagues Steve Daniels, Richard Haight, and John Jacoby who generously shared their ideas about teaching writing with me; my editor, Holt Johnson, who guided me gently and expertly through the trauma of a first book; my typists, Carol Naab and Marcia Richardson, who know the book as well as I do; my wife Sally, who never doubted that I could write it.

David Dillon

A Note to Students and Instructors

One writes out of one thing only—one's own experience. Everything depends on how relentlessly one forces from one's experience the last drop, sweet or bitter, it can possibly give.

James Baldwin

Writing is both an art and a practical skill but the two are seldom combined in schools. The first is usually designated "creative writing," under which fall poems and stories and novels; the second is merely labeled "composition," a nondescript phrase covering essays, reports, examinations, and most other kinds of non-fiction prose. In the first you are free to express yourself, the distinction implies, while in the second you have to stick to the facts. Not only does this give facts a bad name, it discourages students from thinking of their practical prose, which is to say most of their writing, as creative. Consequently, instead of trying to speak honestly and naturally about what they know, they strive to be serious and sophisticated. Formality becomes a first principle that almost precedes thought, and obscurity becomes a kind of virtue. The results are often an affront to literacy:

> The committee felt that the feedback to its input had meaningful connotations for all concerned. It was emphasized that we should address ourselves to total concerns and reexamine ourselves the goals of the university, with no preconceived notions as to where the priorities should be. Not only must avenues for student input be open but the students must be willing to accept the responsibility of having a responsible option to put in.

. . .

> The relative emphasis on the highway as a means to leisure activities has led to the emergence of the freeway culture of drive-in-food dispensaries as an

aspect of middle-class culture (as are artifacts of prepackaged or frozen foods—reflecting the middle-class, future-oriented belief that "time is money").

.   .   .

In this poem [Blake's *I Saw a Chapel All of Gold*] the chapel is stringently stainless. The serpent probes a supposedly sincere group's probity. . . .The narrator compounds the assemblage's impotence by submitting to the poison, to the sty, and eventually to the ground where he could lay tightfisted with the soil. The pillars, the altar, and the bread all-white were improbed by a slimy serpent with thews because of the congregations's truant sinews.

Such prose is worse than bad—it's inhuman. The language is vague, abstract, pretentious, the thinking muddled, not necessarily because the writers themselves are, but because they have completely muffled their own voices. Like ventriloquist's dummies they speak a language they neither comprehend nor control.

One goal of *Experience and Expression,* therefore, is to help you to develop your own voices (the plural is intentional since we all have more than one) by encouraging you to consider your own experience—sensory, emotional, intellectual, social—as the primary, though certainly not the only, source of your writing. Often this will involve applying so-called creative writing techniques to standard composition topics in order to expose you to some of the genuine pleasures of language and writing.

Equally important is the idea of *generating writing.* Many texts are organized according to grammatical and rhetorical principles that have little to do with the actual process of writing. In other words, they concentrate on the analysis of the finished product, not on its making. Now being able to spot a comma splice and a dangling participle or to differentiate between compound and complex sentences is a useful skill, particularly for editing and revising a piece of writing, but it does not put words on paper. And yet putting words on paper, clear, honest, felt words, is what writing is about. *Experience and Expression,* therefore, is a manual for *doing* that begins with simple word games and goes on to more demanding exercises in narrative, autobiography, biography, and exposition. This arrangement has a number of advantages: (1) it is logical in that it begins where human perception begins, the senses, and works outward to more abstract modes of discourse; (2) it is also sequential, which means that you are able to develop your writing skills, and confidence, by building on what you have learned previously; (3) because most of the readings and exercises are related in some way to your own experience, it provides a practical context for discussing such involved topics as tone, voice, audience, and point of view.

Each chapter in the book, with the exception of Chapters 4 and 7, contains an introduction, exercises, readings, and summaries. The introductions describe the kind of writing to be done, discuss several ways of doing it and, whenever relevant, explain its relationship to other kinds of writing in the book. The readings, drawn from students and professionals, illustrate the comments about style and structure found in the introductions. They are not, however, models for imitation in any narrow sense but are simply points of reference, literary polestars, by which you can chart your own course. They are supplements to your own work, in other words, and not the primary texts for the course. The exercises furnish opportunities for practicing basic skills in fresh and interesting ways. Like the book as a whole, they are designed to generate writing, lots of writing.

The genesis of *Experience and Expression* was a two-semester writing workshop at Southern Methodist University that was similar to the one described in Appendix 1. But although a workshop is an extremely useful addition to an introductory writing course it is not a requirement for using this book. Nor is it imperative that the chapters be studied in the order in which they are presented. The word games, for example, can be played anytime during the course; journals might be discussed as a unique kind of writing. Description, of course, is at home anyplace. The readings and exercises are varied enough to allow instructors to devise their own course or else to follow the plan of the book without feeling that they are on a treadmill. A good text should work for you, not you for it. *Experience and Expression* has been written with that idea in mind.

Contents

WRITING: *Experience and Expression*

1 | Getting Started

The truth is that productive logical thinking, even in the most exact sciences, is far more closely related to the type of mind of the artist and the child than the ideal of the logician would lead us to suppose.

Herbert Read

Word-play is as much a part of learning to write as of learning to speak, although this fact is generally ignored in composition courses. As infants we listened to what our parents said and then babbled imitations until at last our grunts and gurgles turned into words that could be understood. Gradually we learned how to verbalize feelings and needs and by the age of five had mastered the basic grammar and syntax of English, all without teachers or textbooks. How did we do it? By listening and imitating and experimenting. Language was a tool for exploring the world, and because we weren't self-conscious about rules and making mistakes we often used it boldly and imaginatively. "This grass is chiggering me," a neighbor's child complained to me. "Ya," said her friend, "and it makes your legs feel like an Alka Seltzer too." It's no secret that children tend to be more playful and inventive in their use of language than adults, nor is it a secret that the best writers retain a childlike fascination with words and the exciting and mysterious things that can be done with them. And while they realize that there is more to writing than sparkling images and snappy comparisons—clarity and logic and a sense of form, for instance—they also know, as students usually do not, that writing is a process of growth and discovery in which one often stumbles into meaning. In order to create you have to be open to the unexpected and be willing to fool around.

Word games are opportunities for fooling around as well as for learning something about metaphor and concreteness and repetition, the cold cash of expressive writing. Do them faithfully but not solemnly and don't be disturbed if most of what you write ends up in the wastebasket. You are simply limbering up, not trying to write the Gettysburg Address. Be satisfied if after

1

a few weeks your paragraphs occasionally contain an image or a comparison that is not secondhand.

Comparisons

Although we may not realize it, we think and speak in figurative terms constantly. When we refer to slivers of information and torrents of abuse, to eyes of hurricanes and tongues of fire, to hitting the roof and feeling under the weather, we are speaking imaginatively rather than literally. Unlike a comparison between two washing machines or two brands of margarine, a figurative comparison relates two essentially dissimilar things on the basis of one or more similarities. It is not a trick, but an apt connection that hasn't been noticed before, one that simultaneously reduces vagueness and increases connotations. To say that your dorm room is small and stuffy is to say very little; to say that it is "snug as a shoebox and humid as a steam laundry" is to bring your discomfort to life. We can begin to see and feel how "small" and "stuffy" it really is.

The most familiar forms of comparison are simile, metaphor, and analogy. A simile is an *explicit* comparison containing the words *like* or *as* ("There was a roaring in my ears like the rushing of rivers"—Stephen Vincent Benét) whereas a metaphor is an *implicit* comparison without *like* or *as* ("The policeman bulled his way through the crowd."). A metaphor is tighter and less self-conscious than a simile because it expresses a relationship in the form of an identification; the policeman *is* a bull, not *like* a bull.

An analogy is an *extended* comparison used to clarify a complex idea or process by relating it to something simpler and more familiar. For example, writing an essay might be compared to building a house or a political campaign to a marathon or a game of chess. Since analogies can be sustained for paragraphs and even pages, they help to explain, persuade, and prove as well as to show.

As a first exercise, turn six ordinary comparative phrases ("As hot as," "as slow as," "as angry as," "as slippery as," etc.) into fresh, expressive similes.

As slippery as a cooked noodle on a drainboard.

As sturdy as an aluminum beer can.

As stubborn as an alarm clock.

As ordinary as blue jeans.

Long as an anteater's tongue.

As wordy as an unabridged dictionary.

Even if you are unusually sensitive to language, at least a few of your comparisons will be clichés, that is, trite, overworked, sapless expressions that long ago lost their energy: light as a feather, happy as a lark, good as gold, flat as a pancake, ugly as sin. They deaden writing by substituting formula for thought. They are knee-jerk expressions (cliché?). **Make a list of descriptive clichés like the ones above and rewrite as many as you can:**

Light as a feather	Light as an empty eggshell
Quiet as a mouse	Quiet as a flea's breathing
Skinny as a rail	Skinny as a slice of luncheon meat
White as snow	White as newly cut teeth

You might take this exercise a step further by writing a descriptive-narrative paragraph composed entirely of cliché comparisons.

> Jane and I had been chummy as two peas in a pod. Well, this particular night we were sitting in my room, happy as larks it seemed to me, when, like a bolt from the blue, she announced she was getting married to a guy back home. You could have knocked me over with a feather. . . .

When drawing comparisons keep these principles in mind: (1) A comparison is not an equation or an identification. "Stingy as a miser" and "Dumb as a moron" are meaningless statements because in each case the second term is virtually a synonym for the first. There should be an imaginative stretch from one to the other. (2) A comparison must be appropriate not only for the subject and the context but for the audience. "Tough as the roast beef sandwiches at Bozo's" would not make sense to people who'd never eaten at Bozo's. A comparison shouldn't be so private that only the author understands it. (3) In an effective comparison images and connotations blend rather than clash. The following metaphors are mixed to the point of absurdity.

> I maintain that the honorable senator is trying to lead his constituents over the brink with his head in the sand.

> I realize that I face an uphill battle, but at least I can make a few waves and set the ball of action in motion.

Be sure you understand what's being compared to what.

Now expand a metaphor or simile into a paragraph. In the first of the following examples, a beleaguered child is compared to a hunted animal, in the second a base stealer is compared primarily to a tightrope walker and secondarily to a bounced ball and an ecstatic bird. Consider the relationships among these comparisons.

> At school he was a desperate and hunted little animal. The herd, infallible in its banded instinct, knew at once that a stranger had been thrust into it, and it was merciless at the hunt. As the lunch-time recess came, Eugene, clutching his

big grease-stained bag, would rush for the playground pursued by the yelping pack. The leaders, two or three big louts of advanced age and deficient mentality, pressed closely about him, calling out suppliantly, "You know me, Gene. You know me"; and still racing for the far end, he would open his bag and hurl to them one of his big sandwiches, which stayed them for a moment, as they fell upon its possessor and clawed it to fragments, but they were upon him in a moment more with the same yelping insistence, hunting him down into a corner of the fence, and pressing it with outstretched paws and wild entreaty. He would give them what he had, sometimes with a momentary gust of fury, tearing away from a greedy hand half a sandwich and devouring it. When they saw he had no more to give, they went away.

Thomas Wolfe, *Look Homeward, Angel*

The Base Stealer

Poised between going on and back, pulled
Both ways taut like a tightrope walker,
Finger tips pointing the opposites,
Now bouncing tiptoe like a dropped ball
Or a kid skipping rope, come on, come on,
Running a scattering of steps, sidewise.
How he teeters, skitters, tingles, teases
Taunts them, hovers like an ecstatic bird,
He's only flirting, crowd him, crowd him,
Delicate, delicate, delicate, delicate—now!

Robert Francis

Abstract and Concrete

Examine the following words and phrases carefully: mode of transportation, wheeled vehicle, automobile, blue Pontiac GTO in my garage. The first is so general that it could refer to anything from roller skates to a hot-air balloon. The last is extremely specific in that it refers, not to a category of things, but to a single automobile.

Now examine this sequence: discomfort, pain, burned tongue, eating a green chile pizza with garlic salt. The first word is the most abstract because it refers to a concept only, the last is very concrete because it identifies a particular kind of discomfort.

Obviously we couldn't get along without words like "discomfort," "anxiety," or maybe even a phrase like "mode of transportation." In certain circumstances they express what we mean or need to say. On the other hand, it is easier for most of us to state an abstract idea than it is to describe an object that can be seen and touched. Good writing appeals to the senses as well as to the intellect. Even when we write about *freedom* and *love* we need images and examples to bring these concepts to life. To say that *love* is "the infinity of the soul" is to sacrifice feeling to philosophy. To define it as "working a whole year on someone's Christmas present" is to speak less grandly but more clearly.

In Chapter 2 we will discuss ways of increasing the sensory quality of your writing. Here we are concerned only with giving abstractions and generalizations some flesh and blood.

Charlie Brown informed us that *Happiness is a warm puppy*. **Using his definition as your model, give concrete definitions of common abstract terms like courage, anxiety, temptation, anger.**

Happiness is a roommate with a year's subscription to *Playboy*.

Temptation is noticing a letter from another girl on your boyfriend's dresser; discipline is not reading it.

Courage is a Chihuahua barking at a Great Dane.

Pessimism is like a good dinner; it humors you into doing nothing.

Frustration is the last letter in a crossword puzzle.

Anxiety is watching a trembling nurse trying to draw blood from your arm.

Terror is looking out the window at midnight and seeing another face looking in.

At times we compound the problem by coupling an abstract noun to an equally abstract adjective, as in "personal considerations," "basic needs," "realistic possibilities." **Make a list of similar clichés and then define them more accurately.**

Our daily conversation is also filled with words and phrases like "far out," "uptight," "ripped off," and "straight" which seem to refer to something concrete and specific but which are often used in vague, imprecise ways. One year everything is "cool," the next "out of sight." **Make a list of such expressions and give them more precise definitions.**

Straight is a jock doing a skit at a pep rally.

Far out is waking up and discovering that the escalator you were riding all night doesn't exist.

Ripped off is pushing the Coke button and getting a Sugar-Free Dr. Pepper.

Spaced out is a mouth full of novocain.

Oppositions

In our thought and conversation we rely as much on oppositions as on comparisons. Someone says *up*, we say *down*, someone says *fat* we say *thin*. *Fast* makes us think of *slow*, *hot* of *cold*, *day* of *night*. Such simple oppositions are mechanical and predictable, but what is the opposite of *Cadillac*, for example, or *soccer* or *doughnut*? The poet Richard Wilbur played a game with his family in which words were turned upside down to find their proper opposites. Here are some results in the form of poems:

> There's more than one way to be right
> About the opposite of white,
> And those who merely answer black
> Are very, very single track.
> They make one want to scream, "I beg
> Your pardon but within an egg
> (fact known to the simplest folk)
> The opposite of white is yolk."
>
> . . . .
>
> The opposite of doughnut? Wait
> A minute while I meditate.
> This isn't easy, Ah, I've found it!
> A cookie with a whole around it.

Fortunately, you don't have to be a poet to discover and use opposites. Advertisements are a rich source of clever oppositions, good and bad, as are the graffiti one finds on fences, sidewalks, and the walls of buildings. **Can you add to this list?**

Remember when air was clean and sex was dirty?

Virtue is its own punishment.

Where will your congressman stand when he takes his seat?

Let's put some life in our funerals.

An entire essay can be built around a single strong opposition. At this point, however, we are concerned primarily with sentences and paragraphs. Note how oppositions unify and tighten the following paragraph and enable the writer to say more with less. Some are the black-white variety while others are considerably more subtle.

> DON JUAN. Pooh! why should I be civil to them or to you? In this Palace of Lies a truth or two will not hurt you. Your friends are all the dullest dogs I know. They are not beautiful: they are only decorated. They are not clean: they are only shaved and starched. They are not dignified: they are only fashionably dressed. They are not educated: they are only college passmen. They are not religious: they are only pewrenters. They are not moral: they are only conventional. They are not virtuous: they are only cowardly. They are not even vicious: they are only "frail." They are not artistic: they are only lascivious. They are not prosperous: they are only rich. They are not loyal, they are only servile; not dutiful, only sheepish; not public spirited, only patriotic; not courageous, only quarrelsome; not determined, only obstinate; not masterful, only domineering; not self-controlled, only obtuse; not self-respecting, only vain;

not kind, only sentimental; not social, only gregarious; not considerate, only polite; not intelligent, only opinionated; not progressive, only factious; not imaginative, only superstitious; not just, only vindictive; not generous, only propitiatory; not disciplined, only cowed; and not truthful at all: liars every one of them, to the very backbone of their souls.

George Bernard Shaw, *Man and Superman*

Think of a person, place, or object that you like very much, then think of another that you dislike intensely. Make lists of opposing qualities and write a paragraph or two in which you get these oppositions talking to one another. Instead of merely identifying them, make them interact.

But opposition involves more than finding "opposites." It is combining ideas, images, facts, and events in ways that surprise a reader into fresh perceptions. When a police officer helps an old lady across the street nobody notices, but when an old lady helps a police officer across the street everyone does. Why? Surprise. A conventional situation has been given a new twist. The expected has become the unexpected. This is the essence of effective opposition, a creative tension between the familiar and the unfamiliar that teases as it delights. As I was walking to class one morning I saw an elderly woman, impeccably dressed in a wool pants suit, take a crash helmet from a shopping bag and jump on a Honda. This incongruity made me smile; it also made me want to know more about the woman. Subsequently, I asked my students to record five interesting oppositions (visual, verbal, physical) and share them with the class. Here are samples of what they found:

> I was standing in line at the Burger King when I heard someone behind me whistling the MacDonald jingle.
>
> The morning after the first frost I looked out the window and saw a Monarch butterfly frozen to the glass.
>
> The manager of the Majestic movie theater watching television in his office.
>
> I was walking towards the student center yesterday when a woman in front of me slipped on a patch of ice. Her purse flew in one direction, her books and papers in another. I rushed over to help her. She took my hand but as soon as she was on her feet said indignantly, "There's really no need for this, young man. I know how to fall."
>
> A washing machine running with no clothes in it.
>
> A Lincoln Continental sitting in a field with an alder growing through its roof.

None is exceptional, perhaps, but each reveals a sense of contrast that is essential for effective writing. **Start keeping your own list of interesting oppositions.**

Repetition

If someone accused you of being redundant you wouldn't feel flattered since the word refers to a form of mental and verbal slovenliness. But there is an important difference between redundancy and repetition, especially in writing. One is the thoughtless and excessive use of the same words and phrases, the other the purposeful use of the same words and phrases for coherence and emphasis. One weakens writing, the other makes it clearer and more vigorous. Winston Churchill roused the English spirit with this famous declaration:

> We shall not flag or fail. We shall fight in France, we shall fight on the seas and oceans, we shall fight with growing confidence and growing strength in the air, we shall defend our island, whatever the cost may be. We shall fight on the beaches, we shall fight on the landing grounds, we shall fight in the fields and in the streets, we shall fight in the hills; we shall never surrender.

The phrase "we shall fight" gains power each time it is repeated until at the end it seems to explode with resolve. Churchill uses repetition to drive his point home, like a skilled carpenter driving in a spike. He is being emphatic, not redundant.

Repetition usually involves single words and phrases that sew the different parts of a paragraph together.

> All the more strange, then, is it that we should wish to know Greek, to try to know Greek, feel forever drawn back to Greek, and be forever making up for some notion of the meaning of Greek, though from what incongruous odds and ends, with what slight resemblance to the real meaning of Greek, who shall say?
>
> Virginia Woolf, *On Not Knowing Greek*

> What is history for? . . . My answer is that history is "for" human self-knowledge. It is generally thought to be of importance to man that he should know himself: where knowing himself means knowing not his merely personal peculiarities, the things that distinguish him from other men, but his nature as man. Knowing yourself means knowing, first, what it is to be a man; secondly, knowing what it is to be the kind of man you are; and thirdly, knowing what it is to be the man *you* are and nobody else is. Knowing yourself means knowing what you can do; and since nobody knows what he can do until he tries, the only clue to what man can do is what man has done. The value of history, then, is that it teaches us what man has done, and thus what man is.
>
> R. G. Collingwood, *The Idea of History*

The second passage contains more parallelism, which is repetition at the level of structure, but in both cases single words ("Greek," "knowing," "man") unify the whole. We have variety and order simultaneously.

Paragraphs are frequently unified by the repetition of related, as distinguished from identical, words and phrases. Notice how Dickens presents the Dedlock estate by means of interlocking images of dampness and dreariness:

> The waters are out in Lincolnshire. An arch of the bridge in the park has been sapped and sopped away. The adjacent low-lying ground, for half a mile in breadth, is a stagnant river, with melancholy trees for islands in it, and a surface punctured all over, all day long, with falling rain. My lady Dedlock's "place" has been extremely dreary. The weather, for many a day and night, has been so wet that the trees seem wet through, and the soft loppings and prunings of the woodsman's axe can make no crack or crackle as they fall. The deer, looking soaked, leave quagmires where they pass. The shot of a rifle loses its sharpness in the moist air, and its smoke moves in a tardy little cloud towards the green rise, coppice-topped, that makes a background for the falling rain. The view from my lady Dedlock's own window is alternately a lead-coloured view and a view in Indian ink. The vases on the stone terrace in the foreground catch the rain all day; and the heavy drops fall, drip, drip, drip, upon the broad, flagged pavement called, from old time, the Ghost's Walk, all night. On Sundays the little church in the park is mouldly; the oaken pulpit breaks out into a cold sweat; and there is a general smell and taste as of the ancient Dedlocks in their graves.
>
> *Bleak House*

The atmosphere is relentlessly grey and dank. An arch of the bridge is "sapped and sopped away," the surrounding ground is like a "stagnant river," neither axe nor rifle sounds with customary sharpness. Even the pulpit sweats. Each word is enriched and extended by those around it and all reinforce the same general impression. Dickens doesn't have to explain his meaning; we can see it.

So far we have discussed only functional repetition. Here is an example of purposeless repetition:

> The members of the university Dramatic Society met Sunday evening for the first time this semester. The purpose of this initial meeting was to arrange and outline this season's program of dramatic offerings. Thirty aspiring Thespians were in attendance to hear Mrs. Loretta Barnes promise to make this year's program the most interesting and exciting in the school's history, not only for the participants themselves but for each and every member of the university community as well. At the conclusion of Sunday's meeting our young stars and starlets vowed to devote a great deal of energy and enthusiasm to the upcoming productions.

The paragraph is bloated with extraneous words. Note the numerous paired redundancies like "each and every," "arrange and outline," and "energy and enthusiasm." We are told twice that this was the first meeting of the year and three times that the "aspiring Thespians"—the writer would do anything to avoid using a homely word like actors or players—are going to present "dramatic offerings" in the coming year. Did we expect karate or flamenco dancing? The repetition is mindless and boring. We feel as though we're wading in a vat of taffy.

Reread some of your daily writing and eliminate any pointless repetitions like those shown above. Also, practice reinforcing main ideas in a paragraph by repeating a key word or phrase in some systematic way.

Or, describe a particular feeling or emotional condition (fear, loneliness, disgust) by assembling related sense impressions, as Dickens does in the passage from "Bleak House." You might begin by free-associating (See Appendix 2) **for a few minutes or else by doing one of the definition exercises on page 5. Once you have a fund of impressions to draw upon, write a coherent paragraph that conveys the feeling you have in mind.**

2 | Description

The body, the senses, must conspire with the mind. Expression is the act of the whole man, that our speech may be vascular. The intellect is powerless to express thought without the aid of the heart and the liver.

Thoreau

SECTION 1 Coming to Your Senses

Description is the precise arrangement of details in space. Defined less formally, it is communication through the senses, a way of uniting the material and conceptual worlds, objects and ideas. And no matter how sophisticated it becomes it always depends ultimately on close observation. When was the last time you really looked at a flower or listened to the wind or, like the old man in this taverna, really examined a glass of wine?

> I received my greatest lesson in esthetics from an old man in an Athenian taverna. Night after night he sat alone at the same table, drinking his wine with precisely the same movements. I finally asked him why he did this, and he said, "Young man, I first look at my glass to please my eyes, then I take it in my hand to please my hand, then I bring it to my nose to please my nostrils, and I am just about to bring it to my lips when I hear a small voice in my ears, 'How about me?' So I tap my glass on the table before I drink from it. I thus please all five senses."
>
> Constantin Doxiadis

Such ordinary sensations are what give writing body and texture. Think for a moment about how our vocabularies are bloated with words like "interesting," "nice," "swell" and "terrific." Sometimes they allow us to get across the general idea we have in mind but used repeatedly they make both our speech and our writing bloodless because they suggest we are concerned *only* with general ideas and not with distinctive qualities. Yet rendering distinctive qualities is what makes a passage of description work. To say "Yesterday was an uncomfortable day" is to say nothing unless your reader

11

happens to know what you mean by "uncomfortable." Too hot? Too damp? Too cold? "Yesterday was a warm day" is slightly more descriptive because there is mention of a specific quality of the day, although we might still be puzzled about the difference between warm and hot. But to say "Yesterday was hotter than the mouth of a blast furnace" clears up any uncertainties. We can picture the white-orange flames and maybe even a pair of gaping jaws belching fire and smoke. The sharper the sensory detail the more vivid the picture in the imagination.

As we noted in Chapter 1, we all think and speak in comparisons, most of which contain some sense impression. Metaphors and similes generally contain images, word pictures, that let us see what we are trying to understand.

> Her hair was gathered up in a coil like a crown on her head.
>
> D. H. Lawrence

> All London had poured into the park, draining the cup of summer to its dregs.
>
> John Galsworthy

The cognitive function of images is more dramatically clear in haiku, traditional three-line, seventeen-syllable Japanese poems. A haiku condenses the impressions of several senses into a compact image, usually of a scene or event in nature that has especially moved the poet. A haiku is always a representation of an emotion rather than a discussion of it, and words that do not enhance the image—most articles, relative pronouns, and transitional phrases of a purely grammatical nature—are usually eliminated.

> The ragged phantom
> of a cloud ambles after
> a slim dancing moon.

First note the number of "oppositions" here. The moon, bright and silvery, is pursued by a dark *phantom* which *ambles* as it *dances*. The cloud is *ragged* and rather bulky whereas the moon is *slim* and hard-edged. We are reminded of Halloween or maybe of a villain in a black cape pursuing some innocent young girl. Whatever our impression, it is conveyed by image, not statement. We understand by seeing.

Images are probably the most conspicuous sensory details in writing but they are certainly not the only ones. Sound and rhythm, which complement one another like piano and bass, are equally important.

Certain words like "buzz," "humm," "screech," and "crack," referred to technically as onomatapoetic words, define themselves on the ear. Their sound *is* their meaning. Many others derive a large part of their meaning from their sound. "Calliope" literally pipes its gaiety. "Marshmallow" feels and sounds sticky; we clean our teeth as we say it. Writers who are sound conscious are often able to re-create the effects they want. They are not restricted to silent adjectives like "loud" and "soft"; they use sound to make writing physical. There is a concrete poem by Aram Saroyan that consists of one word, "crickets," repeated over and over. Say it aloud a dozen times to get the effect. Or read this poem by James Stephens in which sound and rhythm are combined with exceptional skill:

> *The Main-Deep*
>
> The long, rolling
> Steady-pouring
> Deep-trenched
> Green billow:
>
> The wide-topped,
> Unbroken
> Green-glacid
> Slow-sliding
> Cold-flushing,
> On-on-on
> Chill-rushing
> Hush-hushing
>
> Hush-hushing.

The first stanza is dominated by *l, o,* and *n* sounds that represent the boiling and cresting of a wave; *s* sounds dominate the second stanza as the wave breaks and disperses itself. Each line has two accents except the tenth, which has a third to suggest the wave's extending itself, in successively smaller ripples, towards the shore. By repeating the phrase "hush-hushing," and by separating the second from the first by an extra space, Stephens also captures the wave's final, dying sounds. Read in a single breath, the poem has continuous forward movement, which is intensified by the use of hyphenated words and present participles. Using commas and past participles exclusively (hushed, rolled, rushed) would have produced a more abrupt rhythm that would have spoiled the effect. The poem re-creates a simple event exclusively in terms of sensation. It is not "about" anything except a sequence of images and sounds.

Touch, taste, and smell cannot be appealed to as directly as sight and hearing, but we can suggest them by using figurative comparisons ("This room smells like a wet sneaker," "Her skin is rougher than #4 sandpaper") or by enumeration (Note in the excerpt from *Look Homeward, Angel* on page 19, how Eugene Gant catalogues the smells in his father's store), and sometimes we describe the physical and psychological *effects* of a sensation instead of the sensation itself.

He began to look for a cheap restaurant, making his way into darker, less crowded streets. Though it had not rained during the day, the ground was damp, and Mersault had to pick his way among black puddles glimmering between the infrequent paving stones. A light rain started to fall. The busy streets could not be far away, for he could hear the newspaper vendors hawking the *Narodni Politika*. Mersault was walking in circles now, and suddenly stopped. A strange odor reached him out of the darkness. Pungent, sour, it awakened all his associations with suffering. He tasted it on his tongue, deep in his nose. Even his eyes somehow tasted it. It was far away, then it was at the next street corner, between the now-opaque sky and the sticky pavement it was there, the evil spell of the nights of Prague. He advanced to meet it, and as he did so it became more real, filling him entirely, stinging his eyes until the tears came, leaving him helpless. Turning a corner, he understood: an old woman was selling cucumbers soaked in vinegar, and it was their fragrance which had assaulted Mersault. A passer-by stopped, bought a cucumber which the old woman wrapped in a piece of paper. He took a few steps, unwrapped his purchase in front of Mersault and, as he bit into the cucumber, its broken, sopping flesh released the odor even more powerfully. Mersault leaned against a post, nauseated, and for a long moment inhaled all the alien solitude the world could offer him.

Albert Camus, *A Happy Death*

Describing the actual smell of vinegar-soaked cucumbers would be impossible so Camus concentrates on Mersault's responses—stinging eyes, nausea, feelings of loneliness and helplessness. We smell the cucumbers more through their associations than through a precise delineation of their properties. But we smell them nonetheless.

Not every sentence or paragraph must be a cascade of images and sounds, of course, but expressive writing, writing that grabs a reader by the lapels and forces him to pay attention, is writing that relates concepts to things. To paraphrase Flannery O'Connor, writing begins where human perception begins—with the senses. Refining your sense perceptions is a first step in making your writing "vascular."

SUMMARY

Description, the arrangement of physical details in space, appeals to the intellect through the senses. By presenting pictures to the imagination it connects ideas to concrete objects and sensations. Few passages appeal to every sense but the "perceptions" of every sense make the difference between lively and bloodless writing, whether we are speaking of a sonnet to spring or an expository essay on nuclear fission. Good description comes from meticulous, loving attention to the world around us, not from some innate creative spark. It is a basic tool for discovering and rediscovering that world and for sharing our findings with a reader.

EXERCISES

1. (a) Briefly describe a few of the following: the taste of cotton candy, the smell of fresh bread or coffee, the sound of wind blowing, rain falling, a child laughing, the texture of skin, a girl dancing. Use metaphors and similes ("Cotton candy tastes like a wad of cinnamon fiberglass") as well as clusters of random impressions and associations.

   (b) For ten to fifteen minutes concentrate on a single sense and the various ways it is stimulated. Begin by simply jotting down your sense impressions, then later try to express them in similes and metaphors.
       Or, write a brief paragraph on a single color or a single kind of sound—the greens in nature, the sounds made by different motors.

   (c) Description draws on all the senses, not sight alone. As an experiment in sensory awareness, try to describe your room in terms of sound only or a cafeteria in terms of smells. Next, blindfold yourself and describe what you can "see" by listening and touching and smelling. Describing the impressions of one sense in terms of another is known technically as synaesthesia (Donne speaks of "a loud perfume" and Heine of "words as sweet as moonlight and delicate as the scent of a rose."). You needn't strive to blend sense impressions this way, but be open to the possibility.

   (d) Describe the sound of a fire crackling, a snake slithering through the grass, a train going through a tunnel, a percolator, a jackhammer, a power lawnmower. If you can't think of the word you want make one up as Lewis Carroll does in *Jabberwocky* on page 18.

   > The sound starts far away; you hear a "hee-ya," a slap on the horse's rump, and off he goes. The sound builds slowly as it comes closer. You hear more slaps on the rump and more "hee-ya go-boys" and four "ya-ka-tumpas," louder and faster. As they pass you hear a "whoo, boy, whoa"; "ya-ka-tump, ha-ka-tump" slows to "clip-clop, clip, clop" and ends in a whinny of delight.
   >
   > Lynn Gibbs

2. Find an object that especially intrigues you and write a brief physical description of it. Next, write a reflection inspired by the object ("This object reminds me of," "This object makes me think of . . ."). Finally, write a brief narrative involving the object.

3. One way of viewing a familiar object in a new way is to *become* the object. Become a washing machine, for example. What kind of personality do you have? What amuses and irritates you? What sounds do you make? Identifying with an object is one version of the writer's favorite game, *What if?* The following piece was written by a high-school junior:

Wow, am I wrung out! You'd be too if you'd just gone over the pile of dishes I have. We dishrags get no relief. We're either doing breakfast dishes and drying out, or doing lunch dishes and drying out, not to mention all those supper and Sunday dishes. Sunday's no day of rest for us.

We've got the reputation for being drips. I know you've heard the expression "limp as a dishrag." Well, you'd be limp too if you got squeezed and stretched as I do. Really, we dishrags are so unappreciated! People are always hiding us under the sink or tossing us into a stack of gummed up dishes.

We feel that some recognition of our service to mankind is long past due. The invention of automatic dishwashers has freed us from some of the old boring routines, and we're out to create a new image for ourselves. We've started a movement called "dishrag Lib"; we're out to make "Dishrag Power" a household phrase. Some of our more radical cousins, the dish towels, have even made themselves into curtains.

You can't stop us now. We're headed for the top. No more gunky sink bottoms for us.

Carol MacLennan

4. (a) Write three haiku, preferably ones that deal with some aspect of the natural world. Adhere to the three-line structure, which gives haiku symmetry on the page as well as in the imagination, but don't feel bound by the 5-7-5 syllable division since there is no real equivalence between English and Japanese syllable counts. Remember that haiku present pictures, not concepts, and that they attempt to say a great deal in as few words as possible. Words that don't contribute to the central image must be eliminated. If the tight form gives you problems you might try writing complete sentences first, and then gradually cutting out the nonvisual words.

(b) We generally think of writing as a reflective activity in that the words we put on paper represent our thoughts and experiences mulled over, edited, and arranged for a particular purpose. As an experiment, perform some simple physical task (doing sit-ups, washing clothes, kneading bread) and write about it as soon as you've finished. Record all the thoughts, sensations, and emotions you were aware of at the time without trying to analyze or explain them.

(c) Write a second account of the experience the following day and compare the two versions. Is one more coherent than the other? More vivid and dramatic? How did the different perspectives affect the style and tone of your writing? Is there anything in the first version you would include in the second? Is there anything you would exclude?

READINGS

Winter

When icicles hang by the wall,
    And Dick the shepherd blows his nail,
And Tom bears logs into the hall,
    And milk comes frozen home in pail,
When blood is nipped, and ways be foul,
Then nightly sings the staring owl:
                "To-who!
Tu-whit, tu-who!" a merry note,
While greasy Joan doth keel the pot.

When all aloud the wind doth blow,
    And coughing drowns the parson's saw,
And birds sit brooding in the snow,
    And Marian's nose looks red and raw,
When roasted crabs hiss in the bowl,
Then nightly sings the staring owl:
                "To-who!
Tu-whit, tu-who!" a merry note,
While greasy Joan doth keel the pot.

William Shakespeare

Superball

I hear the Superball
That's bouncing and bouncing
"Boing," "boing," it went into the street
"Zoom," "put," "put," a taxi knocked it down the block

I chased after it and "slush"
I fell into a puddle
Down the sewer it went
With a "splash" and then it boinged up again

Down the block I ran
With a "clash," "clash," "clash"
In that puddle again
I fell down with a "swap"

I finally got tired and stopped

And sat on the bench
Then I heard a little "boing" "boing" from far off
And before I knew it, it fell in front of my feet
With a "swoosh" plus a little "boing."

Eric Sebbane

Jabberwocky

'Twas brillig, and the slithy toves
    Did gyre and gimble in the wabe;
All mimsy were the borogoves,
    And the mome raths outgrabe.

"Beware the Jabberwock, my son!
    The jaws that bite, the claws that catch!
Beware the Jubjub bird, and shun
    The frumious Bandersnatch!"

He took his vorpal sword in hand:
    Long time the manxome foe he sought—
So rested he by the Tumtum tree,
    And stood awhile in thought.

And as in uffish thought he stood,
    The Jabberwock, with eyes of flame,
Came whiffling through the tulgey wood,
    And burbled as it came!

One, two! One, two! And through and through
    The vorpal blade went snicker-snack!
He left it dead, and with its head
    He went galumphing back.

"And hast thou slain the Jabberwock?
    Come to my arms, my beamish boy!
O frabjous day! Callooh! Callay!"
    He chortled in his joy.

'Twas brillig, and the slithy toves
    Did gyre and gimble in the wabe;
All mimsy were the borogoves,
    And the mome raths outgrabe.

Lewis Carroll

From *Look Homeward, Angel*

Out of this strange jumbled gallery of pictures the pieced-out world was expanding under the brooding power of his imagination: the lost dark angels of the Doré "Milton" swooped into cavernous Hell beyond this upper earth of soaring or toppling spires, machine wonder, maced and mailed romance. And, as he thought of his future liberation into this epic world, where all the color of life blazed brightest far away from home, his heart flooded his face with lakes of blood.

He had heard already the ringing of remote church bells over a countryside on Sunday night; had listened to the earth steeped in the brooding of dark, and the million-noted little night things; and he had heard thus the far retreating wail of a whistle in a distant valley, and faint thunder on the rails; and he felt the infinite depth and width of the golden world in the brief seductions of a thousand multiplex and mixed mysterious odors and sensations, weaving, with a blinding interplay and aural explosions, one into the other.

He remembered yet the East India Tea House at the Fair, the sandalwood, the turbans, and the robes, the cool interior and the smell of India tea; and he had felt now the nostalgic thrill of dew-wet mornings in Spring, the cherry scent, the cool clarion earth, the wet loaminess of the garden, the pungent breakfast smells and the floating snow of blossoms. He knew the inchoate sharp excitement of hot dandelions in young Spring grass at noon; the smell of cellars, cobwebs, and built-on secret earth; in July, of watermelons bedded in sweet hay, inside a farmer's covered wagon; of cantaloupe and crated peaches; and the scent of orange rind, bitter-sweet, before a fire of coals. He knew the good male smell of his father's sitting-room; of the smooth worn leather sofa, with the gaping horse-hair rent; of the blistered varnished wood upon the hearth; of the heated calf-skin bindings; of the flat moist plug of apple tobacco, stuck with a red flag; of wood-smoke and burnt leaves in October; of the brown tired autumn earth; of honey-suckle at night; of warm nasturtiums; of a clean ruddy farmer who comes weekly with printed butter, eggs and milk; of fat limp underdone bacon and of coffee; of a bakery-oven in the wind; of large deep-hued stringbeans smoking-hot and seasoned well with salt and butter; of a room of old pine boards in which books and carpets have been stored, long closed; of Concord grapes in their long white baskets.

Yes, and the exciting smell of chalk and varnished desks; the smell of heavy bread-sandwiches of cold fried meat and butter; the smell of new leather in a saddler's shop, or of a warm leather chair; of honey and of unground coffee; of barrelled sweet-pickles and cheese and all the fragrant compost of the grocer's; the smell of stored apples in the cellar, and of orchard-apple smells, of pressed-cider pulp; of pears ripening on a sunny shelf, and of ripe cherries stewing with sugar on hot stoves before preserving; the smell of whittled wood, of all young lumber, of sawdust and shavings; of peaches stuck with cloves and pickled in brandy; of pine-sap, and green pine-needles; of a horse's pared hoof; of chestnuts roasting, of bowls of nuts and raisins; of hot cracklin, and of young roast pork; of butter and cinnamon melting on hot candied yams.

Yes, and of the rank slow river, and of tomatoes rotten on the vine; the smell of rain-wet plums and boiling quinces; of rotten lilypads; and of foul weeds rotting in green marsh scum; and the exquisite smell of the South, clean but funky, like a big woman; of soaking trees and the earth after heavy rain.

Yes, and the smell of hot daisy-fields in the morning; of melted puddling-iron in a foundry; the winter smell of horse-warm stables and smoking dung; of old oak and walnut; and the butcher's smell of meat, of strong slaughtered lamb, plump gouty liver, ground pasty sausages, and red beef; and of brown sugar melted with slivered bitter chocolate; and of crushed mint leaves, and of a wet lilac bush; of magnolia beneath the heavy moon, of dogwood and laurel; of an old caked pipe and Bourbon rye, aged in kegs of charred oak; the sharp smell of tobacco; of carbolic and nitric acids; the coarse true smell of a dog; of old imprisoned books; and the cool fern-smell near springs; of vanilla in cake dough; and of cloven ponderous cheeses.

Yes, and of a hardware store, but mostly the good smell of nails; of the developing chemicals in a photographer's dark-room; and the young-life smell of paint and turpentine; of buckwheat batter and black sorghum; and of a negro and his horse, together; of boiling fudge; the brine smell of pickling vats; and the lush undergrowth smell of southern hills; of a slimy oyster-can, of chilled gutted fish; of a hot kitchen negress; of kerosene and linoleum; of sarsaparilla and guavas; and of ripe autumn persimmons; and the smell of the wind and the rain; and of the acrid thunder; of cold starlight, and the brittle-bladed frozen grass; of fog and the misted winter sun; of seed-time, bloom, and mellow dropping harvest.

Thomas Wolfe

Cheese

I was once the Big Cheese,
Much admired for my holes.
Forgotten now,
I rest bored upon my board.

My holes advertised, "Entrances to ecstasy,
Portholes to a Sea of Pleasure
Where undulating waves engulf."
I seduced with my lusty smell and taste.
"Hurry, hurry," I called, and
Sucked admirers
Into the depths of my soft center.

Today, unused, aging in the air,
My extremities darkening,
My holes amount to nothing,
Mute mouths puckering
While the annotating ants
Etch the tale of my decay.

Peyton Davis

A Deserted Barn

I am a deserted barn—
                           my cattle robbed from me,
    My horses gone,
Light leaking in my sides, sun piercing my tin roof
    Where it's torn.
    I am a deserted barn.

    Dung's still in my gutter.
It shrinks each year as side planks shrink,
Letting in more of the elements,
                           and flies.

Worried by termites, dung beetles,
    Maggots, and rats,
    Visited by pigeons and hawks,
No longer able to say what shall enter,
                           or what shall not,
    I am a deserted barn.

    I stand in Michigan,
A gray shape at the edge of a cedar swamp.
    Starlings come to my peak,
Dirty, and perch there;
                     swallows light on bent
    Lightning rods whose blue
    Globes have gone to

A tenant's son and his .22.
    My door is torn.
It sags from rusted rails it once rolled upon,
    Waiting for a wind to lift it loose;
Then a bigger wind will take out
    My back wall.

    But winter is what I fear,
                     when swallows and hawks
Abandon me, when insects and rodents retreat,
    When starlings, like the last of bad thoughts, go off,

And nothing is left to fill me
Except reflections—
                    reflections, at noon,
From the cold cloak of snow, and
Reflections, at night, from the reflected light of the moon.

L. Woiwode

From *More Cricket Songs*

Drifting, feathery
flakes of snow cover the white
mounds of sleeping geese.

The ragged phantom
of a cloud ambles after
a slim dancing moon.

Slanting, windy rain . . .
umbrella, raincoat, and rain
talking together . . .

Snow, softly, slowly,
settles at dusk in a dance
of white butterflies.

Japanese haiku translated by Harry Behn

Haiku

Jagged yellow tips of fire
      wave and bounce
In their own warmth.

Pinholes of brightness
      In a piece of black cardboard:
Moonless night sky.

Dusty blue math book
      On a bright green folder:
The equations stir.

The willow tree weeps
      Splinters of glass in a stream
Cutting sharp, blue holes.

Anonymous students

When you think of a concrete object, you think wordlessly, and then, if you want to describe the thing you have been visualizing you probably hunt about until you find the exact word that seems to fit. When you think of something abstract you are more inclined to use words from the start, and unless you make a conscious effort to prevent it, the existing dialect will come rushing in and do the job for you, at the expense of blurring or even changing your meaning.

George Orwell

SECTION 2   Matters of Fact

"Go in fear of abstraction," Ezra Pound urged, and we'd do well to follow his suggestion. Inexperienced writers assume that an essay always starts with a well-defined *topic* or *thesis*, whereas professionals know that it can begin with an image, a fact, a snatch of conversation. Many of them keep notebooks in order not to lose the suggestive fragments of their daily experience. They scavenge among the commonplace and the apparently trivial searching for raw materials. In *Run Over*, for example, James Agee makes an ordinary event, the death of a cat, into an emblem of courage and tenacity, not by moralizing abstractly but by describing the cat's last agonies with grim precision. A less dramatic example is Alfred Kazin's description of his old neighborhood in Brownsville:

> The smell of damp out of the rotten hallways accompanies me all the way to Blake Avenue. Everything seems so small here now, old mashed-in, more run-down than I remember it, but with a heartbreaking familiarity at each door that makes me wonder if I can take in anything new, so strongly do I feel in Brownsville that I am walking in my sleep. I keep bumping awake at harsh intervals, then fall back into my trance again. In the last crazy afternoon light the neons over the delicatessens bathe all their wares in a cosmetic smile, but strip the street of every personal shadow and concealment. The torches over the pushcarts hold in a single breath of yellow flame the acid smell of half-sour pickles and herrings floating in their briny barrels. There is a dry rattle of loose newspaper sheets around the cracked stretched skins of the "chiney" oranges. Through the kitchen windows along every ground floor I can already see the containers of milk, the fresh round poppy-seed evening rolls. Time for supper, time to go home. The sudden uprooting I always feel at dusk cries out in a crash of heavy wooden boxes; a dozen crates of old seltzer bottles come rattling up from the cellar on an iron roller. Seltzer is still the poor Jew's dinner wine, the mild luxury infinitely prized above the water out of the faucets; there can be few families in Brownsville that still do not take a case of it every week. It sparkles, it

can be mixed with sweet jellies and syrups; besides, the water in Europe was often unclean.

A Walker in the City

Like Agee, Kazin avoids making generalizations about childhood and the past to explain his feelings; he lets the eerie neon lights, sour pickles, and rattling seltzer bottles do it for him. Furthermore, he concentrates on details that evoke the strongest feelings and memories instead of trying to record everything he saw and heard. In all effective description selectivity goes hand in hand with concreteness.

When you ignore the concrete details of daily experience you risk making your writing totally mental. The matter is as simple, and complex, as that. Consequently in the exercises in this section you are asked to put aside issues and ideas momentarily in order to explore the physical world around you. Get yourself dusty. Try to see familiar things in a new way. Learn their names so that if you're fortunate enough to drink a bottle of Lafite Rothschild, 1961, you won't call it "red wine," or refer to the bordello red velour upholstery on your sofa as "fabric." Examine shapes, colors, textures, movement; they are the mortar of effective description. Experiment with comparisons and oppositions since they can make the difference between laundry-list prose and genuinely expressive writing. Note the number of metaphors and similes in *Run Over*, for example, or the subtle connections Kazin makes between the Old World and the New, the neighborhood as remembered and as actually seen. In short, penetrate your subject, get inside and walk around in it so that eventually you'll be able to *show* your meaning to your reader.

Nouns identify things, adjectives identify their qualities. Together with verbs they make description possible. Without things—the word is used broadly here—there is no subject for description. And yet things alone make for dull writing. No one gets very excited about stock lists, tables of contents, or the telephone book. More interesting nominal prose (prose characterized by a high percentage of nouns) can be found in guidebooks and road atlases:

Oklahoma City (pop. 363,225, alt. 1,276 ft.)

Capital of the state, Oklahoma City was founded in 1889 and settled almost overnight by 10,000 people when this territory was opened for settlement.

A leading wholesale and distributing point for the entire state, the city ranks as one of the eight primary livestock markets in the country. There are more than 855 manufacturing concerns here, including packing plants, flour mills, printing and publishing houses, electronic firms, and machine works.

Oklahoma City is noted as the location of two of the largest high gravity oilfields in the world. Over 200 wells, some more than a mile deep, adjoin or are within the city limits. . . .

AAA Tour Book 1971-72

The author is interested only in giving us basic facts about Oklahoma City, not in describing its physical features and atmosphere. The passage contains no images, figurative comparisons, or personal interjections and none of the adjectives (e.g., "entire," "leading," "primary") is visually expressive. The style is heavily nominal and almost totally objective.

Euell Gibbons, however, wants us to be able to identify an Eastern Bay Scallop and to distinguish it from other species. Therefore, he combines technical information with exact physical description:

> Scallops are worldwide in distribution, and there are over two hundred species, but they all have enough family resemblance to be easily recognized. The common Eastern Bay Scallop, *Aequinectan irradians,* found from New England to Cape Hatteras, is a fairly typical species. A bit on the small side, when compared to some of the huge deep-sea scallops, the Bay Scallop is from 2½ to 3 inches across as a full-grown adult, but this is large enough for it to be of commercial importance, and thousands of pounds are dredged up each year and sold on the market. It is almost circular in outline, with 17 to 20 ribs and 2 equal "ears" forming a straight hinge line two-thirds of the width of the shell. It habitually rests on one side, and the upper valve is more convex and darker than the lower one.
>
> *Stalking the Blue-Eyed Scallop*

Here we are told something about the size, shape, and configurations of a Bay Scallop. Several literal comparisons and one figurative one ("ears") make the picture even clearer. Nevertheless, like the preceding passage, this one is primarily expository. What matters is the subject, not the writer's opinions and impressions of it. Explanation takes precedence over interpretation.

Adjectives appeal to our senses directly and therefore make writing physical; they also make it personal by connecting physical details to a writer's consciousness. As we saw earlier, sometimes these connections are invisible and insignificant. Either Oklahoma is a "leading wholesale and distributing point" with two of the "largest high gravity oilfields in the world" or it isn't. The adjectives reveal nothing about the writer. But had he described Oklahoma City as a "slick, glossy metropolis as characterless as a turbine" we would have been aware of a voice and an attitude. The words convey impressions as well as facts and identify the description as *his* alone.

In the next passage, from the opening of *The Way to Rainy Mountain,* Scott Momaday describes not only a place but an attitude. The objective and the subjective are integrated.

A single knoll rises out of the plain in Oklahoma, north and west of the Wichita range. For my people, the Kiowas, it is an old landmark, and they gave it the name *Rainy Mountain*. The hardest weather in the world is there. Winter brings blizzards, hot tornadic winds arise in the spring, and in summer the prairie is an anvil's edge. The grass turns brittle and brown, and it cracks beneath your feet. There are green belts along the rivers and creeks, linear groves of hickory and pecan, willow and witch hazel. At a distance in July or August the steaming foliage seems almost to writhe in fire. Great green and yellow grasshoppers are everywhere in the tall grass, popping up like corn to sting the flesh, and tortoises crawl about on the red earth, going nowhere in the plenty of time. Loneliness is an aspect of the land. All things in the plain are isolate; there is no confusion of objects in the eye, but *one* hill or *one* tree or *one* man. To look upon that landscape in the early morning, with the sun at your back, is to lose the sense of proportion. Your imagination comes to life, and this, you think, is where Creation was begun.

Some adjectives are quite general (old, hot, great, tall) but they are combined skillfully with more figurative comparisons to give a sense of this as a unique place. The prairie is "an anvil's edge" in summer, the steaming foliage "seems to writhe in fire," and grasshoppers "pop up like corn to sting the flesh." This landscape is severe, primitive, but starkly beautiful, communicating to man a sense of both his littleness and his strength. By knowing the place, Momaday suggests, we also know the Kiowas, who are an extension of the land.

A warning about adjectives: too many can be as bad as too few. In the one case the problem is vagueness, in the other excessive particularity. As Momaday demonstrates, "tall," "hot," and "old" can be effective adjectives when they don't have to carry an entire paragraph. The most specific word or phrase is not always the most appropriate. But it is possible to modify a subject to death. The student who wrote this description of an oak tree let his impressions get the better of his sense. The result is a blurred picture:

This magnificent oak pushed out of the ground like a great obelisk—made of the earth and anchored in it. The great trunk of grey knotty bark reaches up and up past old wounds from past days. So wrinkled and folded, so strong, so tall, the thick bark shields the oak from flood and cold. But there, a snapped twig and an old grey in-turning hump with a black cracking center, the remnant of a hiker's path. Above, two branches to the East and West, the cruel remnant of the searing heat of an instantaneous white flash of lightning—a jagged wound charred black and bent but pulsing with life. Then further up through the waving branches a mushroom of rising cloud dusted with fluttering brown. Through those etched and wilted leaves the sun throws its light, dappled with flecks of wandering dust into patterns sent to warm the February chill.

Oaks are certainly "magnificent" but what does "great" do for obelisk? We see the "grey knotty bark" but where, and from what, do these "wounds" come? Are "folded" and "wrinkled" really necessary? When we come to the "searing heat of an instantaneous white flash of lightning" we are out of breath and patience. Details run together wildly; the picture won't stand still long enough for us to see it clearly. We get a psychedelic oak instead of the familiar acorn variety.

Don't overload your reader's circuits. Remember that every image must have a place in the entire paragraph as well as in its own sentence.

SUMMARY

Creativity has been defined as the ability to make what is ordinary seem extraordinary and what is extraordinary seem ordinary. This section deals with the first part of the definition, making something commonplace alive and interesting to a reader. Every kind of experience is grist for a writer's mill. An odd fact or a chance observation can generate as fine a piece of writing as a sophisticated idea, and probably a lot faster. Learn to apply the knowledge and skills you already have: trust your senses; don't overlook what is obvious and familiar merely because it is obvious and familiar; enrich your subject with figurative comparisons and oppositions; show before you tell.

EXERCISES

1. (a) Describe a commonplace activity (e.g., taking an aspirin, using scotch tape, drinking coffee) so that it becomes fresh and interesting to a reader. George Macbeth's poem, *How to Peel an Orange*, (page 31) may suggest some techniques.

   (b) Write a brief essay (250 words) about one of the following: ceilings, drinking fountains, purses, blue jeans, hats, umbrellas, lamps, ashtrays. Here is a student example:

   Tongues

   What would you do without one? You couldn't do simple things like talk, eat, swallow, sing, or whistle. You certainly couldn't stick your tongue out at people. French kissing would be impossible. You couldn't lick stamps, ice cream cones, or your own lips. Without a tongue your molars and bicuspids would drown in saliva. You couldn't taste food or blow up balloons. And what would you burn on steaming hot chocolate—your teeth?

   Elizabeth Moseley

   (c) Describe a familiar object (hat, overcoat, pen) in a way that would distinguish it from others in a group.

   Lemons

   I couldn't believe it the first time I saw her. We were sitting together in a plastic bag. Until that time I thought all lemons were alike, but she stood out and the rest faded into the scenery. I tried to fight, but all my senses compelled me to roll over to her. The first thing I noticed about her that was unique was her stub. It just turned me ripe. The center was brown and surrounded with light green. When I touched her I felt the glossy wax shine that covered her oval body. And I knew we had something in common when I saw her bump. It was as big as mine. I felt that if I didn't win her over I'd turn sweet. But just as I was ready to make my move I was dumped out on a table and picked away, never to see her again.

   Ralph Meyers

   (d) Give another person instructions on how to use one of the following: movie projector, pipe wrench, omelette pan, fly rod, soldering iron, tape recorder. Assume that this person is unfamiliar with what you are describing but that he is intelligent. Make your instructions clear and precise.

2. Adjectives express the qualities of things, the aspects of color, texture,

and size that impinge directly on our senses. They can make the difference between expressive and lifeless writing.

(a) Make a list of anemic adjectives (tall, nice, large, pretty), then a second list of synonyms for each adjective in the first. Use each synonym in a sentence and discuss how it changes the sentence's meaning.

(b) Rewrite an ad for a familiar household product or a menu for a local restaurant. Replace clichés like "New and different" and "taste-tempting" with more expressive descriptive phrases.

(c) Develop a single image—a flower pot sitting on a windowsill, for example—into an extended piece of description by adding physical details. Put flowers in the pot, color in the petals, light in the window. Add details until you feel it is impossible to be any more concrete. Discuss how the different levels of concreteness function in the piece you have written and make any changes that seem appropriate. The readings illustrate many ways of using descriptive detail.

(d) Supply the missing adjectives in the following passage and compare your version with the original printed on page 44. Keep in mind that you are only comparing your choices with the author's, not competing with him.

> About fifteen miles below Monterey, on the _____ coast, the Torres family had their farm, a few _____ acres above a cliff that dropped to the _____ reefs and to the_____ _____ waters of the ocean. Behind the farm the _____ mountains stood up against the sky. The farm buildings huddled like_____ _____ aphids on the mountain skirts, crouched low to the ground as though the wind might blow them into the sea. The _____ shack, the _____ _____ barn were grey-bitten with sea salt, beaten by the damp wind until they had taken on the color of the granite hills. Two horses, a red cow and a red calf, half a dozen pigs and a flock of_____ _____ chickens stocked the place. A little corn was raised on the_____ slope, and it grew _____ and _____ under the wind, and all the cobs formed on the landward sides of the stalks.

> John Steinbeck, *Flight*

3. (a) Get in touch with the place you're in at this moment. If it's your room study its shape and dimensions. Walk around, touch the walls and furnishings, listen to sounds that penetrate. Next, record your impressions in a literal, mechanical style: "Now I am touching the walls. They are white with gold specks and have numerous bumps and depressions. Now I see a fluorescent light over my head. It is

humming and flickering. It casts shadows on the walls." Use no figurative language. Be as objective and impersonal as possible.

(b) Describe the same place subjectively by adding adjectives, similes, metaphors, and other figurative expressions: "I am touching the white antiseptic walls. The depressions in the plaster are like tiny moon craters. My fingers explore them tentatively like astronauts just out of their space capsule." Compare the two versions.

(c) Write a two-part description of a place or event that has both literal and metaphoric or symbolic significance for you. For example, you might describe the local Dairy Queen as a fast-food restaurant and as a symbol of plastic America. Make the differences between the two clear by the details you choose rather than by flat explanatory statements.

READINGS

How To Eat an Orange

First you must roll it in your hands
To loosen the firm outer skin.
Peel this all off. Sealed perfume-glands
Fling their faint sweetness like a thin

Spray on scrubbed air. Palm-cupped, your sun,
Stripped, looks ripe to burst. First ease
Apart the packed liths: lightly run
Washed fingers in: then slowly squeeze

Bunched curves of it. Your joints get wet
With rippling juice: your pared nails meet
In wads of pith. It halves. You whet

Fresh appetite; but set to eat,

Feel the rough tongue twist in your lips
And spit small, bitter, bone-dry pips.

George MacBeth

Stay Put

Something doesn't seem to be behooving
Me to panegyrize the act of moving.
Rather, could I kick with my own foot
My derrière, I'd kick. ONE SHOULD STAY PUT!
(So deeply are my mind and body scarred
And bruised, they could not likely be more marred
By one small kick upon that vital area;
The bruises' color scheme would just be merrier.)
The scars upon my fingers number thirty;
What's more, my hands look permanently dirty.
While as for the condition of my back—
Well, do not try to lift from off a stack
Of four full book-boxes the topmost first one;
You'll slip a disc, or maybe even burst one.
I could say more—Nay, could become an essayist
About such work, this work of all the messiest.
But now all pictures hang (though some awry);
The job is finished, done—and so am I.

Margaret Blum

The Uncommon Cold

When you're afflicted with a fev'rish ague,
You think that you have ills enough to plague you;
Your cough sounds hoarse and hollow, and your sneezes
Aren't reminiscent of last springtime's breezes:
They sound embarrassed, like a blunderbuss
That, once misfired, explodes in thunderfuss.
You languish in your bed, well antihistamined;
Read trash, not caring that your mind's by this demeaned.
You count the sheep of Morpheus, drowsing worriedly
(Your only hope to make the day pass hurriedly).
    Then Inspiration whispers, "Check your mail.
    A jaunt downstairs might just make joy prevail
    By bringing news of filial visitation,
    Or possibly a party invitation."
But no. Instead you find a bill from your physician—
Not large enough, this time, to cause severe attrition
To your account (whose chronic ills know no remission).
Yet even so you find the bill annoying
When ev'ry sinus is itself enjoying
(They all claim independence from the rest of you,
And work concertedly to get the best of you).
Now from the envelope a green form flutters,
A missive to make howlings out of mutters!
Red eyes (steaks cooked too rare in germy air)
Must view—a questionnaire from MEDICARE!
What boots it that your doctor's cheerful nurse
Has read your age's digits in reverse?
    Your mind's distraught, you have this thought,
    Profound and deep as darkest Styx:
    "Oh, what the hell! I might as well
    Be sixty-five as fifty-six!"

                       Margaret Blum

Nail Clippings

Think about nail clippings for a moment—fingers or toes, it makes no difference. Think about the many different sizes, shapes, colors, and textures, not to mention the history behind each one.

If you begin to look more closely at each clipping you'll discover subtle but distinct differences among them. Some are thick and sturdy and can be bent all the way back; others are thin and flakey and will split with the slightest pressure. Some have been cut, filed, and neatly buffed while others are cracked, split, and obviously neglected. Some have pulled tacks out of walls or unscrewed screws, others got stubbed off on sidewalks, closed in doors, coated with polish, covered with dirt, split by a frisbee, chewed by a dog.

There are, sad to say, a few insensitive types who bite their nails before they've had a chance to mature, as though nail clippings were nothing more than annoying bits of plastic to step on in your bare feet. If only they'd think of them as little pieces of forgotten memories, bits of history, fragments of the past.

Raymond Remmel

A Watch

The small gilded buckle is corroded slightly, and the brown alligator strap is worn and blackened by fifty-three years of use. The crystal has been shattered, leaving long thin cracks across the face and a small hole along the right edge, where two glass chips have been dislodged. The face, probably once light silver or grey, is now scarred and discolored. Two narrow, sharply pointed hands inlaid with green enamel swing methodically over the twelve arabic numerals on the inside edge. Just above the central axis is the manufacturer's stamp, "International Watch Co." Finely engraved on the back is the name Frank D. Stout and a date, 1921.

Anonymous student

Central Park

March 1956

On the afternoon of the first day of spring, when the gutters were still heaped high with Monday's snow but the sky itself was swept clean, we put on our galoshes and walked up the sunny side of Fifth Avenue to Central Park. There we saw:

Great black rocks emerging from the melting drifts, their craggy skins glistening like the backs of resurrected brontosaurs.

A pigeon on the half-frozen pond strutting to the edge of the ice and looking a duck in the face.

A policeman getting his shoe wet testing the ice.

Three elderly relatives trying to coax a little boy to accompany his father on a sled ride down a short but steep slope. After much balking, the boy did, and, sure enough, the sled tipped over and the father got his collar full of snow. Everybody laughed except the boy, who sniffled.

Four boys in black leather jackets throwing snowballs at each other. (The snow was ideally soggy, and packed hard with one squeeze.)

Seven men without hats.

Twelve snowmen, none of them intact.

Two men listening to the radio in a car parked outside the Zoo; Mel Allen was broadcasting the Yanks-Cardinals game from St. Petersburg.

A tahr (*Hemitragus jemlaicus*) pleasantly squinting in the sunlight.

An aoudad absently pawing the mud and chewing.

A yak with its back turned.

Empty cages labelled "Coati," "Orang-outang," "Ocelot."

A father saying to his little boy, who was annoyed almost to tears by the inactivity of the seals, "Father [Father Seal, we assumed] is very tired; he worked hard all day."

Most of the cafeteria's out-of-doors tables occupied.

A pretty girl in black pants falling on them at the Wollman Memorial Rink.

"BILL & DORIS" carved on a tree. "REX & RITA" written in the snow.

Two old men playing, and six supervising, a checkers game.

The Michael Friedsam Foundation Merry-Go-Round, nearly empty of children but overflowing with calliope music.

A man on a bench near the carrousel reading, through sunglasses, a book on economics.

Crews of shinglers repairing the roof of the Tavern-on-the-Green.

A woman dropping a camera she was trying to load, the film unrolling in the slush and exposing itself.

A little colored boy in aviator goggles rubbing his ears and saying, "He really hurt me." "No, he didn't," his nursemaid told him.

The green head of Giuseppe Mazzini staring across the white softball field, unblinking, though the sun was in its eyes.

Water murmuring down walks and rocks and steps. A grown man trying to block one rivulet with snow.

Things like brown sticks nosing through a plot of cleared soil.

A tire track in a piece of mud far removed from where any automobiles could be.

Footprints around a KEEP OFF sign.

Two pigeons feeding each other.

Two showgirls, whose faces had not yet thawed the frost of their makeup, treading indignantly through the slush.

A plump old man saying "Chick, chick" and feeding peanuts to squirrels.

Many solitary men throwing snowballs at tree trunks.

Many birds calling to each other about how little the Ramble has changed.

One red mitten lying lost under a poplar tree.

An airplane, very bright and distant, slowly moving through the branches of a sycamore.

John Updike

Run Over

I was rounding the corner into asylum avenue, ambling home in the middle of the afternoon, and there at the curb was a crowd and there in the middle of the crowd was a big thin black cat with wild red blood all over its face and its teeth like long thorns and its tongue curled like that of a heraldic lion. Right across the middle it was as flat as an ironed britches leg. Purple guts stained the pavement and a pale bloody turd stood out under its tail. Its head was split open like a melon; against the black fur, its crushed skull was like an egg. This cat was not lying still, nor keeping still: it was as lively as if it were on a gridiron and it was yelling and gasping satanically, the yells sounding like something through a horn whose reed is split: never getting to its feet but flailing this way and that, lying still and panting hardly five seconds at a time: people sidestepping the tatters of blood and slime and closing in again when he was off in another direction. The people were fairly quiet; talking in undertones and not saying much, but never looking away. Something respectful in every one of them. Someone said he had nine lives. It was the first I had ever heard of that, and I believed it. Other people were speculating how many of them he'd lost by now: nobody agreed on that, but they were mostly defending the cat as if against libel: he had plenty more left to go through yet.

Not that anyone there was fool enough to think he'd come out of this and get well, with two or three lives up his sleeve to spare for later contingencies, but he was putting up one whale of a fight, and though there was now and then a murmur about putting him out of his misery which no voice was raised against, nobody ventured to interfere with the wonderful processes of nature. (Things like this are happening somewhere on the earth every second.)

James Agee

From *Life On The Mississippi*

THE HOUSE BEAUTIFUL

We took passage in a Cincinnati boat for New Orleans; or on a Cincinnati boat—either is correct; the former is the Eastern form of putting it, the latter the Western.

Mr. Dickens declined to agree that the Mississippi steamboats were "magnificent," or that they were "floating palaces"—terms which had always been applied to them; terms which did not over-express the admiration with which the people viewed them.

Mr. Dickens's position was unassailable, possibly; the people's position was certainly unassailable. If Mr. Dickens was comparing these boats with the crown jewels; or with the Taj, or with the Matterhorn; or with some other priceless or wonderful thing which he had seen, they were not magnificent—he was right. The people compared them with what *they* had seen;

and, thus measured, thus judged, the boats were magnificent—the term was the correct one; it was not at all too strong. The people were as right as was Mr. Dickens. The steamboats were finer than anything on shore. Compared with superior dwelling-houses and first-class hotels in the valley, they were indubitably magnificent; they were "palaces." To a few people living in New Orleans and St. Louis they were not magnificent, perhaps; not palaces; but to the great majority of those populations, and to the entire populations spread over both banks between Baton Rouge and St. Louis, they were palaces; they tallied with the citizen's dream of what magnificence was, and satisfied it.

Every town and village along that vast stretch of double river-frontage had a best dwelling, finest dwelling, mansion—the home of its wealthiest and most conspicuous citizen. It is easy to describe it: large grassy yard, with paling fence painted white—in fair repair; brick walk from gate to door; big, square, two-story "frame" house, painted white and porticoed like a Grecian temple—with this difference, that the imposing fluted columns and Corinthian capitals were a pathetic sham, being made of white pine, and painted; iron knocker; brass door-knob—discolored, for lack of polishing. Within, an uncarpeted hall, of planed boards; opening out of it, a parlor, fifteen feet by fifteen—in some instances five or ten feet larger; ingrain carpet; mahogany center-table; lamp on it, with green-paper shade—standing on a gridiron, so to speak, made of high-colored yarns, by the young ladies of the house, and called a lamp-mat; several books, piled and disposed, with cast-iron exactness, according to an inherited and unchangeable plan; among them, Tupper, much penciled; also, *Friendship's Offering*, and *Affection's Wreath*, with their sappy inanities illustrated in die-away mezzotints; also, Ossian; *Alonzo and Melissa*, maybe *Ivanhoe*; also "Album," full of original "poetry" of the Thou-hast-wounded-the-spirit-that-loved-thee breed; two or three goody-goody works—*Shepherd of Salisbury Plain*, etc.; current number of the chaste and innocuous *Godey's Lady's Book*, with painted fashion-plate of wax-figure women with mouths all alike—lips and eyelids the same size—each five-foot woman with a two-inch wedge sticking from under her dress and letting on to be half of her foot. Polished air-tight stove (new and deadly invention), with pipe passing through a board which closes up the discarded good old fireplace. On each end of the wooden mantel, over the fireplace, a large basket of peaches and other fruits, natural size, all done in plaster, rudely, or in wax, and painted to resemble the originals—which they don't. Over middle of mantel, engraving—"Washington Crossing the Delaware"; on the wall by the door, copy of it done in thunder-and-lightning crewels by one of the young ladies—work of art which would have made Washington hesitate about crossing, if he could have foreseen what advantage was going to be taken of it. Piano—kettle in disguise—with music, bound and unbound, piled on it, and on a stand near by: "Battle of Prague"; "Bird Waltz"; "Arkansas Traveler"; "Rosin the Bow"; "Marseillaise Hymn"; "On a Lone Barren Isle" (St. Helena); "The Last Link Is Broken"; 'She Wore a Wreath of Roses the Night When Last We Met"; "Go, Forget Me, Why Should Sorrow o'er That Brow a Shadow Fling"; "Hours That Were to Memory Dearer"; "Long, Long Ago"; "Days of Absence"; "A Life on the Ocean Wave, a Home on the Rolling Deep"; "Bird at Sea"; and spread open on the rack where the plaintive singer has left it, "*Ro*-holl on, silver *moo* -hoon, guide the *trav*-el-err on his *way*," etc. Tilted pensively against the piano, a guitar—guitar capable of playing the Spanish fandango by itself, if you give it a start. Frantic work of art on the wall—pious motto, done on the premises, sometimes in colored yarns, sometimes in faded grasses: progenitor of the "God Bless Our Home" of modern commerce. Framed in black moldings on the wall, other works of art, conceived and committed on the premises, by the young ladies; being grim black-and-white crayons; landscapes, mostly: lake, solitary sailboat, petrified clouds, pregeological trees on shore, anthracite precipice; name of criminal conspicuous in the corner. Lithograph, "Napoleon Crossing the Alps." Lithograph, "The Grave at St. Helena." Steel plates, Trumbull's "Battle of Bunker Hill," and the "Sally from Gibraltar." Copper plates, "Moses Smiting the Rock," and "Return of the Prodigal Son." In big gilt frame, slander of the family in oil: papa holding a book ("Constitution of the United States"); guitar leaning against mamma, blue ribbons fluttering from its neck; the young ladies, as children, in slippers and scalloped pantalettes, one embracing toy horse, the other beguiling kitten with ball of yarn, and both simpering up at mamma, who simpers back. These persons all fresh, raw, and red—apparently skinned. Opposite, in gilt frame, grandpa and grandma at thirty and twenty-two, stiff, old-fashioned, high-collared, puff-sleeved, glaring pallidly out from a background of solid Egyptian night. Under a glass French clock dome, large bouquet of stiff flowers done in corpsy-white wax. Pyramidal what-not in the corner, the shelves occupied chiefly with bric-à-brac of the period, disposed with an eye to best effect; shell, with the Lord's Prayer carved on it; another shell—of the long-oval sort, narrow, straight orifice, three inches long, running from end to end—portrait of Washington carved on it; not well done; the shell had Washington's mouth, originally— artist should have built to that. These two are memorials of the long-ago bridal trip to New Orleans and the French Market. Other bric-à-brac: Californian "specimens"—quartz, with gold wart adhering; old Guinea-gold locket, with circlet of ancestral hair in it; Indian arrow-heads, of flint; pair of bead moccasins, from uncle who crossed the Plains; three "alum" baskets of various colors—being skeleton-frame of wire, clothed on with cubes of crystallized alum in the rock-candy style—works of art which were achieved by the young ladies; their doubles and duplicates to be found upon all what-nots in the land; convention of desiccated bugs and butterflies pinned to a card; painted toy dog, seated upon bellows attachment—drops its under-jaw and speaks when pressed upon; sugar-candy rabbit—limbs and features merged together, not strongly defined; pewter presidential-campaign medal; miniature cardboard wood-sawyer, to be attached to the stovepipe and operated by the heat; small Napoleon, done in wax; spread-open daguerreotypes of dim children, parents, cousins, aunts, and friends, in all attitudes but customary ones; no templed portico at back, and manufactured landscape stretching away in the distance—that came in later, with the photograph; all these vague figures lavishly chained and ringed—metal indicated and secured from doubt by stripes and splashes of vivid gold bronze; all of them too much combed, too much fixed up; and all of them uncomfortable in inflexible Sunday clothes of a pattern which the spectator cannot realize could ever have been in fashion; husband and wife generally grouped together—husband sitting, wife standing, with hand on his shoulder—and both preserving, all these fading years, some traceable effect of the daguerreotypist's brisk "Now smile, if you please!" Bracketed over what-not—place of special sacredness—an outrage in water-color, done by the young niece that came on a visit long ago, and died. Pity, too; for she might have repented of this in time. Horsehair chairs, horsehair sofa which keeps sliding from under you. Window-shades, of oil stuff, with milkmaids and ruined castles stenciled on them in fierce colors. Lambrequins dependent from gaudy boxings of beaten tin, gilded. Bedrooms with rag carpets; bedsteads of the "corded" sort with a sag in the middle, the cords needing tightening; snuffy feather-bed—not aired often enough; cane-seat chairs, splint-bottomed rocker; looking-glass on wall, school-slate size, veneered frame; inherited bureau; wash-bowl and pitcher, possibly—but not certainly; brass candlestick, tallow candle, snuffers. Nothing else in the room. Not a bathroom in the house; and no visitor likely to come along who has even seen one.

That was the residence of the principal citizen, all the way from the suburbs of New Orleans to the edge of St. Louis. When he stepped aboard a big fine steamboat, he entered a new and marvelous world: chimney-tops cut to counterfeit a spraying crown of plumes—and maybe painted red; pilot-house, hurricane-deck, boiler-deck guards, all garnished with white wooden filigree-work of fanciful patterns; gilt acorns topping the derricks; gilt deer-horns over the big bell; gaudy symbolical picture on the paddle-box, possibly; big roomy boiler-deck, painted blue, and furnished with Windsor armchairs; inside, a far-receding snow-white "cabin"; porcelain knob and oil-picture on every stateroom door; curving patterns of filigree-work touched up with gilding, stretching overhead all down the converging vista; big chandeliers every little way, each an April shower of glittering glass-drops; lovely rainbow-light falling everywhere from the colored glazing of the skylights; the whole a long-drawn, resplendent tunnel, a bewildering and soul-satisfying spectacle! In the ladies' cabin a pink and white Wilton carpet, as soft as mush, and glorified with a ravishing pattern of gigantic flowers. Then the Bridal Chamber—the animal that invented that idea was still alive and unhanged, at that day—Bridal Chamber whose pretentious flummery was necessarily overawing to the now tottering intellect of that hosannahing citizen. Every stateroom had its couple of cozy clean bunks, and perhaps a looking-glass and a snug closet; and sometimes there was even a wash-bowl and pitcher, and part of a towel which could be told from mosquito-netting by an expert—though generally these things were absent, and the shirt-sleeved passengers cleansed themselves at a long row of stationary bowls in the barber shop, where were also public towels, public combs, and public soap.

Take the steamboat which I have just described, and you have her in her highest and finest, and most pleasing, and comfortable, and satisfactory estate. Now cake her over with a layer of ancient and obdurate dirt, and you have the Cincinnati steamer awhile ago referred to. Not all over—only inside; for she was ably officered in all departments except the steward's.

But wash that boat and repaint her, and she would be about the counterpart of the most complimented boat of the old flush times: for the steamboat architecture of the West has undergone no change; neither has steamboat furniture and ornamentation undergone any.

Mark Twain

It is all a question of choice and arrangement.

Graham Greene

SECTION 3 Putting Things in Perspective

Description is the arrangement of details in space but the nature of this arrangement depends, first of all, on the writer's physical relationship to his subject, which is the most literal meaning of "point of view." When you are ten feet away from something you notice details that would be invisible at a hundred yards; on the other hand, at a hundred yards you might have an overview that would be impossible from ten feet. Depending on your intention, you can also adjust your point of view as you would a zoom lens. If you want to heighten the drama of a situation, for example, you might use close-ups, as James Dickey does in describing Ed's climb up the face of the cliff (page 80). If you are more interested in conveying an overall sense of mood and atmosphere you might prefer a sequence of panoramic shots like those in Twain's description of the sunrise on the Mississippi. The patterns are as varied as our ways of looking at the world. What matters in description is that there be a pattern and that it be clear to a reader.

Here is a paragraph from a popular field guide that begins with the smallest details and ends with the largest:

> Douglas Fir (*Pseudotsuga menziesii*) needles, 1 to 1.5 inches long, stick out in all directions from the branches. Cones, 3 to 4 inches long, have 3 pointed bracts, extending beyond ends of scales. Buds "cigar shaped." Bark of young trees smooth and grey, with resin blisters; on mature trees, thick and furrowed, black to reddish brown outside and marbled cream-and-brown beneath. The compact, conical crown has drooping side branches. Forest trees have long, clear trunk. Grows rapidly, attaining greatest size—250 feet tall, 8 feet in diameter—in moist Pacific Coast region.
>
> C. Frank Brockman, *Trees of North America*

In this next passage everything is related to a single object—a massive bed in the center of the room:

> The red room was a spare chamber, very seldom slept in; I might say never, indeed, unless when a chance influx of visitors at Gateshead hall rendered it necessary to turn to account all the accommodation it contained; yet it was one of the largest and stateliest chambers in the mansion. A bed supported on massive pillars of mahogany, hung with curtains of deep red damask, stood out like a tabernacle in the center; the two large windows, with their blinds always drawn down, were half shrouded in festoons and falls of similar drapery. The carpet

was red, the table at the foot of the bed was covered with a crimson cloth, the walls were a soft fawn color, with a blush of pink in it; the wardrobe, the toilet table, the chairs, were of darkly-polished old mahogany: out of these deep surrounding shades rose high, and glared white, the piled up mattresses and pillows of the bed, spread with a snow Marseilles counterpane. Scarcely less prominent was an ample cushioned easy-chair near the head of the bed, also white, with a footstool before it; and looking, as I thought, like a pale throne.

Charlotte Brontë, *Jane Eyre*

Quite different from these exact, catalogue-like descriptions is Norman Mailer's account of the riots at the 1968 Democratic National Convention. Since from the nineteenth floor small details are impossible to detect, he draws a series of figurative comparisons that give a sense of the general movement of the crowd. From his vantage point the scene is less like a riot than a clash of elemental forces:

The police attacked with tear gas, with Mace, and with clubs; they attacked like a chain saw cutting into wood, the teeth of the saw the edge of their clubs, they attacked like a scythe through grass, lines of twenty and thirty policemen striking out like an arc, their clubs beating, demonstrators fleeing. Seen from overhead, from the nineteenth floor, it was like wind blowing dust, or the edge of waves riding foam on the shore.

The police cut through the crowd one way, then cut through them another. They chased people into the park, ran them down, beat them up: they cut through the intersection at Michigan and Balbo like a razor cutting through a head of hair, and then drove columns of new police into the channels, who in turn pushed out, clubs flailing, on each side, to cut new channels, and new ones again. As demonstrators ran, they reformed in new groups only to be chased by the police again. The action went on for ten minutes, fifteen minutes, with the absolute ferocity of a tropical storm, and watching it from a window on the nineteenth floor, there was something of the detachment of studying a storm at evening through a glass, the light was a lovely gray-blue, the police had uniforms of gray-blue, even the ferocity had an abstract elemental play of forces of nature at battle with other forces, as if sheets of tropical rain were driving across the street in patterns, in curving patterns which curved upon each other again.

Miami and the Siege of Chicago

Knowing where you stand in relation to your subject, and therefore knowing what you can and cannot see, is essential for writing convincing description. (A student in my fiction class once wrote several pages about the reflections in his own eyes, never realizing that he couldn't possibly see them without a mirror.) You are allowed to shift your point of view, of course, provided that your transitions are clear and logical. But don't make so many shifts that you blur the picture. Restrain the impulse to record everything.

When you have completed a draft of your piece, you might ask yourself the following questions:

What are the most important details about this place or situation?

Are they related to one another in any organic way? If so, have I made these relationships clear to my reader?

What principle of organization am I using? Am I using it consistently?

Am I considering my subject singly or in relation to others? If the latter, have I made these relationships clear?

SUMMARY

Description helps to clarify *what* we see and *how* we see. It is more than a catalogue of sense impressions and concrete physical details; it is a fresh, suggestive arrangement of them.

A writer's eye may be compared to a camera lens with multiple settings. For some subjects close-up shots are appropriate while others require middle-distance or wide-angle shots. Sometimes we remain stationary, other times we move from place to place. We are not restricted to one point of view in even the simplest descriptive pieces, but we must be sure that any changes in focus are clear and consistent. If we begin at the middle of a scene we should work towards the periphery; if we start at the periphery we should move gradually towards the center, and so forth. Good description should be coherent as well as vivid.

EXERCISES

1. Spend a few hours taking an inventory of a familiar place or activity. Initially, record whatever interests you without worrying about its place in a finished essay. Later, edit your material into a coherent descriptive essay using one of the methods of organization discussed in the introduction. The readings should suggest additional possibilities.

2. Describe one place at two different times of day or under significantly different circumstances. For example, describe the Greyhound terminal at noon and at three in the morning, or a gymnasium before and after a basketball game.

3. Find a description of a local landmark or historical site in a chamber of commerce pamphlet or a guidebook. Determine the point(s) of view from which it was written and then rewrite it from a substantially different point of view. Compare your version with the "official" one for clarity and coherence.

4. Describe a place or structure on campus without mentioning it by name. Give your description to another person in the class who must not only find *what* you've described but the *exact spot* from which you've described it.

5. Describe a single event (concert, rally, lecture) from three different physical points of view. Or, attend such an event with two other people, each of whom writes his own account. Afterwards, compare the descriptions and discuss how your different points of view influenced what you wrote.

READINGS

From *Hard Times*

COKETOWN

The streets were hot and dusty on the summer day, and the sun was so bright that it even shone through the heavy vapor drooping over Coketown, and could not be looked at steadily. Stokers emerged from low, underground doorways wiping their swarthy visages, and contemplating coals. The whole town seemed to be frying in oil. There was a stifling smell of hot oil everywhere. The steam engines shone with it, the dresses of the hands were soiled with it, the mills throughout their many stories oozed and trickled it. The atmosphere of those fairy palaces was like the breath of the simoon; and their inhabitants, wasting with heat, toiled languidly in the desert. But no temperature made the melancholy mad elephants more mad or more sane. Their wearisome heads went up and down at the same rate, in hot weather and cold, wet weather and dry, fair weather and foul. The measured motion of their shadows on the walls was the substitute Coketown had to show for the shadows of rustling woods; while for the summer hum of insects, it could offer, all the year round, from the dawn of Monday to the night of Saturday, the whir of shafts and wheels. Drowsily they whirred all through the summer day, making the passenger more sleepy and more hot as he passed the humming walls of the mills. Sunblinds and sprinklings of water a little cooled the main streets and the shop; but the mills and the courts, and alleys, baked at a fierce heat. Down upon the river that was black and thick with dye, some Coketown boys who were at large—a rare sight there—rowed a crazy boat which made a spumous track upon the water as it jogged along, while every dip of an oar stirred up vile smells.

Charles Dickens

From *Flight*

About fifteen miles below Monterey, on the wild coast, the Torres family had their farm, a few sloping acres above a cliff that dropped to the brown reefs and to the hissing white waters of the ocean. Behind the farm the stone mountains stood up against the sky. The farm buildings huddled like little clinging aphids on the mountain skirts, crouched low to the ground as though the wind might blow them into the sea. The little shack, the rattling rotting barn were grey-bitten with sea salt, beaten by the damp wind until they had taken on the color of the granite hills. Two horses, a red cow and a red calf, half a dozen pigs and a flock of lean, multicolored chickens stocked the place. A little corn was raised on the sterile slope, and it grew short and thick under the wind, and all the cobs formed on the landward sides of the stalks.

John Steinbeck

Pentwater

The beach at Pentwater, on Lake Michigan, is one of the most peaceful places in the world. The sand is soft and fine as a baby's hair, the water is clear and cool, with no dead fish or seaweed to make it smell. The bottom of the lake is covered with sandy ripples, like potato chips. There are sandbars everywhere, and even if you were to swim out to the third bar you could stand up and see your feet.

When you look down the beach to your right you see no seawalls stretching out into the lake like fences to keep people out. It is a clear beach that welcomes people in its openness. About twenty miles farther down is Ludington, resting in the water like a whale. The smoke from the hydro-electric plant is like the whale's spout. Even this looks peaceful.

To the left you see Pentwater pier, and if you look carefully you can see people walking back and forth along it, making it look like a comb with all its teeth broken down to nubs, except at the end where there is a single tooth—the lighthouse.

Behind you, inland, are sand dunes covered with dune grass bent over by the wind.

Susan Herndon

London, 1940

Early September morning in Oxford Street. The smell of charred dust hangs on what should be crystal pure air. Sun, just up, floods the once more inno-cent sky, strikes silver balloons and the intact building-tops. The whole length of Oxford Street, west to east, is empty, looks polished like a ball-room, glitters with smashed glass. Down the distances, natural mists of morning are brown with the last of smoke. Fumes still come from the shell of a shop. At this corner where the burst gas main flaming floors high made a scene like a hell in the night, you still feel heat. The silence is now the enormous thing—it appears to amaze the street. Sections and blocks have been roped off; there is no traffic; the men in the helmets say not a person may pass (but some sneak through). Besides the high explosives that did the work, this quarter has been seeded with timebombs—so we are herded, waiting for those to go off. This is the top of Oxford Street, near where it joins the corner of Hyde Park at Marble Arch.

We people have come up out of the ground, or out from the bottom floors of the damaged houses: we now see what we heard happen through-out the night. Roped away from the rest of London we seem to be on an island—when shall we be taken off? Standing, as might the risen dead in the doors of tombs, in the mouths of shelters, we have nothing to do but yawn at each other or down the void of streets, meanwhile rubbing the smoke-smart deeper into our eyes with our dirty fists. . . . It has been a dirty night. The side has been ripped off one near block—the open gash is nothing but dusty, colourless. (As bodies shed blood, buildings shed mousey dust.) Up there the sun strikes a mirror over a mantelpiece; shreds of a carpet sag out over the void. An A.R.P. man, like a chamois, already runs up the debris; we stare. The charred taint thickens everyone's lips and tongues—what we want is bacon and eggs, coffee. We attempt little sorties—"Keep BACK, please! Keep OFF the street!" The hungry try to slake down with smoking. "PLEASE—that cigarette *out*! Main gone—gas all over the place—d'*you* want to blow up London?" Cigarette trodden guiltily into the trodden glass. We loaf on and on in our cave-mouths; the sun goes on and on up. Some of us are dressed, some of us are not: pyjama-legs show below overcoats. There are some Poles, who having lost everything all over again sit down whenever and wherever they can. They are our seniors in this experience: we cannot but watch them. There are two or three unmistakable pairs of disturbed lovers—making one think "Oh yes, how odd—love." There are squads of ageless "residents" from aquarium-like private hotels just round the corner. There are the nomads of two or three nights ago who, having been bombed out of where they were, pitched on this part, to be bombed out again. There is the very old gentleman wrapped up in the blanket, who had been heard to say, humbly, between the blasts in the night, "The truth is, I have outlived my generation. . . ." We are none of us—except perhaps the Poles?—the very very poor: our predicament is not a great predicament. The lady in the fur coat has hair in two stiff little bedroomy grey plaits. She appeals for hair-pins: most of us have short hair—pins for her are extracted from one of the Poles' heads. Girls stepping further into the light look into pocket mirrors. "Gosh," they say remotely. Two or three people have, somehow, begun walking when one time-bomb goes off at Marble Arch. The street puffs itself empty; more glass splinters. Everyone laughs.

It is a fine morning and we are still alive.

Elizabeth Bowen

From *The Adventures Of Huckleberry Finn*

Two or three days and nights went by; I reckon I might say they swum by, they slid along so quiet and smooth and lovely. Here is the way we put in the time. It was a monstrous big river down there—sometimes a mile and a half wide; we run nights, and laid up and hid daytimes; soon as night was most gone we stopped navigating and tied up—nearly always in the dead water under a towhead; and then cut young cottonwoods and willows, and hid the raft with them. Then we set out the lines. Next we slid into the river and had a swim, so as to freshen up and cool off; then we set down on the sandy bottom where the water was about knee-deep, and watched the day-light come. Not a sound anywheres—perfectly still—just like the whole world was asleep, only sometimes the bullfrogs a-cluttering, maybe. The first thing to see, looking away over the water, was a kind of dull line—that was the woods on t'other side; you couldn't make nothing else out; then a pale place in the sky; then more paleness spreading around; then the river softened up away off, and warn't black any more, but gray; you could see little dark spots drifting along ever so far away—trading-scows, and such things; and long black streaks—rafts; sometimes you could hear a sweep screaking; or jumbled-up voices, it was so still, and sounds come so far; and by and by you could see a streak on the water which you know by the look of the streak that there's a snag there in a swift current which breaks on it and makes that streak look that way; and you see the mist curl up off of the water, and the east reddens up, and the river, and you make out a log cabin in the edge of the woods, away on the bank on t'other side of the river, being a wood-yard, likely, and piled by them cheats so you can throw a dog through it anywheres; then the nice breeze springs up, and comes fanning you from over there, so cool and fresh and sweet to smell on account of the woods and the flowers; but sometimes not that way, because they've left dead fish lay-ing around, gars and such, and they do get pretty rank; and next you've got the full day, and everything smiling in the sun, and the song-birds just going it!

A little smoke couldn't be noticed now, so we would take some fish off the lines and cook up a hot breakfast. And afterwards we would watch the lonesomeness of the river, and kind of lazy along, and by and by lazy off to sleep. Wake up by and by, and look to see what done it, and maybe see a steamboat coughing along up-stream, so far off towards the other side you couldn't tell nothing about her only whether she was a stern-wheel or side-wheel; then for about an hour there wouldn't be nothing to hear nor nothing to see—just solid lonesomeness. Next you'd see a raft sliding by, away off yonder, and maybe a galoot on it chopping, because they're most always doing it on a raft; you'd see the ax flash and come down—you don't hear nothing; you see that ax go up again, and by the time it's above the man's head then you hear the k'chunk!—it had took all that time to come over the water. So we would put in the day, lazying around, listening to the still-ness. Once there was a thick fog, and the rafts and things that went by was beating tin pans so the steamboats wouldn't run over them. A scow or a raft went by so close we could hear them talking and cussing and laughing— heard them plain; but we couldn't see no sign of them; it made you feel crawly; it was like spirits carrying on that way in the air. Jim said he believed it was spirits; but I says:

"No; spirits wouldn't say, 'Dern the dern fog.' "

Soon as it was night out we shoved; when we got her out to about the middle we let her alone, and let her float wherever the current wanted her to; then we lit the pipes, and dangled our legs in the water, and talked about all kinds of things—we was always naked, day and night, whenever the mosquitoes would let us—the new clothes Buck's folks made for me was too good to be comfortable, and besides I didn't go much on clothes, nohow.

Sometimes we'd have that whole river all to ourselves for the longest time. Yonder was the banks and the islands, across the water; and maybe a spark—which was a candle in a cabin window; and sometimes on the water you could see a spark or two—on a raft or a scow, you know; and maybe you could hear a fiddle or a song coming over from one of them crafts. It's lovely to live on a raft. We had the sky up there, all speckled with stars, and we used to lay on our backs and look up at them, and discuss about whether they was made or only just happened. Jim he allowed they was made, but I allowed they happened; I judged it would have took too long to *make* so many. Jim said the moon could 'a' *laid* them; well, that looked kind of reasonable, so I didn't say nothing against it, because I've seen a frog lay most as many, so of course it could be done. We used to watch the stars that fell, too, and see them streak down. Jim allowed they'd got spoiled and was hove out of the nest.

Once or twice of a night we would see a steamboat slipping along in the dark, and now and then she would belch a whole world of sparks up out of her chimbleys, and they would rain down in the river and look awful pretty; then she would turn a corner and her lights would wink out and her pow-wow shut off and leave the river still again; and by and by her waves would get to us, a long time after she was gone, and joggle the raft a bit, and after that you wouldn't hear nothing for you couldn't tell how long, except maybe frogs or something.

Mark Twain

3 | Narration

I was trying to write . . . and found the greatest difficulty, aside from knowing truly what you really felt, rather than what you were supposed to feel, and had been taught to feel, was to put down what really happened in action; what the actual things were which produced the emotion that you experienced. In writing for a newspaper you told what happened and, with one trick and another, you communicated the emotion aided by the element of timeliness, which gives a certain emotion to any account of something that happened on that day; but the real thing, the sequence of motion and fact which made the emotion and which would be as valid in a year or in ten years or, with luck and if you stated it purely enough, always, was beyond me and I was working very hard to try to get it.

Ernest Hemingway

SECTION 1   Getting Down to Basics

Narration, broadly defined, is the arrangement of ideas and events in time sequence. It occurs in virtually every kind of writing and invariably answers the question, What happens next? Recipes, for example, are capsule narratives in which the steps of a continuous process are presented as a compact, tightly-integrated series. Rearrange the steps and you are likely to ruin the meal. Most instructions follow a similar pattern.

Methods of Sprouting

First read the directions for the individual seed for special instructions and the selection of the proper method of sprouting.

Measure seeds and pick them over carefully, retaining only good whole seeds for sprouting. Broken seeds tend to ferment. Wash seeds well and place in a bowl or jar with lukewarm water. Use four cups of water to one cup of seeds. Soak overnight. Drain, retaining soaking liquids to be used as stock in soups and beverages. Do not soak seeds which are to be sprouted by the sprinkle method. . . .

Put seeds in sprouting container, if not there already, and rinse thoroughly. Drain off all excess water. Keep seeds in a warm area where temperature will remain even. Size of container will depend on amount of seeds to be sprouted. Container must be large enough for growth and air circulation. . . .

After the sprouts have grown to desired length, the chlorophyll content of the leaves can be increased by placing sprouts in the light until leaves become green. This "greening" process takes only a few hours if the sprouts are placed in artificial light or in indirect sunlight.

Karen Cross White, *The Complete Sprouting Cookbook*

When we want to explain a complex natural or mechanical process we often rely on simple narration. Here is an account of how hurricanes are formed in which each sentence recounts one stage in the total process:

A hurricane is born in a hot moist air mass over the ocean. The cyclonic motion is often started as opposing trade winds whirl around each other. This can occur only when the ITCZ [intertropical convergence zone] is displaced from the equator so that the twisting effect of the earth's rotation can take place. The rotating low pushes air toward its center, forcing hot moist air there to lift. Lifting causes moisture to condense. Heat thrown off as the moisture condenses further warms rotating air, which becomes even lighter and rises more swiftly. As more and more moist tropical air sweeps in to replace the rising air, more and more condensation takes place. So air inside the storm rises faster and faster. . . . Surrounding air sweeps in rapidly until the hurricane is a giant wheel of violent winds.

Burnett, Lehr, Zim, *Weather*

Once again the basic narrative pattern is chronological. The first sentence describes the birth of a hurricane, the last describes its mature fury. But within the paragraph details are also arranged *causally* and *emphatically*. Event A precedes event B and in some way brings it about. Event A is also related to event B as walking might be related to doing cartwheels. In other words, there is a climactic order that goes from the simple to the complex.

Whenever we want to explain how we reached a conclusion or solved a problem we observe similar narrative patterns. Here is Soren Kierkegaard's account of why he decided to become a writer and philosopher:

It is now about four years ago that I got the notion of wanting to try my luck as an author. I remember it quite clearly; it was on Sunday, yes, that's it, a Sunday afternoon, I was seated as usual, out-of-doors at the Cafe in the Fredericksberg Garden. . . . There I sat and smoked my cigar until I lapsed into thought. Among other thoughts I remember these: "you are going on," I said to myself, "to become an old man, without being anything, and without really undertaking to do anything: On the other hand, wherever you look about you, in literature and in life, you see the celebrated names and figures, the precious and much heralded men who are coming into prominence and are much talked about, the many benefactors of the age who know how to benefit mankind by making life easier and easier, some by railways, others by omnibuses and steamboats, others by the telegraph, others by easily apprehended compendiums and short recitals of everything worth knowing, and finally the true benefactors of the age who make spiritual existence in virtue of thought easier and easier, yet more and more significant. And what are you doing?" Here my soliloquy was interrupted, for my cigar was smoked out and a new one had to be lit. So I smoked again, and then suddenly this thought flashed through my mind: "You must do something, but inasmuch as with your limited capacities it will be impossible to make anything easier than it has become, you must, with the same humanitarian enthusiasm as the others, undertake to make something harder." The notion pleased me immediately, and at the same time it flattered me to think that I, like the rest of them, would be loved and esteemed by the whole community. For when all combine in every way to make everything easier, there remains only one possible danger, namely, that the ease becomes so great that it becomes altogether too great; then there is only one want left, though it is not yet a felt want, when people want difficulty. Out of love for mankind, and out of despair at my embarrassing situation, seeing that I had accomplished nothing and was unable to make anything easier than it had already been made, and moved by a genuine interest in those who make everything easy, I conceived it my task to create difficulties everywhere.

Concluding Unscientific Postscript

Even though his account is extremely abbreviated we understand clearly how one idea led to another. This is the first criterion for evaluating any piece of narration. Are the relationships among events clear? Is there a definite progression from A to B to C and so on?

Whenever we talk about sequence, therefore, we are speaking about narration of some kind. It is the process more than the subject matter that distinguishes it from other forms of writing.

The basic organizational devices in narration are always the clock and the calendar, and they can be used in many different ways. In diaries and journals, for example, they are usually only mechanical conveniences that enable us to group our thoughts for easy reference. Continuity between entries is not especially important. But in novels it invariably is, as we can see in the selection from *Deliverance* (page 80). Time is virtually a subject. We want to know whether or not Ed will make it to the top of the cliff and therefore ask ourselves constantly, "What's going to happen next?" To add to the suspense, the climb itself is presented as a single continuous sequence of movements and thoughts until, after a while, Ed's climbing time and our reading time seem to coincide. It's as though we were climbing along with him. This is an extremely particular chronological narrative. Quite different is John Dos Passos' portrait of Robert LaFollette (page 194) in which an entire career is compressed into a few pages. Decades pass between paragraphs, and chronology serves a dual purpose of providing a general historical framework for the narrative and of underscoring the central truth of LaFollette's whole life: from *beginning* to *end* he was a feisty, tough-minded, independent Populist who fought courageously against corrupt party and government machines.

But the passage of time alone cannot sustain a narrative without the help of other structural and stylistic devices common to all types of writing. Repetition, for example (see Chapter 1 also) is extremely important for connecting ideas and events in a series. The following paragraph, which is really more expository than narrative, illustrates several basic kinds of repetition: *key terms* (New York, city), *reference pronouns* (it, its, this), and *parallel sentence structure.*

> There are roughly three New Yorks. There is, first, the New York of the man or woman who was born here, who takes the city for granted and accepts its size and its turbulence as natural and inevitable. Second, there is the New York of the commuter—the city that is devoured by locusts each day and spat out each night. Third, there is the New York of the person who was born somewhere else and came to New York in quest of something. Of these three cities the greatest is the last—the city of final destination, the city that is a goal. It is this third city that accounts for New York's high-strung disposition, its poetical deportment, its dedication to the arts, and its incomparable achievements. Commuters give the city its tidal restlessness; natives give it solidity and continuity; but the settlers give it passion. And whether it is a farmer arriving from Italy to set up a small grocery store in a slum, or a young girl arriving from a small town in Mississippi to escape the indignity of being observed by her neighbors, or a boy arriving from the Corn Belt with a manuscript and a pain in his heart, it makes no difference: each embraces New York with the intense excitement of first love, each absorbs New York with the fresh eyes of an adventurer, each generates heat and light to dwarf the Consolidated Edison Company.
>
> E. B. White, *Here is New York*

As important as repetition are various transitional words and phrases, the most familiar of which are the coordinating conjunctions *and, but, or, nor.* Generally speaking, these indicate similarity, difference, or equality between two sentences or two clauses. Sometimes they are used to connect several independent clauses that might stand as separate sentences. But a word like *and,* and occasionally *or* and *then,* can also be used to propel clauses and sentences ahead at a brisk, tumbling pace, thereby increasing the momentum and excitement of a piece of writing. Here are the opening paragraphs from one of Pat Dirane's stories in Synge's *The Aran Islands* in which the entire sequence of actions and events is linked, in a rather breath-less manner, by the conjunction *and:*

> One day I was travelling on foot from Galway to Dublin, and the darkness came on me and I ten miles from the town I was wanting to pass the night in. Then a hard rain began to fall and I was tired walking, so when I saw a sort of a house with no roof on it up against the road, I got in the way the walls would give me shelter.
>
> As I was looking round I saw a light in some trees two perches off, and think-ing any sort of a house would be better than where I was, I got over a wall and went up to the house to look in at the window.
>
> I saw a dead man laid on the table, and candles lighted, and a woman watching him. I was frightened when I saw him, but it was raining hard, and I said to myself, if he was dead he couldn't hurt me. Then I knocked on the door and the woman came and opened it.

Here is a list of additional transitional expressions and their functions:

To indicate a conclusion or a result: *thus, therefore, accordingly, in conclu-sion, to sum up, in brief.*

To introduce a contrast or qualification: *but, however, yet, nevertheless, though, although, still, in spite of, instead.*

To express continuity with or amplification of something that has been said previously: *again, in addition, furthermore, also, moreover, finally.*

To indicate the passage of time: *presently, shortly, since, afterwards, there-after, in the meantime, meanwhile, lately.* These obviously have very direct application to narration.

To introduce an example: *for example, for instance, in particular, thus.*

Only with practice will you be able to use transitions flawlessly, but there are several rules of thumb that will help you to use them with increased proficiency: (1) Review the function of each expression you use so that you won't confuse *consequently* with *furthermore* or *thus* with *therefore*; (2) Don't rely on the same few expressions all the time. Experiment with different ones to increase your flexibility; (3) Avoid overusing transitions. If the mean-ing of a passage is clear without one, omit it. Remember that there are other devices for achieving coherence in your writing, especially repetition and parallel structure.

Brevity is the soul of narration as well as wit. "I came, I saw, I con-quered" was Caesar's concise summary of his victory at Pontus, "Rain, no game" one wit's version of the shortest short story. Both illustrate brevity carried to extremes, perhaps, but they do suggest an important narrative principle: tell your reader all that is necessary but not more than is neces-sary, and never what he can easily figure out for himself. Begin as close to the crucial event as possible so that your reader doesn't have to wade through a bog of tedious preliminary details. In other words, catch an action on the rise or as it's about to turn a corner and follow it through to the end. Pat Dirane's introduction, quoted earlier, is so effective because it identifies the setting and the basic situation, indicates his (Pat's) relationship to both, and makes us want to know what will happen next. He doesn't tell us about his past life or give a capsule history of the region because such information is irrelevant to his story. And when he comes to the climactic moment, in which the husband, who has been feigning death, finally kills his wife's lover, he is equally crisp and economical:

> We went in and saw them lying together with her head on his arm.
> The dead man hit him a blow with the stick so that the blood out of him leapt up and hit the gallery.

What could be more expressive, and conclusive, than this single violent image? It makes further commentary unnecessary.

The virtues of conciseness are illustrated even better in the ballad *Sir Patrick Spens* (page 58), a model of clear, spare narrative.

The first stanza recounts the foolish and ultimately fatal request of the king, the last stanza describes the drowning of Sir Patrick and the other Scots lords "Haf owre to Aberdour." We begin and end with a critical event. In between is a series of brief dramatic scenes, composed primarily of description and dialogue, that tell us all we *need* to know, as distinguished from all we *might* know, about the king, life at court, Sir Patrick's character and the reasons for his noble obedience. There are no digressions, no unnecessary transitions from scene to scene, no explanation of the "moral" of the story, which can be inferred from Sir Patrick's words and the pointed contrasts between his cold death and the ease of the court ladies "wi thair fans into thair hands." Additional background information would only detract from the drama of the story without increasing our understanding of it. In a story, as in life, we can sometimes know too much.

Now let's suppose that your're planning to write a thousand-word narrative essay about a recent weekend in New York City, and you want to arrange events chronologically. You got up, ate breakfast, and took a cab to the airport. The air was crisp and clear, the sun was glancing brilliantly off ice-covered trees. Such an exquisite moment deserves at least a paragraph, you say to yourself. On the plane you sat next to an eccentric Hungarian cellist, and the ensuing conversation was so intriguing that you must devote a paragraph to it as well. Then there was a mix-up with your luggage which took an hour to unravel and which also gets a paragraph. By now you've used half your word allotment and not said a thing about the city. "But all of this actually happened," you say, "just as I described it." True, but no reason to preserve every detail. Unless the preliminary events were more interesting to you than the actual visit to New York City—in which case you have a new topic—you will have to sharpen your focus in order to write a readable essay. You might compress the introductory material into a single paragraph just to set the tone for the rest of the essay; or you might begin the essay with your arrival in the city; or you might concentrate on one incident that epitomized the entire experience for you. The object is to get from A to B smoothly and efficiently, which means including only information related to your focus and excluding what is extraneous to it. Narrative time has to be an abridgment of clock time; days and hours must be covered in a paragraph or a sentence. Otherwise, a simple trip to the laundromat becomes an epic journey that exhausts both writer and reader.

SUMMARY

Narration, the arrangement of events and ideas in some form of time sequence, highlights the movement from one high point in a situation to another, not the laborious trudging in between. It is crucial to select the type of sequence (chronological, emphatic, cause-effect) that best fits your materials, and also to know where to begin and end your account. Try never to tell a reader more than he needs to know or things that he can figure out for himself. Condense background details to essentials, keep description precise and spare, avoid redundant illustrations, make transitions clear and consistent.

EXERCISES

1. (a) Write a factual case history of a simple daily event such as making breakfast, walking to class, or going to the supermarket. Record what you do, see, and say in a spare notational style that keeps the focus squarely on the event. See Chapter 2, Section 2 for additional suggestions.

   (b) Write a narrative account of a more extended project such as learning to drive, reading *War and Peace*, or rehearsing a part for a play. Since you will be dealing with more incidents than in the previous exercise you will have to pay particular attention to transitions and other structural devices for maintaining narrative flow and continuity. You may also have to experiment with different kinds of narrative sequences (e.g., causal, chronological, climactic) to find the most appropriate one for your subject.

2. (a) Write a 250-word summary of a complicated natural or mechanical process like photosynthesis or internal combustion. Textbooks and encyclopedias will provide you with raw information but the summary itself should reflect your own estimation of what is most essential for a layman to know.

   (b) Condense a newspaper or magazine article of some length into a series of twenty-second "spots" that could be used in a newscast. How does this severe compression of background detail affect the focus and tone of the original article?

3. (a) Thoreau comments in his *Journal* that "thoughts accidentally thrown together become a frame in which more may be developed and exhibited." To test this idea, keep meticulous notes on what you do, say, and think during a single day. Don't force your material into a preconceived pattern but keep in mind that ultimately it must have a focus and a point of view. At the end of the day write a brief summary (1–2 paragraphs) that would give a reader an accurate, if only partial, idea of how you spent your time.

   (b) Now keep a personal journal for a week, following the same basic procedures as before. Let things simmer at the back of your mind until a suitable narrative framework suggests itself. And remember that strict chronology is only one of the patterns available to you. At the end of the week write a narrative essay (500–750 words) that could stand as some sort of permanent record of this segment of your life. More will be said about journals in Chapter 4.

4. Narration starts with an idea or event that is about to turn a corner in a

new and perhaps unforseen direction. Almost anything can become the subject of narrative if it is handled properly.

(a) Write an essay about a unique personal experience in which the uniqueness is conveyed through a sequence of motion and fact rather than by interpretative commentary. Some possible topics: The wildest party I ever attended; The most exotic meal I ever ate; The most frustrating experience of my life.

(b) Write a brief narrative account of a shift from one mood, feeling, or point of view to another. You will be focusing on an internal "event" which, as we shall see, is often what we mean by plot in autobiography.

(c) Think of a critical moment in your life when you were forced to examine your attitudes and assumptions carefully, a moment in which you had to make an important decision, for example, or in which you found yourself in conflict with some form of established authority. Write an essay about this moment that contains an introduction, a description of the crisis, and some type of resolution. The readings in this section and in Chapter 5, Section 3 should give you further guidance.

5. Newspapers sometimes print leads and headlines that suggest fascinating and even bizarre stories. I found this on the front page of a local newspaper: "Cannibal marriage won't last, son predicts." The statement is open to various interpretations, any one of which could be the basis of an amusing sketch or story. Make your own list of such statements and write a story based on one of them. Let your imagination run free.

6. Construct an outline for a story that includes a brief description of the main character, perhaps yourself, a setting, a basic situation, and the first line. Give the outline to another member of the class to develop as best he can. That person then gives the story, containing his additions, to a third person and so on until six people have contributed. The last contributor must end the story in an appropriate manner. A "group fiction" is an excellent way to study the basics of narration, particularly strategies for developing ideas and situations and for maintaining consistency in style, tone, and point of view.

READINGS

After Ever Happily
or
The Princess and the Woodcutter

And they both lived happily ever after. . .
The wedding was held in the palace. Laughter
Rang to the roof as a loosened rafter
Crashed down and squashed the chamberlain flat—
And how the wedding guests chuckled at that!
"You, with your horny indelicate hands,
Who drop your haitches and call them 'ands,
Who cannot afford to buy her a dress,
How dare you presume to pinch our princess—
Miserable woodcutter, uncombed, unwashed!"
Were the chamberlain's words (before he was squashed).
"Take her," said the Queen, who had a soft spot
For woodcutters. "He's strong and he's handsome. Why not?"
"What rot!" said the King, but he dare not object;
The Queen wore the trousers—that's as you'd expect.
Said the chamberlain, usually meek and inscrutable,
"A princess and a woodcutter? The match is unsuitable."
Her dog barked its welcome again and again,
As they splashed to the palace through puddles of rain.
And the princess sighed, "Till the end of my life!"
"Darling," said the woodcutter, "will you be my wife?"
He knew all his days he could love no other,
So he nursed her to health with some help from his mother,
And lifted her, horribly hurt, from her tumble.
A woodcutter, watching, saw the horse stumble.
As she rode through the woods, a princess in her prime
On a dapple-grey horse . . . Now, to finish my rhyme,
I'll start it properly: Once upon a time—

Ian Serraillier

Sir Patrick Spens

The king sits in Dumferling toune,
    Drinking the blude-reid wine:
"O whar will I get guid sailor,
    To sail this schip of mine?"

Up and spak an eldern knicht,
    Sat at the kings richt kne:

"Sir Patrick Spens is the best sailor,
  That sails upon the se."

The king has written a braid letter,
  And signed it wi his hand,
And sent it to Sir Patrick Spens,
  Was walking on the sand.

The first line that Sir Patrick red,
  A loud lauch lauched he;
The next line that Sir Patrick red,
  The teir blinded his ee.

"O wha is this has don this deid,
  This ill deid don to me,
To send me out this time o' the yeir,
  To sail upon the se?

"Mak hast, mak haste, my mirry men all
  Our guid schip sails the morne."
"O say na sae, my master deir,
  For I feir a deadlie storme.

"Late, late yestreen I saw the new moone,
  Wi the auld moone in her arme,
And I feir, I feir, my deir master,
  That we will cum to harme."

O our Scots nobles wer richt laith
  To weet their cork-heild schoone;
Bot lang owre a' the play wer playd
  Their hats they swam aboone.

O lang, lang may their ladies sit,
  Wi thair fans into their hand,
Or eir they se Sir Patrick Spens
  Cum sailing to the land.

O lang, lang may the ladies stand,
  Wi thair gold kems in their hair
Waiting for thair ain deir lords,
  For they'll se thame na mair.

Haf owre, haf owre to Aberdour,
  It's fiftie fadom deip;
And thair lies guid Sir Patrick Spens,
  Wi the Scots lords at his feit.

Anonymous

From *The Aran Islands*

One day I was travelling on foot from Galway to Dublin, and the darkness came on me and I ten miles from the town I was wanting to pass the night in. Then a hard rain began to fall and I was tired walking, so when I saw a sort of a house with no roof on it up against the road, I got in the way the walls would give me shelter.

As I was looking round I saw a light in some trees two perches off, and thinking any sort of a house would be better than where I was, I got over a wall and went up to the house to look in at the window.

I saw a dead man laid on a table, and candles lighted, and a woman watching him. I was frightened when I saw him, but it was raining hard, and I said to myself, if he was dead he couldn't hurt me. Then I knocked on the door and the woman came and opened it.

"Good evening, ma'am," says I.

"Good evening kindly, stranger," says she. "Come in out of the rain."

Then she took me in and told me her husband was after dying on her, and she was watching him that night.

"But it's thirsty you'll be, stranger," says she. "Come into the parlour."

Then she took me into the parlour—and it was a fine clean house—and she put a cup, with a saucer under it, on the table before me with fine sugar and bread.

When I'd had a cup of tea I went back into the kitchen where the dead man was lying, and she gave me a fine new pipe off the table with a drop of spirits.

"Stranger," says she, "would you be afraid to be alone with himself?"

"Not a bit in the world, ma'am," says I; "he that's dead can do no hurt."

Then she said she wanted to go over and tell the neighbours the way her husband was after dying on her, and she went out and locked the door behind her.

I smoked one pipe, and I leaned out and took another off the table. I was smoking it with my hand on the back of my chair—the way you are yourself this minute, God bless you—and I looking on the dead man, when he opened his eyes as wide as myself and looked at me.

"Don't be afraid, stranger," said the dead man; "I'm not dead at all in the world. Come here and help me up and I'll tell you all about it."

Well, I went up and took the sheet off of him, and I saw that he had a fine clean shirt on his body, and fine flannel drawers.

He sat up then, and says he—

"I've got a bad wife, stranger, and I let on to be dead the way I'd catch her goings on."

Then he got two fine sticks he had to keep down his wife, and he put them at each side of his body, and he laid himself out again as if he was dead.

In half an hour his wife came back and a young man along with her.

Well, she gave him his tea, and she told him he was tired, and he would do right to go and lie down in the bedroom.

The young man went in and the woman sat down to watch by the dead man. A while after she got up and "Stranger," says she, "I'm going in to get the candle out of the room; I'm thinking the young man will be asleep by this time." She went into the bedroom, but the divil a bit of her came back.

Then the dead man got up and he took one stick and he gave the other to myself. We went in and saw them lying together with her head on his arm.

The dead man hit him a blow with the stick so that the blood out of him leapt up and hit the gallery.

That is my story.

John Millington Synge

From *The Man Who Walked Through Time*

When I began to set up camp by the flickering light of my little fire, I quickly found myself dropping into back-packing routines that I have evolved over the years. In themselves, the acts I performed were trivial and unimportant. But they too signaled simplicity. And I knew that they, or variations of them, would form the daily framework of my journey. Soon that framework would exist almost unnoticed. But now, on this first evening, the freshness of renewed familiarity stamped every act on my conscious mind.

Even before I began searching for firewood, I had from habit propped up the pack with my long bamboo walking staff by angling the staff's butt into the soft gravel and jamming its head under the top crossbar of the aluminum pack frame. Now, with the fire well alight (though needing constant replenishment, for desert firewood burns like forest tinder), I positioned the pack more carefully, up at the head of the little patch of open gravel I had chosen. And I dug the butt of the staff more deeply into the gravel, so that the pack would stand firm even when I used it, as I always do, for a back rest.

Then I undid the flap of the big gray pack bag and took out everything I would need for the night. As usual, I had packed the gear so that the things I expected to need at the next halt would come out in roughly the order I needed them.

First I took out two half-gallon water canteens (there were two more further down) and laid them on the gravel, close beside the pack.

Then I unpacked and immediately put on the light, down-filled jacket that was the only warm upper garment I had brought. The evening was not cold yet, not at all cold. And there was nothing that could quite be called a breeze. But already I could feel—especially where my shirt clung damply to the small of my back—the slight downhill air movement that you so often find at night in desert canyons.

Next I took from the pack a blue coated-nylon poncho that on this trip, when I expected no rain after the first two or three weeks, would have to triple as raincoat, sun awning, and groundsheet. The poncho was brand-new, and tough, and I hoped it would not develop big holes too quickly from being used as a groundsheet. I spread it out flat, in front of the pack, with its left edge about three feet from the fire.

Next I lifted out of the pack the big plastic laundry bag that held all the food I would need for the next twenty-four hours. (The balance of the week's rations was in another big bag, down at the bottom of the pack.) I put the food bag on the groundsheet, on the side nearest the fire. Then I took out my two nesting aluminum pots—old and rather battered friends of many years' cooking—and removed the plastic bag that always wraps them and tucked it in securely between pack frame and pack bag, where no sudden gust of wind could whisk it away during the night and where I would reach for it quite automatically in the morning. Back on Hualpai Hilltop I had emptied into the smaller pot a four-ounce package of diced dehydrated potatoes, half a cup of water, and some salt, so that by dinnertime the potatoes would be rehydrated and would need only about ten minutes of cooking, not half an hour. Now I emptied the vegetables into the big pot and washed the last clinging dice free with water that would be needed anyway for cooking the potatoes.

Next I took my little Svea stove out of the pack, removed the stove from its plastic bag, and tucked this bag too between pack frame and pack bag. Then I inserted the stove handle into its socket, grasped the handle between finger and thumb, and held the stove about a foot above the fire. After a moment or two I set the stove down just beside the groundsheet, twisted it a couple of times to bed it firmly in the gravel, and opened the jet valve a half turn. Liquid gasoline, warmed by the fire, welled up out of the nozzle, ran down the stem, and began to collect in a hollow at its base. When I could see in the bright beam of my flashlight that the hollow was almost full, I closed the valve and put a match to the gasoline. A blue-and-yellow flame enveloped the stem of the stove. Cupping my hands, I shielded it from the air movement. When the flame began to subside, I opened the valve. The stove roared into life. It was good, I found, to hear that familiar roar. Good to hear it once more against the silence of the night. Against the huge, soft, black, familiar silence.

I put the pot with the potatoes and water onto the stove and went back to setting up camp. (This freedom to do other things while food cooks is one reason I rarely cook over a campfire. Other advantages include speed, ease of control, and avoidance of collecting firewood—except when you want a fire for warmth or cheer or both. Also—and this is no fiddle-faddle—a stove does not begrime your pots, and so they never coat hands or clothing or equipment with a layer of soot that is invisible at night but can be an unholy nuisance.)

When I had added a few sticks to the fire and then stepped a couple of paces away from it to take a quick look out into the night (just enough of a look to see that a faint paleness still hung along the high western horizon, up above the wall of the Canyon), I took my hip-length air mattress out of the pack and began to blow it up. I inflated the main section hard and the pillow section soft (the reverse of the way I would want it for sleeping on), so that it would make a comfortable chair when propped against the pack with the pillow downward.

Finally I unrolled my new ultralightweight, down-filled, mummy-type sleeping bag and draped it over the air mattress. Its bright orange nylon shell shone warmly in the flickering firelight.

The firelight also showed, now, clouds of steam billowing out from under the lid of the cooking pot on the stove. I turned the stove dead low. The roar abated; but it still shut off, like a massive studded door, the silence of the night.

I sat down on the mummy bag and took off my boots and put them beside the groundsheet on the side away from the fire. I took off my socks too, and hung them half in and half out of the boots. Then I anointed my feet sparingly with rubbing alcohol from a small plastic bottle, taking great care to keep it well away from the fire. The alcohol felt as delightfully refreshing as a dive into a swimming pool after an August day in the city. As soon as it had dried, I unzippered the mummy bag part way, pushed my feet down into it, pulled the bag up loosely around my waist, and leaned back. It was very comfortable like that, with my butt cushioned on the pillow of the air mattress and my back leaning against the firmly inflated main section, which in its turn leaned against the now almost empty pack. I sat there for several minutes, content, relaxed, drifting—hovering on the brink of daydreams without ever achieving anything quite so active.

Colin Fletcher

The Track Meet

"MacIlvaine up, McMahon on deck, Jones in the hole."

The scent of honeysuckle seemed to linger in the air and joined itself with the sweet odor of freshly cut grass. In the distance trees danced in a warm wind. It was the sort of day which melted colors and images and mellowed one's senses so that nature, for a moment at least, might be perceived, only to be lost in the complexity of it the next. Before me stretched a carpet of grass upon which was impeccably detailed the shadow of my tree. I stood beneath an elm. From the vertex of the triangle which outlined the foul lines of the javelin field, I counted off steps back to where I would begin my takeoff and approach, and made two marks. A slight wind blew head-on, as if funneled into the triangle. Much to my advantage I thought. Above me leaves rustled and late afternoon birds called back and forth.

It occurred to me that these creatures, on wings perfectly suited for flight, glide through the air masters of technique by instinct. Far from a master of technique, I am to hurl a metal rod eight feet in length that is also perfectly suited for flight. Yet this rod fights and mocks the inexperienced.

I slipped out of my bright red sweats and flung them to the base of the tree. I picked up the javelin, stuck point down in the turf. The cross which hung about my neck swung back and forth in its freedom as I stretched my arms with the javelin behind my neck. Out of habit, I stood and held the javelin in my left hand, and with the thumb of my right forced small clumps of dirt from the tip. I searched for a target. Picking a spot in a cloud moving towards me I cocked the javelin above my shoulder and regulated my breathing. My right foot was placed on the first mark and my left rested behind, on my toes. My eyes were focused on one abstract point in the sky. Pierce it. I built up energy. Slowly, my legs flowed in motion, like pistons waiting for full power and speed. I could feel my legs churning faster, the muscles rippling momentarily, only to be solidified when foot and turf met like gears. Hitting the second mark, I escaped from the shadow of the tree and was bathed in sunlight. . . . . .Left foot forward . . . . javelin back, straight back, ... turn now, five steps . . . . . three, four . . . . . stretch, the clouds, the point . . . . . turn back, throw the hips . . . . chest out . . . explode through the javelin . . . . terminate forward motion, release.

The muscles of my right leg divided in thirds just above my knee, as the full weight of my body in motion was left to its support. Skipping, I followed through and watched the quivering javelin climb as it floated in the oncoming wind. My cross swung. For a moment, it reflected the sunlight and I lost sight of the javelin. It landed quickly, piercing the ground. I heaved in exhaustion, and perspiration flowed from my face and hands. Before me the field stretched and I attempted to evaluate my throw. I was pleased. The smell of honeysuckle again drifted into my senses and somehow, I had a feeling of accomplishment I could just as easily have experienced had I thrown poorly.

Cheers invaded my thoughts and for the first time since my call, I returned to consciousness.

"McMahon up, Jones on deck, MacIlvaine in the hole."

W. Rodman MacIlvaine

Excitement is simple: excitement is situation, a single event. It mustn't be wrapped up in thoughts, similes, metaphors. A simile is a form of reflection, but excitement is of the moment when there is no time to reflect. Action can only be expressed by a subject, a verb, and an object, perhaps a rhythm—little else. Even the adjective slows the pace or tranquilizes the nerve.

Graham Greene

SECTION 2   Actions Speak Louder

In Section 1 we concentrated on the structure of narrative; in this section we are concerned mainly with its style, although most of the discussion is directly applicable to other kinds of writing as well.

As Graham Greene points out, the simple sentence (one main clause and no subordinate clauses) is the most effective means for conveying action because it is short and compact and has a steady ongoing rhythm that carries the reader through from beginning to end without interruption. It differs from compound and complex sentences the way an express bus differs from a local.

Schabb saw the Greek crouch. He saw the Greek's right hand flash back towards his belt, then forward again with a revolver. He saw Torrey's right arm stiffen. Torrey's body was at a different angle, turned slightly away from the right. Schabb saw the Greek's hand pick up, then down.

Schabb saw Torrey reel slightly. Schabb saw the Blackhawk briefly as it pointed towards the sky. Schabb saw the Greek crouch at the left rear fender of the Bird. He saw the Greek's hand kick up with the revolver, then kick down again. He heard shots. He saw Torrey stagger back. He saw the Blackhawk pointing towards the sky. He saw the Greek's right hand kick upward again. He saw Torrey's body lurch in its stride. He saw the Greek straighten up. He heard the shot. He saw the Greek point the black revolver at Torrey, as Torrey's body recovered its balance again. The Blackhawk flew out of Torrey's hand. Schabb saw the Greek's right hand kick up, then down. Schabb saw a white piece fly away from Torrey's head, in the back. Schabb heard the shot. Schabb saw Torrey reel backward again. Schabb jammed the accelerator to the floor. The motor leaped widly. Schabb jerked the transmission out of PARK. The Impala leaped forward as Torrey came down on the grass. Schabb rolled the wheel over to miss a white Plymouth Fury at the kerb, one door down from the Greek's. The Impala slewed. Schabb hauled the wheel over hard. The Impala slewed to the right. Schabb got the Impala straightened out.

George V. Higgins, *The Digger's Game*

The excitement of the passage comes from the blunt simple sentences that jolt us like a series of left jabs. There are almost no adjectives and only an occcasional adverb ("Schabb saw Torrey reel slightly") or prepositional phrase ("The Impala slewed to the right") to slow the pace.

Now the strict subject-verb-object construction has its limitations, as any reader of Dick and Jane knows; yet there are ways to make it livelier and more expressive without diluting its energy. Taking "John drove his car" as our core sentence, we could modify the subject with adjectives:

> John, sullen and angry, drove his car.

or insert a participial phrase:

> John, flushed with anger, drove his car.

Or we might, like Higgins, modify the predicate by adding a prepositional phrase:

> John drove his car down Highland Avenue.

or by combining the verb with an adverb:

> John drove his car erratically down Highland Avenue.

or by modifying the direct object:

> John drove his sleek blue car down Highland Avenue.
> John drove his car, the pride of his life, down Highland Avenue.

Finally, we might use a compound predicate:

> John fumed, cursed, and drove his car down Highland Avenue.

Of course, there's a limit to the amount of modification a sentence can carry before it begins to sway and buckle from its own weight. Greene observes that comparisons tend to impede action and "tranquilize the nerve." Considering the importance given to figurative language in the previous two chapters, this remark may be puzzling. Actually, it introduces a necessary refinement. Because metaphors, similes, adjectives, and adverbs add color and texture to our writing, and thereby diminish vagueness, we cannot get along without them. Nevertheless, every time a reader makes a comparison, every time he says to himself, "This is like that," he pauses. The more often he pauses the slower he reads, and the slower he reads the more inclined he is to ponder the individual attributes and qualities of things than to be carried along by an action. In narration, and other forms of writing as well, we try to strike a balance between sensory details, which imprint pictures on our imagination, and the underlying progression of events and ideas. A superb example of this type of integration is the opening paragraph of *A Farewell to Arms:*

> In the late summer of that year we lived in a house in a village that looked across the river and the plain to the mountains. In the bed of the river there were

pebbles and boulders, dry and white in the sun, and the water was clear and swiftly moving and blue in the channels. Troops went by the house and down the road and the dust they raised powdered the leaves of the trees. The trunks of the trees too were dusty and the leaves fell early that year and we saw the troops marching along the road and the dust rising and leaves, stirred by the breeze, falling and the soldiers marching and afterward the road bare and white except for the leaves.

We could spend several pages discussing the repetition alone ("white," "dust," "leaves") but more important for our purposes is the way Hemingway creates what he calls "a sequence of motion and fact." Two things stand out: (1) Except for "powdered" no verb is especially striking, and yet the entire passage has an urgent, almost breathless rhythm because of the way the individual clauses are joined by "and." This simple connective makes the passage seem like a single smooth, continuous sentence; (2) Although there are many modifiers in the passage they don't impede its forward movement because they are generally plain, familiar, and follow the nouns so as to become part of the general flow of things. Notice what happens to the second sentence when we rearrange the modifiers: "In the bed of the river there were dry, white pebbles, and there was clear, blue, swiftly moving water in the channels." Now the rhythm is halting. Adjectives and adverbs become hurdles that we have to clear in order to get to the nouns. Which is not to say that modifiers should always follow nouns or that clauses should always be linked by "and." The point of the explication is to show you what can be accomplished with a subject, a verb, and a few ordinary modifiers.

Like all writing, narration depends on its verbs to express action and to help support the rest of the sentence. Generally speaking, the stronger the verbs the better the writing. We all rely too heavily on *to be, to have,* and their anemic next of kin like *to make, to do,* and *to look.* These are all essential, serviceable, and in many instances unavoidable verbs. But they are always colorless and sometimes inaccurate as well. "I had a good time at the party" is a feebler version of "I enjoyed the party" or "I loved the party." "It is my opinion that John's explanations were unconvincing" may be a spineless way of saying "John lied." Few of us can get as much mileage out of *is* and *was* as Hemingway. We depend on strong, expressive verbs to carry our meaning. To see how verb consciousness can improve writing, study the following paragraphs. The first is the original draft, the second the revision:

It seems to me that not very many people get out and exercise often enough. Looking around, wherever I go, I see people who look out of shape. For instance, the natatorium is run by a man who is 5′ 9′ tall and must weigh 300 pounds. His stomach is extremely large and full of fat. I really don't think he could swim one length of the pool. When I see someone in this condition such as his I think to myself, how uncomfortable that person must be. He is made very unattractive to others by his weight and more important an unnecessary strain is put on his heart and lungs. If he had a regular exercise program he would not be as overweight as he is and he would look and feel much better. Exercise would definitely brighten up his life.

. Few people exercise enough. Wherever I go I see people as out of shape as sacks of dirty laundry. The supervisor of the natatorium stands 5′ 9′ tall and weighs 300 pounds. His stomach is round and fat, as though he'd swallowed a beach ball. He probably couldn't swim one length of the pool. How uncomfortable he must be. Being overweight makes him unattractive to others and strains his heart and lungs unnecessarily. Exercise would reduce his weight, improve his health, and brighten his life.

Although not dazzling, the revised version is certainly tighter and more expressive than the original. The author has added two similes that brighten his idea and has also put his verbs to work. Specifically, he has moved several of them from middle position in a sentence, where they are lost among other words and phrases, to first and second position, thereby eliminating many useless introductory phrases and clauses; he has eliminated parts of the verbs *to be* and *to have* and strengthened other verbs, particularly in the final sentence; he has changed several sentences from *passive voice*, in which the subject is the receiver of the action, to *active voice*, in which the subject is the doer of the action.

Like the adjectives "good" and "interesting," passive voice has many legitimate uses. It is pointless to try to eliminate it completely. "The *New York Times* first published excerpts from the Pentagon Papers" is a sentence in active voice. "Excerpts from the Pentagon Papers were first published in the *New York Times*" is in passive voice. If we want to emphasize who did the publishing we use the first version; if we want to emphasize what was published we use the second. Nevertheless, there are several reasons for using passive voice cautiously and sparingly: (1) Active voice is dramatic because it keeps action going forward from subject to object and because it emphasizes the subject. Passive voice throws action on its back, gives it a reverse spin so to speak, and stresses the object instead of the subject; (2) Passive voice automatically introduces more words than you need. In the sample sentence above, the second version is two words longer than the first. In the student paragraph, passive voice bred clauses like rabbits; (3) Passive voice reduces an author's responsibility for what he says and also gives his statements a false sense of authority. "All memos are to be typed" is good bureaucratic passive.

SUMMARY

Because narration deals with events in time sequnce, it requires a style that can express movement, particularly urgent forward movement.

Strong active verbs are essential ("The discus *hurtled* through space and *smacked* the soft earth"; Fred *splintered* the pane of glass with his fist.") as are a generous number of simple subject-verb-object sentences. Passive voice and subordinate constructions tend to impede action and make writing sluggish. So does densely figurative language, which often calls attention to a writer's cleverness at the expense of his subject. In this section, therefore, concentrate on developing a lean, compact style that can support any load you may eventually put on it.

EXERCISES

1. Narration is action and action is verbs. The stronger the verbs the more effective the narration.

   (a) Make a list of ten common verbs (walk, talk, look) and then a second list of vigorous, expressive synonyms for each one. Write several sentences using each of the synonyms. Refer to a thesaurus if you get stuck.

   (b) Revise any piece of narrative writing you did in Section 1 by replacing all parts of the verb *to be* with strong active verbs. Do the same thing with the auxiliary *have*. Study the effects of these revisions closely.

   (c) Write a straightforward narrative account of a single dramatic incident (a fire, a fight, an automobile accident) without using any subordinate clauses, periodic constructions, or adjectival and adverbial modifiers. For example: "He tossed the pistol to Annie. She pointed it at the window. A figure moved. She pulled the trigger. Glass shattered." Write several pages in this bare, cryptic style until you develop a feel for its blunt, hard rhythms. The selections from Dickey (page 80) and Smith (page 77) may be helpful here.

   (d) Repeat the previous exercise but this time add subordinate clauses, passive voice and periodic constructions, and figurative language. How do the two versions differ? What is gained and lost by the changes?

   (e) Select any descriptive or narrative essay you have written and try to change its mood and tone by changing the structure of the sentences. If the majority of them were short, make them longer, if complex, simple, if loose, periodic.

2. (a) Think about some prolonged activity you have witnessed or participated in, such as building a cabin or riding cross-country on a bus, and recount it from beginning to end in one page. Reduce background information and narrative detail to a minimum; pack each sentence with meaning by using strong, expressive verbs, compound predicates, and absolute constructions.

   (b) Repeat the exercise, focusing now on an emotional or psychological event. Think of a time you felt threatened, for example, or were making a crucial decision about your life. How do you maintain narrative flow and coherence when you are writing about an internal event?

3. Write a brief action narrative (500 words) about some competitive activity from the point of view of a participant instead of a bystander. What would it feel like to play goal in ice hockey or drive a stock car? Pick an activity you know first-hand and try to *reproduce* your actual thoughts and sensations.

READINGS

Corsicana

Travelling south on Interstate 45, down where the Dallas skyline stands as only a glimmer against the late afternoon sky, you notice that people lead quieter lives.

Fluttering clothesline ghosts replace neon city signs and you're likely to see a horse in someone's front yard, nuzzling a patch of grass on the other side of a barbed wire and wood post fence.

Broken white highway stripes disappear under the front of the car, and if you let up a little on the gas pedal, the engine whine becomes more of a steady drone, the rolling hills don't run together quite so fast, the furrows in the fields become more distinct, and the expressions on the faces of the farmers don't flicker away before you can settle into your stare.

Trips like this are only good when the weather has settled into autumn, when the temperature is cool enough that the windows can be rolled up tight. Open a vent, and the gentle rush of the wind buffeting against the glass becomes a roar, muffling even the conversations of close friends.

Wide-hipped farm women in thin cotton dresses cup their hands over their eyes in a careless salute to a dull red sun slipping low in the pearl sky. Their stoop-backed husbands shuffle around clapboard houses, nudging sweaty brimmed hats back from their foreheads with one hand, and with the other, ruffling the necks of their rangy hounds.

Businesses aren't the slick type, here. Instead, a couple of hardware stores, Mom and Pop groceries and garages hug the narrow strips of highway that slice through the town. The local drivein restaurant is crowded with old, rusting pickup trucks, filled with browned, muscular farm hands.

But even small towns have their specialty stores, where the locals can get a taste of the exotic. Like a Stuckey's, all blue and white and fluorescent, filled with pecan logs and the most outrageously priced milkshakes Americana can offer.

Or the antique shop, an old house filled with 19th-century curios, fading photographs, broken jugs, a slightly out of tune piano with a great looking cabinet, and sun-bleached steers' heads hung in prominent display on a tall wooden fence.

When the car crawls onto the pathway, gravel spitting up from beneath the wheels, the shop's owner comes out.

He's dressed carelessly, and if you were a casting director, you'd want to give him the role of the slightly addled, kindly old geezer.

"Hahwa y'al?" he demands of no one in particular. "Fine day, ain't it?"

We answer with a 2-part chorus of noncommittal "uh huh's" and finger the quilted coverlets, smooth the dust from the vintage glass Texaco bubble, run our hands along the cold brass bedsteads.

My fellow explorer gives in to the owner's coaxing to try out the piano.

So he picks out a tinny-sounding ragtime while our host extolls the virtues of the instrument.

"It's a fine little piece of furniture. The cabinet alone is worth the price," he says in a scratchy voice.

Then he burps. Loud.

So my friend and I look at each other, roll our eyes to the ceiling, in a gesture of hopelessness, and stifle the urge to laugh.

"Y'all come on back when you're ready." Another chorus of okays, and we go back to prowling among the boy scout hats, broken picture frames and decoy ducks.

In the kitchen, three people had pulled themselves up to a bare wooden table, listening to a radio show. They shoot us sidelong glances when we whisper too long about a particular find.

On the other side of a leaded glass window is a pack of howling dogs—the owner's. And they weren't about to allow us to pet them—it was that kind of dog.

So we rapidly lose interest, pass up the vintage glass Texaco bubble, the quilts, the brass beds, even the sun-bleached steers' heads. The owner calls out a twangy farewell, and bids us come back "Next time you get down this way from up there in Dallas."

Back into the car, adjusting our newly bought straw cowboy hats, we settle into the ride home.

If you blur your eyes, and look at the hills, you could be anywhere, even the St. Vrain Valley if your imagination was vivid enough to conjure up the Rockies to the west.

And the steady drone of the engine became more of a whine, and the wind rushing through the open vent muffles even the conversations of close friends.

Jan Carroll

From *Listening To America*

ON THE ROAD IN EAST TEXAS

I turned north up the Texas forest trail and headed for Marshall, my home town, in the northeast corner of the state. There were still two hours of daylight in the sky when my eye was drawn to a large crowd in the football stadium of the high school in Kirbyville, an inconspicuous but pleasant little town of about two thousand surrounded by piny woods. Deciding to investigate, I found a parking place among the pickup trucks and the yellow schoolbuses and joined the throng in the "Home of the Kirbyville Wildcats." The meeting turned out to be the annual gathering of the Jasper-Newton Rural Electric Cooperative. From all over the two counties families had come for an evening of food, entertainment, and progress reports. There were four generations in some families. Grandmothers with faces like hard pastry dipped snuff while their false teeth clicked, and tall pubescent boys in high-heeled boots sneaked away to the schoolbuses for a smoke. I observed that down here women over forty seem to have abandoned girdles as women under forty have abandoned bras in New York. The men pushed straw stetsons back on their heads and talked about the one subject that farmers always talk about: the weather.

And there was food—four long tables of barbecued chicken, beef, baked beans with thick juice like melted jelly, raw onions and pickles, home-made fried pies. I picked up an empty plate and someone slapped half a pound of sliced beef on it. Kids were throwing scraps under the stadium to the fattest, sleekest country red dog I have ever seen, the kind of dog that travels from one REA affair to another in the summer and sleeps it off all winter.

"Where you goin'?" a woman inquired of her husband.

"Git me 'nother one of them fried pies."

"Lord, Farrell, you done had three."

"Yeah, but I didn't eat but two helpin's' beef."

Ten years ago there would have been no Negroes here. They were abundantly present tonight. One white child and a middle-aged black woman reached at the same time for the spoon in the beans. The little girl looked up and her mother said: "Say you're sorry, honey." She did.

In the middle of the football field a flatbed trailer had been parked, decorated with green and gold crepe paper. The mayor of Kirbyville tapped on the microphone, looked around the field, and said: "Folks say things never happen around here but they sure can't say that tonight."

Another man introduced visitors and especially welcomed home "Mr. Willie Whitehead, who moved to Conroe and has come back to be with us tonight." Conroe is about a hundred miles to the west. Whistling and clapping, the crowd seemed happy to see Willie Whitehead again.

Mrs. Lilly Walker—I think that is what the mayor called her—had arranged the program for the evening, and the first performer was a preacher who sang "Galveston." The man sitting in front of me said: "Glen Campbell wrote that one." His wife replied: "I'd give two of my blackberry pies to see Glen Campbell in person."

Brother Jess Harper, Jackie Harper, and Betty Bass sang and played "Jesus is Coming Soon" and "Jesus, I Believe What You Say" on the piano and the electric bass guitar. Brother Harper then told the audience: "It's not exactly Western and it's not exactly a hymn, so we're going to sing a country Western gospel song, Johnny Cash's 'Papa Sing Bass.' "

After their final number Brother Harper asked the people to stand and sing the national anthem. "Everybody now," he said. "I want to see everybody sing. I was in the position for about eleven months where it was forbidden to sing this song and I'd like to hear everybody sing it like you appreciate it." It has been a long time since I have heard an audience sing the national anthem with so much enthusiasm.

While the co-op members went about their business I sought Brother

Jess Harper behind the platform. A tall man with a distinguished mustache, he wore a dark blue shirt, a white tie, and a blue tie pin. I asked him where he had been during those eleven months when he could not sing "The Star-Spangled Banner."

"I was in a stalag in northern Poland. Got there by being marched for three months, three miserable months. Until recently I couldn't sing that song without choking up. Now, I'm not in accord with everything that's going on in this country but I still think we got to believe some of them folks in Washington know what they are doing. This isn't a perfect country and the government is made up of just folks, but I tell you—this is still a mighty good place to live."

What about the kids?

"They don't know, the ones who're spitting on the flag. They just don't know what price some folks have paid for it. They don't know what it stands for when we might have lost it. I don't hate 'em—they're our kids. But they're wrong when they spit at the flag and try to tear the country down instead of trying to change it 'n make it better. Better to light a candle than to curse the darkness, I say. You spend eleven months in a stalag, Mister, and that song means something to you."

Bill Moyers

Carry Nation

A deafening medley of voices that merged into a terrific "Hurrah for Carry Nation!" A mob of thousands, beating this way and that, tearing, trampling each other for a sight of that squat, determined little figure, marching on with the exaltation of a conquering hero, and the Kansas Smasher was steered straight into the arms of three burly New York policemen and promptly "pinched."

It happened at Devery's corner, Twenty-eighth Street and Eighth Avenue, at 5:30 yesterday afternoon. The dauntless Carry unmolested had:

Precipitated a riot in three saloons.

Invaded two Sunday concert halls.

Paraded the highways and byways with a tumultuous rabble at her heels.

It was only when she invaded the district of the Big Chief that the arm of the law became effective.

"I am not disturbing the peace," asserted Mrs. Nation indignantly, whisking about in her Quakerish linen gown with its quaint cape, and fixing on the bluecoats an invincible eye.

"You are raising a crowd and creating a riot, and I arrest you," was the response of one of her captors, while the two others closed in about her and the procession started for the West Twentieth Street Station.

At Twenty-fourth Street, satisfied by Mrs. Nation's friends that she was about to return to her hotel, the policemen released her and put her on a car amid a volley of "Hurrahs!"

Mrs. Nation arrived from Danbury, Illinois, at 9:30 yesterday morning to fulfill her lecture engagement at Carnegie Hall last night. She went immediately to the Victoria Hotel, loudly declaring that she had traveled in a "saloon on wheels."

Giving herself only time to exchange her linen duster for a fresh white piqué frock (plain in cut and finished with the invariable cape, with a small hatchet in her buttonhole) and fortifying herself with a service at the Cathedral, the crusader started out to purify New York. With characteristic directness she went straight to the Democratic Club.

"I want to get in," she said to the servant who barred her path.

"No ladies admitted!"

"But I want to see a member who can admit me," went on the imperturbable Carry, while a crowd gathered about the steps.

"I'm one, madam," from an elderly gentleman just inside the door, "and I repeat it is against the rules."

"Break 'em," responded the Smasher, one foot on the threshold.

The Superintendent rushed forward to the rescue.

"Have you got anything in here you don't want me to see? I would like to hold a Sunday-school lesson and a Bible reading in here."

"The club was not organized for that purpose," put in the Superintendent hastily.

"Don't you know," and she pushed her way past, only to be politely thrust out again, "that God said it isn't good for men to be alone?"

"Who are you, madam?" in wrathful tones.

"I'm Carry Nation, and I tell you that this must be a mighty bad place if you can't let a woman in."

At Fiftieth Street and Seventh Avenue Mrs. Nation saw the side door of a saloon open, and dashed in, attended by a crowd that filled the place.

"Oh me! Oh my!" she cried, making way for the "barkeep," who, paralyzed with terror at the unexpected onslaught, turned a sickly white.

"Look at him! Look at his white face! Nervous, ain't you?" and with a gleeful laugh Carry launched out for a bottle of whisky and raised it to hurl it to the floor, but the man was too quick for her, and disarmed, she turned to the loungers drinking at the tables.

"Ain't you 'shamed, boy, to be drinking up what you ought to give to your family?" she inquired from a bulletheaded youth.

"Ain't got none," was the laconic reply.

"Give her a highball, Peter, and I'll stand treat," cried a voice from the rear before the employees of the place could come to their senses and endeavor to clear the place.

The Smasher's progress down Broadway after this escapade was a veritable triumphal procession.

A short luncheon, and Mrs. Nation was in fine fettle for her afternoon campaign.

"Take me to some more hellholes," she demanded of her escort. Darting into a saloon at Twenty-ninth Street and Sixth Avenue, she cried:

"Ain't this against the law? Where are the police? I am Carry Nation, and I protest against the selling of that hell broth."

"We are selling lemonade," insisted the barkeeper.

"Lemonade!" echoed the reformer scornfully. "It's beer!" and walking over to a table where some sailors were drinking, she seized one of the steins and took a sip. "I know the taste of beer as well as you do, and you men are disgracing Uncle Sam's uniform every drop you drink."

At Thirty-first Street and Sixth Avenue she effected an entrance and intrepidly faced the danger of a rough handling.

Her further progress was "tipped off." Wide-open places were mysteriously closed at a moment's notice, and the Smasher was confronted by a series of closed doors, with anxious faces peeping from behind drawn curtains.

Half a dozen times en route she was obliged to take a car to escape the crowds, but her enthusiasm never flagged, and while her escort lagged and faltered she never turned a hair.

At the Apollo Music Garden—the French quarter of Eighth Avenue, with a legend that reads *Entrée libre en Café Chantant*—she went in search of women sinners, but quiet reigned and an irritable proprietor turned her out of his "private house."

Further down she investigated The Abbey, No. 416, another music hall, with similar results. It was here that the crowds running from every direction swelled into a mighty sea of humanity that brought about her encounter with the police.

Mrs. Nation did not confine her attention to the saloon abuse and cigarettes. She discovered in the lobby of the Victoria Hotel a subject for her hatchet that roused her to fury.

"Look at that image," she cried, pointing to a figure of Diana, clothed simply in a bow and arrow—"she ain't got a thing on. Where's the hotel proprietor?"—and she rushed up to the desk.

"There's a woman over there," she announced to the astonished clerk, "without any apparel on her. It ain't respectable. Would you like your wife to see that?" pointing an accusing finger. "Now, I'd like you to put a little something on her right away or there may be a little 'hatchetation' around here."

The clerk hurriedly promised the matter should be looked to, and Carry retired to rest for her lecture.

Corsets came in for her denunciation from the platform of Carnegie, where her talk was constantly interrupted by shouts of laughter, storms of applause, and audible comment. She bade girls avoid making their "hearts and livers into one solid lump." She likened herself to Moses, who, she said, was the first smasher when he broke up the golden calf.

⊙

Today she goes to Steeplechase Park, Coney Island, and will make the Bowery her chief concern while here.

New York *World*, September 2, 1901

From *Report From Engine Co. 82*

As I slide the pole the bells come in—Box 4746—Prospect Avenue and Crotona Park East. It's a job. The telephone alarm and the location give me a feeling that we'll have a worker. It's like a sixth sense.

It is 8:20 P.M. As we turn up Prospect Avenue we can smell the smoke. There is only one smell like this: burning paint, plaster, and wood. We can see the smoke banking down on the avenue before us, but we can't see the fire yet. Ladder 31 is right behind us, so we know we will get the ventilation we need.

As we turn the corner at Crotona Park we can see the fire. Flames are licking out of eight windows on the third and fourth floors of a six-story tenement. There must have been a delayed alarm, and I imagine people alerting other people—alerting everyone but the Fire Department. There is a crowd of people on the sidewalk. Some are in nightclothes. Some are barefoot. Many are simply interested passersby. People are still rushing out of the building, crying, sobbing, or just sullen.

We have to take the heavy two-and-a-half-inch hose for a body of fire like this. Jim Stack takes the nozzle again, and the first length, I take the second, and Carroll the third. Vinny and Carmine head for the mask compartment. *"Take off!"*

People are screaming that there are people trapped on the fifth floor. They are angry and confused because we are not paying any attention to them. They haven't seen Ladder 31 go into the building. But we know if there is a rescue to be made, Ladder 31 will make it.

As we start to hump the hose into the building I notice that Jerry Herbert has already raised the aerial ladder to a fifth-floor window. Richie Rittman and Billy-o are climbing up it.

The lights in the building have blown, and Captain Albergray guides us up the stairs with his portable lamp. He tells us that Chief Niebrock has ordered a second alarm. We'll need the extra help.

We reach the second floor and flake out the hose. We go to the top of the stairs at the third-floor landing. The whole front half of the building is on fire. The flames are in the hallway and shooting up the stairs to the fourth floor.

We have to wait now for the water to come through the hose. It's getting hotter, and Captain Albergray tells us to back halfway down the stairs.

Jim turns to me and Benny, and says, "When we get water we'll hit the hallway and then make a left into the first apartment. It's going to be a hard bend, so keep the hose low. I don't know how far we'll be able to go, but we'll try."

Captain Albergray says, "All right Jim, but don't push too fast. The goddam fire must be through the roof by now, so we'll be here for hours anyway."

We can hear the water gushing through the line. As it reaches the nozzle, Jim says, "Let's go," and he moves up the stairs with us humping the hose behind. I can see Engine 45 moving up the stairs below us with another line. I tell them to move in on the second apartment as soon as they get water, but my words are unnecessary. They'll be there.

It is starting to get smoky now that the water is on the fire. The fire in the hallway goes out quickly. We are putting 250 gallons of water per minute on it. Jim makes the landing, and fights with the hose as he makes the bend. Captain Albergray is next to him. "Beautiful. Easy now. Keep low. Beautiful," he is saying. Carroll and I are behind pulling on the hose to take the strain off Jim's arms. The heat in the walls is radiating out, and my body is dripping and my clothes are saturated with perspiration.

I put my mouth to the floor in an attempt to breathe cool air, and suddenly my throat hurts, like it does after a two-day drunk and a thousand cigarettes. I must have taken in some super-heated air. I forgot about the second apartment. The fire lapping out of it has lit up the hallway again.

"Hey Jim," I shout, "you better turn the line, or else we're going to get caught between it."

Jim struggles to turn the line again, and he hits the fire in the hall. He moves a foot or so into the apartment.

Captain Albergray says, coolly, "The ceiling is down, Jim, and the floor upstairs is beginning to go. Watch it, 'cause it'll come down in pieces."

"Well, let's try to move in just a little more," says Jim. "Then maybe I can hit that room on the left." We push the line in a few feet, and Jim yells, "Ahh, ahh, your mother's ass. . . ." Part of the floor above has given way.

Jim is on his knees, and he wants desperately to get out of the apartment, but he knows better than to shut the nozzle down in a fire like this. The water is our only protection. So I crawl up fast, and take the nozzle from Jim. Vinny and Carmine are down on the floor now. Their masks will make it easier to fight this fire. Vinny takes the nozzle, and I back downstairs to get a mask. Jim is already in the street breathing the clear air heavily. He has multiple burns on the ears, neck, and shoulders. I put my arm around his waist, and say, "You did a beautiful job Jim—like always."

Jim attempts a weak smile, and replies, "It couldn't have been too beautiful, the fire's not out yet, is it?" I laugh a little, and run to the pumper for the masks. I pass a leaking hose connection, and bend low for a drink of water, but I can't swallow. I spit the water out. Valenzio has taken out two masks for me. I put mine on, and throw the other over my shoulder for Captain Albergray.

The second alarm companies are in now. Hose lines—spaghetti—all over the street, up the adjoining building, up the fire escapes, up the aerial ladder. Some are bulging with water, and some haven't yet been charged.

As I return to my company I pass Carroll on the stairs. "What's up, Benny?" I ask.

"I got a goddam cinder down my glove. The back of my hand is all blistered, so I'll have to take up for a while." He sounds defeated.

"Take care of yourself," I murmur as I continue up the stairs. I feel sorry for Benny, because I know he wouldn't leave the action for a burned hand, not unless Captain Albergray ordered him down.

I meet the company on the third-floor landing. They were pushed back. Captain Albergray backs down the stairs a little to put his mask on. Carmine is on the nozzle now, and I ask him how they were pushed out of the apartment. He tells me that Engine 45 had water pressure trouble, and they had to shut down their line. The fire then got into the hall again, and my company was caught between the two fires. A fundamental rule in this business is never to let the fire get behind you, so 82 had to fight their way back to the hall stairs.

I take the nozzle, and tell Carmine to "take a blow." The nob is heavy, and the back pressure makes my arms strain. I know I won't lose control of it though, because Vinny has a firm grip on the hose behind me. We are now keeping the fire inside the two apartments. At least it hasn't crossed the hall.

Engine 45 gets pressure in its line again, and returns to the landing. The fire is now spreading throughout both floors above us.

We yell to Engine 45 to take the second apartment again, and Engine 73 passes us as it humps its hose to the fourth floor. It is still ash hot, but the masks make it a lot easier to breathe. We are now at the door of the first apartment, and Engine 45 is at the second. We move in a little, and 45 moves in. Captain Albergray is next to me, and I say, "The only way to put this fire out is to move in on it. Otherwise, we'll be here all night."

"We're gonna be here all night anyway, so take it slow," he answers.

Vinny moves up and takes the nozzle, and Carmine moves behind Vinny. Deputy Chief Kelsen is on the scene now. He calls the Captain on the walkie-talkie and Albergray tells him our position and progress. Chief Kelsen tells him to hold the position, and not to take any unnecessary risks. We have advanced five feet into the apartment. The fire is burning freely overhead in front of us, and we watch it closely, as closely as anyone would want to watch a fire. We have killed a good part of it in the room on the left, but we can't get it all unless we move up a few feet. But we can't move up because of the fire overhead. We don't want to get directly underneath it. God knows what will fall.

Suddenly, the fire starts pushing in at us. It's coming hard, and our line can't hold it back. We know what it is. A company has opened a line from the front fire escape, and they are pushing the fire toward us. We have to retreat to the hall again. Captain Albergray calls the Chief on the walkie-talkie, and asks him to have that line shut down. In a minute the order is given, and the fire lets up. We can move in once more.

Carmine takes the nozzle from Vinny, and I move behind Carmine. We know now that we'll have to drown this fire, not attack it, and we try to get in the most comfortable position possible. Carmine sits on his heels, and I kneel on both knees.

We start to get sprayed with rebounding water. Engine 73 is above us, and trying to move in. Carmine leans over, puts one hand on top of his helmet, and starts shaking his head. He doesn't say anything, but his head still shakes.

"What's wrong, Carmine?" I ask.

"I think I got burned."

"Where?"

"On the neck."

I ask Captain Albergray for his lamp. Carmine is still moving the nozzle back and forth. I move his helmet up, and pull back his coat. "You did get burned, Carmine. It's all blistered already, about three inches long. It must have been an ember."

Carmine moves out, and Vinny takes the nob. I try to think of something funny to say to Captain Albergray. I can tell that he doesn't feel too happy. "Your company is slowly diminishing, Cap," I say. "Pretty soon there won't be any more Engine 82."

He smiles resignedly, and says, "It's just one of those things. Look at the great job we did earlier. No one got hurt there. This is just one of those fires. They happen from time to time, that's all."

The fire has darkened down. Chief Kelsen calls on the walkie-talkie: "Engine 82, I'm sending Engine 88 to relieve you. Report to me in front of the fire building."

We don't mind giving the line to Engine 88, because it's only a question of holding the position now, and keeping water on the fire. We did our job. The pressure is off and we walk down the stairs to a well-needed break.

Dennis Smith

From *Deliverance*

Everything around me changed. I put my left arm between the bowstring and the bow and slid the bow back over my shoulder with the broadheads turned down. Then I walked to the gorge side and put a hand on it, the same hand that had been cut by the arrow in the river, as though I might be able to feel what the whole cliff was like, the whole problem, and hold it in my palm. The rock was rough, and a part of it fell away under my hand. The river sound loudened as though the rocks in the channel had shifted their positions. Then it relaxed and the extra sound died or went away again into the middle distance, the middle of the stream.

I knew that was the sign, and I backed off and ran with a hard scramble at the bank, and stretched up far enough to get an elbow over the top side of the first low overhang. Scraping my sides and legs, I got up on it and stood up. Bobby and Lewis were directly beneath me, under a roof of stone, and might as well not have been there. I was standing in the most entire aloneness that I had ever been given.

My heart expanded with joy at the thought of where I was and what I was doing. There was a new light on the water; the moon was going up and up, and I stood watching the stream with my back to the rock for a few minutes, not thinking of anything, with a deep feeling of nakedness and helplessness and intimacy.

I turned around with many small foot movements and leaned close to the cliff, taking on its slant exactly. I put my cheek against it and raised both hands up into the darkness, letting the fingers crawl independently over the soft rock. It was this softness that bothered me more than anything else; I was afraid that anything I would stand on or hold to would give way. I got my right hand placed in what felt like a crack, and began to feel with my left toes for something, anything. There was an unevenness—a bulge—in the rock and I kicked at it and worried it to see how solid it was, then put my foot on it and pulled hard with my right arm.

I rose slowly off the top of the overhang, the bow dropping back further over my left shoulder—which made it necessary to depend more on my right arm than my left—got my right knee and then my foot into some kind of hole. I settled as well as I could into my new position and began to feel upward again. There was a bulge to the left, and I worked toward it, full of wonder at the whole situation.

The cliff was not as steep as I had thought, though from what I had been able to tell earlier, before we spilled, it would probably get steeper toward the top. If I had turned loose it would have been a slide rather than a fall back down to the river or the overhang, and this reassured me a little—though not much—as I watched it happen in my mind.

I got to the bulge and then went up over it and planted my left foot solidly on it and found a good hold on what felt like a root with my right hand. I looked down.

The top of the overhang was pale now, ten or twelve feet below. I turned and forgot about it, pulling upward, kneeing and toeing into the cliff, kicking steps into the shaly rock wherever I could, trying to position both hands and one foot before moving to a new position. Some of the time I could do this, and each time my confidence increased. Often I could only get one handhold and a foothold, or two handholds. Once I could only get one handhold, but it was a strong one, and I scrambled and shifted around it until I could get a toe into the rock and pull up.

The problem-interest of it absorbed me at first, but I began to notice that the solutions were getting harder and harder: the cliff was starting to shudder in my face and against my chest. I became aware of the sound of my breath, whistling and humming crazily into the stone: the cliff was steepening, and I was laboring backbreakingly for every inch. My arms were tiring and my calves were not so much trembling as jumping. I knew now that not looking down or back—the famous advice to people climbing things—was going to enter into it. Panic was getting near me. Not as near as it might have been, but near. I concentrated everything I had to become ultrasensitive to the cliff, feeling it more gently than before, though I was shaking badly. I kept inching up. With each shift to a newer and higher position I felt more and more tenderness toward the wall.

Despite everything, I looked down. The river had spread flat and filled with moonlight. It took up the whole of space under me, bearing in the center of itself a long coiling image of light, a chill, bending flame. I must have been seventy-five or a hundred feet above it, hanging poised over some kind of inescapable glory, a bright pit.

I turned back into the cliff and leaned my mouth against it, feeling all the way out through my nerves and muscles exactly how I had possession of the wall at four random points in a way that held the whole thing together.

It was about this time that I thought of going back down, working along the bank and looking for an easier way up, and I let one foot down behind me into the void. There was nothing. I stood with the foot groping for a hold in the air, then pulled it back to the place on the cliff where it had been. It burrowed in like an animal, and I started up again.

I caught something—part of the rock—with my left hand and started to pull. I could not rise. I let go with my right hand and grabbed the wrist of the left, my left-hand fingers shuddering and popping with weight. I got one toe into the cliff, but that was all I could do. I looked up and held on. The wall was giving me nothing. It no longer sent back any pressure against me. Something I had come to rely on had been taken away, and that was it. I was hanging, but just barely. I concentrated all my strength into the fingers of my left hand, but they were leaving me. I was on the perpendicular part of the cliff, and unless I could get over it soon I would just peel off the wall. I had what I thought of as a plan if this should happen; this was to kick out as strongly as I could from the cliff face and try to get clear of the overhang and out into the river, into the bright coiling of the pit. But even if I cleared the rocks, the river was probably shallow near the bank where I would land, and it would be about as bad as if I were to hit the rocks. And I would have to get rid of the bow.

I held on. By a lot of small tentative maneuvers I swapped hands in the crevice and touched upward with my left hand, weighted down by the bow hanging over my shoulder, along the wall, remembering scenes in movies where a close-up of a hand reaches desperately for something, through a prison grate for a key, or from quicksand toward someone or something on solid ground. There was nothing there. I swapped hands again and tried the wall to my right. There was nothing. I tried the loose foot, hoping that if I could get a good enough foothold, I could get up enough to explore a little more of the wall with my hands, but I couldn't find anything there either, though I searched as far as I could with the toe and the knee, up and down and back and forth. The back of my left leg was shaking badly. My mind began to speed up, in the useless energy of panic. The urine in my bladder turned solid and painful, and then ran with a delicious sexual voiding like a wet dream, something you can't help or be blamed for. There was nothing to do but fall. The last hope I had was that I might awaken.

I was going, but anger held me up a little longer. I would have done something desperate if I had had a little more mobility, but I was practically nailed in one position; there was nothing desperate I could do. Yet I knew that if I were going to try something, I had better do it now.

I hunched down into what little power was left in my left leg muscles and drove as hard as it was possible for me to do; harder than it was possible. With no holds on the cliff, I fought with the wall for anything I could make it give me. For a second I tore at it with both hands. In a flash inside a flash I told myself not to double up my fists but to keep my hands open. I was up against a surface as smooth as monument stone, and I still believe that for a space of time I was held in the air by pure will, fighting an immense rock.

Then it seemed to spring a crack under one finger of my right hand; I thought surely I had split the stone myself. I thrust in other fingers and hung and, as I did, I got the other hand over, feeling for a continuation of the crack; it was there. I had both hands in the cliff to the palms, and strength from the stone flowed into me. I pulled up as though chinning on a sill and swung a leg in. I got the middle section of my body into the crevice as well, which was the hardest part to provide for, as it had been everywhere else. I wedged into the crack like a lizard, not able to get far enough in. As I flattened out on the floor of the crevice, with all my laborious verticality gone, the bow slid down my arm and I hooked upward just in time to stop it with my wrist. I pulled it into the cliff with me, the broadheads at my throat.

With my cheek on one shoulder, I lay there on my side in the crevice, facing out, not thinking about anything, solid on one side with stone and open to the darkness on the other, as though I were in a sideways grave. The glass of the bow was cold in my hands, cold and familiar. The curves were beautiful to the touch, a smooth chill flowing, and beside the curves the arrow lay—or stood—rigidly, the feathers bristling when I moved a little, and the points pricking at me. But it was good pain; it was reality, and deep in the situation. I simply lay in nature, my pants' legs warm and sopping with my juices, not cold, not warm, but in a kind of hovering. Think, I said, think. But I could not. I won't think yet; I don't have to for a while. I closed my eyes and spoke some words, and they seemed to make sense, but were out of place. I believe I was saying something about some back advertising Thad and I were not in agreement on, but it might not have been that at all; there is no way to tell.

The first words I really remember were said very clearly. What a view. *What* a view. But I had my eyes closed. The river was running in my mind, and I raised my lids and saw exactly what had been the image of my thought. For a second I did not know what I was seeing and what I was imagining; there was such an utter sameness that it didn't matter; both were the river. It spread there eternally, the moon so huge on it that it hurt the eyes, and the mind, too, flinched like an eye. What? I said. Where? There was nowhere but here. Who, though? Unknown. Where can I start?

You can start with the bow, and work slowly into the situation, working back and working up. I held the bow as tightly as I could, coming by degrees into the realization that I was going to have to risk it again, before much longer. But not now. Let the river run.

And let the moonlight come down for a little while. I had the bow and I had one good arrow and another one I might risk on a short shot. The thought struck me with my full adrenaline supply, all hitting the veins at once. Angelic. Angelic. Is that what it means? It very likely does. And I have a lot of nylon rope, and a long knife that was held at my throat and stuck by a murderer in the tree beside my head. It is not in the tree now; it is at my side. It is not much duller for having been in the river, and if I wanted to shave hair with it, I could. Does it still hurt, where that woods rat, that unbelievable redneck shaved across me with it? I felt my chest, and it hurt. Good. Good. Am I ready? No. No. Not yet, Gentry. It doesn't have to be yet. But soon.

It was easy to say I don't understand, and I did say it. But that was not really relevant. It just came down to where I was, and what I was doing there. I was not much worried. I was about 150 feet over the river, as nearly as I could tell, and I believed that if I could get that far I could get the rest of the way, even though the cliff was steeper here than it was lower down. Let me look, now. That is all there is to do, right at this moment. That is all there is to do, and that is all that needs to be done.

What a view, I said again. The river was blank and mindless with beauty. It was the most glorious thing I have ever seen. But it was not seeing, really. For once it was not just seeing. It was beholding. I *beheld* the river in its icy pit of brightness, in its far-below sound and indifference, in its large coil and tiny points and flashes of the moon, in its long sinuous form, in its uncomprehending consequence. What was there?

Only that terrific brightness. Only a couple of rocks as big as islands, around one of which a thread of scarlet seemed to go, as though outlining a face, a kind of god, a layout for an ad, a sketch, an element of design. It was a thread like the color of sun-images underneath the eyelids. The rock quivered like a coal, because I wanted it to quiver, held in its pulsing border, and what it was pulsing with was me. It might have looked something like my face, in one of those photographs lit up from underneath. My face: why not? I can have it as I wish: a kind of three-quarter face view, set in the middle of the moon-pit, that might have looked a little posed or phony, but was yet different from what any mirror could show. I thought I saw the jaw set, breathing with the river and the stone, but it might also have been a smile of some kind. I closed my eyes and opened them again, and the thread around the rock was gone, but it had been there. I felt better; I felt wonderful, and fear was at the center of the feeling: fear and anticipation—there was no telling where it would end.

I turned back. I turned back to the wall and the cliff, and into my situation, trying to imagine how high the cliff had seemed to be the last time I had seen it by daylight, and trying to estimate where I was on it. I thought I surely must be three quarters of the way up. I believed I could stand upright in the crevice, and this would give me three or four more feet.

Why not? Was there a bulge above me? If I could get on top of that, who knows what might not be possible? I let my hand go up, and it felt the top of the crevice. What are you sending me? I said. It feels good. It feels like something I might be able to work up on top of, if I went to the left, and took one moment of pure death. There is going to be that moment, but that is not bad. I have had so many in the past few hours: so many decisions, so many fingers groping over this insignificant, unwatched cliff, so many muscles straining against the stone.

Where was Drew? He used to say, in the only interesting idea I had ever heard him deal with, that the best guitar players were blind men: men like Reverend Gary Davis and Doc Watson and Brownie McGhee, who had developed the sense of touch beyond what a man with eyes could do. I have got something like that, I said. I have done what I have done, I have got up here mostly by the sense of touch, and in the dark.

Are they below? Is Lewis still twisting into the sand? Is Bobby sitting on the rock beside him trying to think what to do? Is his head in his hands? Or has his jaw set, believing that we can all get out, even now?

Who knows that? But we have laid a plan, and that is all we have been able to do. If that doesn't work, we will probably all be killed, or if I can get back down the cliff when nothing happens, we will all just go a few miles downriver in the canoe, take a few days in the city to recover, report Drew as drowned and get back into the long, declining routine of our lives. But we were cast in roles, and first we must do something about them.

I was a killer. There were deaths involved: one certain murder and probably another. I had the cold glass of the bow in my hand, and I was lying belly-up in a crevice in a cliff above a river, and it could be that everything was with me.

I could get there, in my mind. The whole thing focused, like an old movie that just barely held its own on the screen. The top of the gorge was wild and overgrown and lumpy, and I remembered it also thickly wooded. I wanted to give myself something definite to do when I got to the top, and lying there, I tried to fix on what would be the best thing and the first thing to do when I got there.

I had to admit it: I thought that there was really no danger involved, at least from anything human. I didn't actually believe that the man who had shot Drew would stay around all night for another shot at us, or that he would come back in the early light, either. But then I remembered what I had told Bobby, and I was troubled again. *If it were me* was the main thing I thought. I went over everything in my mind, and as far as I could tell, I was right. There was a lot more reason for him to kill the rest of us than there was for him to let us go. We were all acting it out.

I turned. Well, I said to the black stone at my face, when I get to the top the first thing I'll do will be not to think of Martha and Dean again, until I see them. And then I'll go down to the first stretch of calm water and take a look around before it gets light. When I finish that, I'll make a circle inland, very quiet, and look for him like I'm some kind of an animal. What kind? It doesn't matter, as long as I'm quiet and deadly. I could be a snake. Maybe I can kill him in his sleep. That would be the easiest thing to do, but could I do it? How? With the bow? Or would I put the hardware store knife through him? Could I do it? Or would I like to do it? I asked this.

But the circling—what about that? If I got too far from the river, and the sound of the river, I would almost surely lose myself. And then what? A circle? *What* circle? What principle guides you, when you try to make a circle—a *circle*—in the woods? I didn't have it. Suppose I got inland from the river far enough to lose track of myself? Had I shot the whole thing, right there?

But I could see myself killing, because I had no real notion I would have to. If he was close to the cliff edge, as he would at some place and time have to be, the high-rising sound of water would help me get close enough to him for a killing shot. I wanted to kill him exactly as Lewis had killed the other man: I wanted him to suspect nothing at all until the sudden terrible pain in his chest that showed an arrow through him from behind, come from anywhere.

Oh what a circle, I thought. All in the woods, with the leaves waiting, the wind waiting, for me to draw it. That is leaving too much to chance. It won't work, I knew as I considered it. It will never work.

What then, art director? Graphics consultant? What is the layout? It is this: to shoot him from behind, somewhere on the top of the gorge. He almost certainly would get himself into the prone position in order to shoot down onto the river. There are these various kinds of concentration. While he was deep in his kind, I would try to get within twenty or thirty feet of him and put my one good arrow through his lower rib cage—for what would save the shot would be exactness—and then fall back and run for it into the woods, and sit down and wait until he had time enough to die.

That was as far ahead as I could think. In a way, it seemed already settled. It was settled as things in daydreams always are, but it could be settled only because the reality was remote. It was the same state of mind I had had when I had hunted the deer in the fog. These were worthy motions I was going through, but only motions, and it was shocking to remind myself that if I came on him with the rifle I would have to carry them through or he would kill me.

I slid farther into the crack to draw from the stone a last encouragement, but I was already tired of being there. It would be best to stand up and get on with it.

I got on one knee and went cautiously outward, rising slowly with both hands palm-up on the underside of the fissure top. I was up, slanting backward, and I felt along and around the bulge over my head. To the right there was nothing I could do, but I was glad to be back. To the left the crevice went on beyond where I could reach, and the only thing to do was to edge along it, sidestepping inch by inch until only my toes, very tired again, were in the crack. But I was able to straighten from my back-leaning position to an upright one—really upright—and then to lean surprisingly forward at the waist, as I edged to the left. This was unexpected and exhilarating. The stone came back at me strong. I got on the rock with my knees instead of my toes and fingertips, and had a new body position. With it, I wormed. I went to the left and then to the right, and the river-pit blazed. It was slow going, for the handholds were not good, and the broadheads gored me under the arms a good deal, but there was a trembling and near-perfect balance between gravity—or my version of it—and the slant of the stone: I was at the place where staying on the wall and falling canceled each other out in my body, yet were slightly in favor of my staying where I was, and edging up. Time after time I lay there sweating, having no handhold or foothold, the rubber of my toes bending back against the soft rock, my hands open. Then I would begin to try to inch upward again, moving with the most intimate motions of my body, motions I had never dared use with Martha, or with any other human woman. Fear and a kind of enormous moonblazing sexuality lifted me, millimeter by millimeter. And yet I held madly to the human. I looked for a slice of gold like the model's in the river: some kind of freckle, something lovable, in the huge serpent-shape of light.

Above me the darks changed, and in one of them was a star. On both sides of that small light the rocks went on up, black and solid as ever, but their power was broken. The high, deadly part of the cliff I was on bent and rocked steadily over toward life, and toward the hole with the star in it, where, as I went, more stars were added until a constellation like a crown began to form. I was now able to travel on knees—my knees after all—the bow scraping the ground beside me.

I was crying. What reason? There was not any, for I was really not ashamed or terrified; I was just there. But I lay down against the cliff to get my eyesight cleared. I turned and propped on my elbow like a tourist, and looked at it again. Lord, Lord. The river hazed and danced into the sparkle of my eyelashes, the more wonderful for being unbearable. This was something; it was something.

But eventually you have to turn back to your knees, and on cliffs they carry you better than any other part of the body, on cliffs of a certain slant; I got on my knees.

It was painful, but I was going. I was crawling, but it was no longer necessary to make love to the cliff, to fuck it for an extra inch or two in the moonlight, for I had some space between me and it. If I was discreet, I could offer a kick or two, even, and get away with it.

My feet slanted painfully in one direction or another. Guided by what kind of guesswork I could not say, I kept scrambling and stumbling upward like a creature born on the cliff and coming home. Often a hand or foot would slide and then catch on something I knew, without knowing, would be there, and I would go on up. There was nothing it could do against me, in the end; there was nothing it could do that I could not match, and, in the twinkling of some kind of eye-beat. I was going.

By some such way as this, I got into a little canyon. Yes, and I stood up. I could not see much, but it *felt* like the little draw where I had hunted the deer in the fog. The bottom underfoot—under *foot*—was full of loose rocks and boulders, but I was walking it. At each shoulder, the walls were wanting to come down, but they did not. Instead, they started to fill with bushes and small, ghostly, dense trees. These were solid, and I came up to them, little by little. Then their limbs were above me. I was out.

James Dickey

4 | Journals

To set down choice experiences that my own writings may inspire me and at last I may make wholes of parts. Certainly it is a distinct profession to rescue from oblivion and to fix the sentiments and thoughts which visit all men more or less generally, that the contemplation of the unfinished picture may suggest its harmonious completion. . . . Thoughts accidentally thrown together become a frame in which more may be developed and exhibited. Perhaps this is the main value of a habit of writing, of keeping a journal—that so we remember our best hours and stimulate ourselves.

Thoreau

Most people make notes from time to time on their travels, reading, friendships, business activities, dreams; those who do it regularly usually keep journals. Insofar as they are arranged chronologically journals are a type of narrative, but insofar as their internal structure is really determined by the meanderings of one writer's mind they are a species of autobiography, a device for exploring our lives and explaining ourselves to ourselves. The first and perhaps only "rule" about keeping a journal is that it be honest and your own, meaning that it should be a record of your responses to what happened, not a résumé of *what* happened:

> *September 21, 1974* Up at six. Toast, scrambled eggs, and coffee for breakfast. Skimmed the morning paper. Red Sox beat the Orioles 5–2. Raining as I trudged off to psychology class to find out that I'd made a D on the first exam. Lunch with Karen at HoJo's. Saw the latest James Bond flick at the Gemini after my lab. Fish sticks and two cans of Bud for supper. Read two more chapters of David Copperfield and went to bed at eleven.

As a summary of the day's events this might be adequate but as a journal entry it is an abomination. Is this person a Red Sox or an Orioles fan? Is he in love with Karen? Does *David Copperfield* move him? We don't know because in telling us what happened on September 21, 1974 he has really left himself out.

How might this entry be improved? Well, instead of trying to mention everything that happened during the day the person might have focused on a single incident and described it in detail:

> Had lunch with Karen at HoJos. First we had to wait twenty minutes for a table and then got stuck next to two guys from the business school who wanted to know what I was doing in psychology when I could make $30,000 a year selling real estate. Not feeling too confident about my career today I told them I just like rats better than landlords, which ended the conversation. Then we had to settle for liverwurst instead of pastrami, the waitress spilled coke on my notebook, and then tried to make me pay someone else's check. "We ought to do this more often," Karen said, and she wasn't smiling.

Or else have tried to examine his reactions to something that happened:

> Made a D on the first psychology exam and this isn't even an upper level course. Can I cut it or should I try surfing? I mean, I read the material over three times, took notes and made my five-point outline just like the study guides say, got a good night's sleep, ate a good breakfast—and bombed. My roommate studies a total of twenty minutes with one eye on the textbook and the other on Star Trek and gets an A-. There's a moral there somewhere but I don't want to know what it is.

Or explored an idea that was merely suggested by something he did or saw:

> I detest violence and love James Bond flicks. I was having trouble reconciling these feelings until I realized that it was because of all the gimmicks and stunts. They make the violence look like slapstick comedy or vaudeville and the more fantastic they get the less involved I get. As long as somebody's murdered with a little style nobody really feels threatened.

These entries are improvements on the first one because they have a focus, that is a central event, feeling, or thought, and because they tell us something about the writer. Raw facts are not ends in themselves but the starting points for private dialogue and reflection. Which isn't to suggest that every entry be "confessional" (even soap operas have their light moments) but only that what goes into your journal should count in some way. A good journalist is someone with an eye for what Thoreau calls "choice experiences" and a talent for synthesizing them into personally expressive statements. As you write, therefore, ask yourself these questions: Have I said what I really think and feel about this or only what I'm supposed to think and feel? Have I told not simply what happened but what it means to me? Would this entry make sense to me next year? In five years? Would it make sense to someone else?

The last question implies that a journal is also a public document. It is, to the extent that it is written in a language that other people use and not in some private code, and to the extent that without at least a remote awareness of a listener, an ear for your voice, you probably wouldn't write at all. But the distinguishing feature of a journal is the freedom it allows for experimentation and improvisation. You are not writing *for* that listener finally; you are writing notes to yourself about what matters to you. Nobody else can tell you what to say or how to say it; correctness and consistency do not have the same importance as in an essay, for example, so that depending on your mood and subject you might be whimsical, serious, introspective, coolly matter of fact. One day you may want to write haiku or analogies, the next day letters or definitions or passages of physical description. Neither the length of an entry nor the style in which it is written is particularly important. Besides providing opportunities for reflection, therefore, a journal simply allows you to be yourself.

It does other things as well: (1) Kept regularly—and regularly may mean daily, twice a week, or every Saturday evening at 11:30—a journal sustains the habit of writing. On days when you can't write a coherent sentence or think a coherent thought you can always scribble a few lines in your journal, perhaps on the subject of incoherence. (2) As Thoreau suggests, a journal is a repository for all those fragmentary ideas and odd scraps of information that might otherwise be lost but which someday might lead to more "harmonious" compositions. In this respect a journal can make you more aware of how a longer piece of writing might be generated by a single detail. (3) We all have patterns of thinking and writing that we are unconscious of. Re-reading your journal regularly may reveal what some of yours are. (4) Because journals can accommodate such diverse materials—metaphors, dialogues, descriptions of persons and events, lists—they help to sharpen all our powers of observation.

The following passages illustrate several different types of journal entries: aphorisms (Baudelaire), anecdotes (Butler), factual reports (Janet Flanner) and personal reflections (Merton). They are not intended to be models for imitation as much as examples of things you might do in your own journal.

> Whenever you receive a letter from a creditor, write fifty lines upon some extra-terrestrial subject, and you will be saved.

> What is annoying about Love is that it is a crime in which one cannot do without an accomplice.

> Stupidity always preserves beauty, it keeps away the wrinkles, it is the divine cosmetic.

> We love women in so far as they are strangers to us.

> Baudelaire

Stevedores appeared momentarily against the lighted hold of a barge and jerked quickly out of sight down an invisible incline. . . .

The late sun glinted on the Mississippi flats a mile away. . . .

The first lights of the evening were springing into pale existence. The Ferris wheel, pricked out now in lights, revolved leisurely through the dusk; a few empty cars of the roller coaster rattled overhead. . . .

Seen in a Junk Yard. Dogs, chickens with few claws, brass fittings, T's elbow, rust everywhere, bales of metal 1800 lbs, plumbing fixtures, bathtubs, sinks, water pumps, wheels, Fordson tractor, acetylene lamps for tractors, sewing machine, bell on dinghy, box of bolts (No. 1), van, stove, auto stuff (No. 2), army trucks, cast iron body, hot dog stand, dinky engines, sprockets like watch parts, hinge all taken apart on building side, motorcycle radiators, George on the high army truck.

F. Scott Fitzgerald

Things are looking up for the convicts in France. At any rate, they're taken wherever they're going, if it is only to hard labor for life, in cell-equipped autobuses now, instead of in the old "salad-basket" cars which figured like extra cabooses on freight trains, and allowed prisoners to languish in freight yards days or nights, or even both, if there was much besides jailbirds to unload. The new penitentiary buses have just carried some two hundred "lifers" to La Rochelle, where they embarked for the island prison of St.-Martin-de-Re, next to the *bagne* near Cayenne, the worst that can happen to them, and usually the first step toward it. These sail-offs of convicts attract observers from all over France, in addition, that is, to the mothers and wives, who stand and watch and cry. The stars of this year's embarkation were the prisoner Dr. Laget, "freshly shaven, attired in tortoise-shell glasses, golf suit and cap of pearl grey, and yellow polkadot tie"; a strangler named Morveau, whose accomplice was a motorcycle acrobat named the Death-Defier, since dead of tuberculosis; and young Davin, a rich moron who murdered an American playboy pal for fun and pocket money. Clearly, French criminals do not operate in gangs. Three of Kid Dropper's old mob could stop one of these new cell-buses, with three hands tied behind them. As Davin *mere* said, "My son is a lonely irresponsible." Yet convicts escape from the Devil's Island *bagne* not singly but in groups of ten or fifteen, rather like tropical walking clubs. Dr. Bougrat, one of the most popular poisoners of Marseilles, recently fled from his cell to Caracas, where he now enjoys a flourishing general practice, though nose and throat were his original specialty. It took the cooperation of twenty men to effect his escape. Apparently French criminals learn the value of trade solidity only when it is a little late.

Janet Flanner

We often walk from Rickmansworth across Moor Park to Pinner. On getting out of Moor Park there is a public-house just to the left where we generally have some shandy-gaff and buy some eggs. The landlord had a noble sow which I photographed for him; some months afterwards I asked how the sow was. She had been sold. The landlord knew she ought to be killed and made into bacon, but he had been intimate with her for three years and some one else must eat her, not he.

"And what," said I "became of her daughter?"

"Oh, we killed her and ate her. You see we had only known her eighteen months."

I wonder how he settled the exact line beyond which intimacy with a pig must not go if the pig is to be eaten.

I must get in about the people one meets. The man who did not like parrots because they were too intelligent. And the man who told me that Handel's *Messiah* was "très chic" and the smell of the cyclamens "stupendous." And the man who said it was hard to think the world was not more than 6000 years old, and we encouraged him by telling him we thought it must be even more than 7000. And the English lady who said of some one that "being an artist, you know, of course, he had a great deal of poetical feeling." And the man who was sketching and said he had a very good eye for colour in the light, but would I be good enough to tell him what colour was best for the shadows.

"An amateur," he said, "might do very decent things in water-colour, but oils require genius."

So I said: "What is genius?"

"Millet's picture of the *Angelus* sold for 700,000 francs. Now that," he said, "is genius."

After which I was very civil to him.

Samuel Butler

September 24

This is one of those days when you feel scabby all over. *Iniquitatem meam ego cognosco et peccatum meum contra me est semper.* However, I am glad of it. It makes penance a delight. You look around for something that will kill this leprous image that you have discovered in your soul.

I have been reading about the Carmelites in the *Dictionaire de Spiritualité*. There are some good notes on poverty in the article—something of the idea that struck me the other day: poverty conceived as a function of solitude or "nakedness"—detachment, isolation from everything superfluous in the interior life. Renunciation of useless activity in your natural faculties. All this is what a Carmelite understands by being poor. And I wish I were poor. Yet I do not want to wish I were poor in a way that might imply that I thought myself rich. I

*"For I know my iniquity and my sin is always before me" (Psalm 50).

am not rich. I just sit in my little pawnshop of second-rate emotions and ideas, and most of the time they make me slightly sick.

The one thing I really feel like writing—*The Waters of Siloe*, a book about the history and spirituality of the Order—is lying there half finished, but every time I reach out to take it up again, something else interferes.

Meanwhile, the typewriter assigned to me has gone off to the shop to be repaired again. It is an old rebuilt machine and important parts—the letters, for instance—keep falling off when I am trying to write. I have Father Raymond's typewriter; if he suddenly needs it again I will have nothing to work with at all, because all the other typewriters are needed to handle all the other correspondence.

September 28   Day of Recollection

There was supposed to be no weekend retreat in the guest house but a whole crowd arrived anyway right after the diocesan priests had gone. So I am reading to them about Our Lady of Fatima, although it is our Day of Recollection and we are supposed to be immersed in silence and prayer. The trouble with this reading is that the guests come up and ask me questions and sometimes I go ahead and answer them. One man tried to give me a dollar.

I made a futile effort to find some notes I was writing this time last year, to compare the Days of Recollection then with the Days of Recollection now—as if I could really learn something important by doing so. Really, I do not need to find those notes and I know it. What I was writing then is just about the same as what I am writing now. And yet I know too that somehow my interior life is deeper and that I have more peace and that I am closer to God and more under His control. But do not ask me how I got there because I do not know. Solemn Profession, for one thing, had much to do with it. I could make a long list of the other graces God has given me: but I would never know how to say whether I had made use of them. Somehow, with God's help, they have not been fruitless.

Thomas Merton

5 | Autobiography

There is no description so difficult as describing oneself.
Montaigne

The term autobiography means literally "self + life + writing," the revelation of oneself through language. It is a broad term covering everything from the gilt-edged memoirs of a five-star general to the hasty scribbling we often do in diaries and journals. Much of the writing you've done so far is autobiographical to the extent that it contains *your* observations and reflections on some object, place, or event in the external physical world. In this chapter, however, you will be focusing more on your private experiences, on your memories, anxieties, fantasies, and frustrations. In autobiography *you* are the subject and your job is to give a reader a glimpse of your inner life, to share with him your unique perception of things. The enduring fascination of autobiography is that no two persons and no two lives are ever the same; the constant challenge to the autobiographer is to communicate this uniqueness clearly and forcefully.

Presenting yourself in words never means presenting your whole self. Each of us has different voices and different images for different audiences and situations. Each of the four sections in this chapter calls for a different kind of autobiographical writing. In a monologue, for example, you are speaking primarily to yourself, recording your thoughts and impressions in an apparently random, spontaneous manner. In an autobiographical capsule, on the other hand, you are speaking more publicly, perhaps to an audience of friends and peers, and instead of writing down whatever comes to mind you mention only those details that reinforce a particular image of yourself. Similar adjustments in style and voice must be made in letters and autobiographical sketches. In working through this chapter, therefore, you will discover both how protean "I" can be and how it is controlled by audience and circumstance. For even though autobiographical writing is a means of self-expression and self-discovery, it should not be an excuse for self-indulgence. (Teachers who treat "I" like a four-letter word are not necessarily enemies of individual expression. They may be reacting to the excessive or inappropriate use of the first person.) Like all good writing autobiography demands clarity, precision, and concreteness. It also demands honesty and directness. Since you are the subject, criticism pierces many niceties of style and technique and spears you directly. If your writing is dull or inane or trite you are, in some way, dull or inane or trite also. You can't hide behind objective impersonal facts and borrowed opinions. You are out front all of the time, which is a good reason to say what you really think and feel instead of falling back on the facile cliché and the glib generalization. Your style, more emphatically than in other kinds of writing, is you. Work to be yourself on paper.

By the time anyone learns to write he has already learned how to speak in rather complex ways, and in most schools it is presumed that writing must be taught almost as something totally distinct from speaking.

Roger Sale

SECTION 1 **Monologues**

Every monologue, whether *interior* (one person speaking mainly to himself) or *dramatic* (one person speaking and responding to an audience), is a prolonged utterance, usually in direct address, that reveals something about the speaker's inner life. Prayers are monologues. So are tirades against your English teacher, conversations with your dachshund, and complaints about the state of your love life. Unlike essays, which seem "composed," monologues are chatty and apparently spontaneous outpourings of thoughts and feelings to which a reader is a kind of eavesdropper. They rely on the rhythms and vocabulary of speech and often give the impression that the speaker is living through the events he is describing *as* he describes them. They are usually immediate and always in a state of "becoming."

In writing essays we sometimes forget about our natural voice(s) and start to churn out bland, homogenized prose composed of generalizations, abstractions, and bombast. Instead of engaging a reader in dialogue we try to impress him with big words and loftly sentiments that invariably muffle our voices. Here are two paragraphs from a freshman essay on parental pressure. Although this was a severe problem for this girl—incidentally, would you know the author was a girl unless you were told?—she writes about it in such an impersonal, toneless manner that we're asleep after the first sentence:

> Today's society thinks that a young adult just out of high school should attend college. However, this belief does not hold true for every individual. Some students have a real desire for a higher education while others would prefer to wait for a year or two.
>
> Many parents make the mistake of forcing or pushing their child into college immediately after graduation. Some are afraid of being embarrassed when they are asked to explain what their high-school graduate is doing, while others want their child to have the opportunities they did not have. This is a serious mistake made by parents because the son or daughter may not fully appreciate the value of a college education at the time. Many young adults feel they are wasting both their time and money being at college. Even though a great deal can be learned there about people and issues, this knowledge can also be ac-

quired at other places besides school. It should be remembered that only a small percentage of high school graduates know what they want to study. These usually have a great desire for higher education. For others, an area of study might come from family, friends, or work.

Several sentences begin with abstract or collective nouns ("Today's society," "Many parents," "Many young adults") that neatly divorce the writer from her opinions. Are *her* parents forcing her to go to college? Is *her* life being disrupted? We can't really tell because she never mentions her own experience. This impersonality is reinforced by a monotonous sentence pattern, frequent and unnecessary use of passive voice (see page 68), and the complete absence of contractions, colloquialisms, and direct address that would suggest conversation, or at least a human voice. This is computer prose from a very dull computer.

Here is the opening paragraph of Tom McAfee's story, *This Is My Living Room* (page 104), an extended interior monologue written in "talking" style:

> It ain't big but big enough for me and my family—my wife Rosie setting over there reading recipes in the *Birmingham News,* and my two girls Ellen Jean and Martha Kay watching the TV. I am setting here holding *Life* magazine in my lap. I get *Life,* the *News,* and *Christian Living.* I read a lots, the newspaper everyday from cover to cover. I don't just look at the pictures in *Life.* I read what's under them and the stories. I consider myself a smart man and I ain't bragging. A man can learn a lots from just watching TV if he knows what to watch for and if he listens close. I do. There ain't many that can say that and be truthful. Maybe nobody else in this whole town, which is Pine Springs.

From the beginning we are aware of a voice telling us where to look and what to notice. The space between writer and reader is considerably narrower than in the student sample. Furthermore, we notice many contractions and colloquial expressions ("I ain't bragging," "A man can learn a lots by watching TV," "setting" used for "sitting") that we wouldn't find in formal prose. Most sentences are short, simply constructed—subject, verb, object, with virtually no modifiers—and arranged in a loose tumbling pattern that suggests a mind in motion. The last clause, for example, seems like an afterthought. Periodic sentences and sentences with a number of subordinate clauses are much less common in speech than in writing. Speech also contains fewer noun phrases than formal writing: "I live in Boston" is talk, "My place of residence is Boston" is writing—stuffy writing.

A colloquial style much as McAfee's would obviously be inappropriate for an essay on the Bill of Rights or a résumé for a scholarship. As we shall see in the next section, one's style is invariably determined by one's subject, audience, and intention. A good writer is never arbitrarily chatty or formal. Nevertheless, monologues can be an effective antidote for impersonal, insipid prose for several reasons: (1) They encourage you to put yourself into your writing. And since it is difficult to write about yourself without using "I" or by falling back on anemic expressions like "Many People say" or "It is thought to be true that," you have to develop a more direct, supple, self-expressive style; (2) monologues can open your writing up by making you more conscious of the rhythms and language of conversation. The more you listen to the sound of your own voice the less likely you will be to speak in one that is bogus and borrowed.

SUMMARY

Whether a monologue is *interior* (a person thinking and talking to himself) or *dramatic* (a person thinking and talking to an audience, real or imagined), it depends primarily on the rhythms and language of actual conversation, not on the conventions of the formal essay. A monologue is an immediate, dramatic, and seemingly spontaneous outpouring of thoughts and feelings, a combination daydream and soliloquy that gives us a glimpse of a person's inner life. Practiced judiciously, it can make your writing more supple, expressive, and personal.

EXERCISES

1. (a) Without worrying about grammar or coherence, and in as conversa-
   tional a style as possible, record whatever comes into your mind in a
   five-minute period. In other words, talk on paper as you might talk to
   a friend.

   (b) Repeat the preceding exercise, focusing now on a specific idea, emotion, or event. Concentrate on capturing the actual rhythms of speech
   and thought without attempting to "compose" polished sentences
   and paragraphs. Let the words fall as they may. If you have difficulty
   beginning, introduce a few sentences with "Now I'm thinking" or
   "Now I'm feeling" until you develop an easy, natural prose rhythm.
   You might also consult Appendix 2 on freewriting.

2. (a) Write a monologue in which two halves of your mind, or two sides of
   your personality, discuss an important personal issue.

   (b) Recall a conversation in which you disagreed strongly with another
   person. Present it first as a dialogue (see Chapter 6, Section 2 for
   suggestions) and then as a dramatic monologue in which the other
   speaker's responses are conveyed implicitly in what you say.

   (c) Paraphrase a soliloquy, the stage version of a monologue, from a play
   by Shakespeare or some other dramatist. Respect the tone and intention of the original but translate the ideas into your own language.
   How does this translation affect the speech rhythms?

3. Think about the most restrictive high-school English class you were in
   and write a short paper that, structurally and stylistically, would be appropriate for it. Then rewrite the paper in a style that seems natural to you
   now. Compare the voices in the two versions.

4. We all have fantasies in which we perform incredible feats that, for one
   reason or another, are impossible in our real lives. Perhaps you imagine
   yourself being a goalie for the Bruins, climbing the Matterhorn, or singing in Carnegie Hall. Live out one of your favorite fantasies in the form of
   a monologue. Tell what it's like to have people firing pucks at you, for
   example. What goes through your mind?

READINGS

The Debate

I really don't want to be here, stuck inside this foreign high school waiting for two other debaters to join me in verbal warfare. Maybe they won't come. If no one enters the room by four-thirty we win by forfeit. I say "we" because I have a partner for the debate. But he doesn't exactly inspire confidence as he sits next to me biting his nails while sweat drips off his forehead.

I can just visualize what the other team will look like. They'll be wearing three-piece suits, gold watch chains, white shirts, narrow ties, short hair, and horn-rimmed glasses. They'll be accompanied, of course, by five or six file boxes full of evidence. I can only stare at our lone recipe box containing our total knowledge of the debate topic. One of our opponents will undoubtedly smoke a pipe. I hope we don't offend them by our appearance. Maybe tennis shoes and patched bluejeans weren't quite right for this occasion. I wish my partner had combed his hair.

As I look around the room, I spot two possible exits in case things get difficult. I have to give an eight minute speech! I don't even know what I'll say until I hear what the other team argues. What if I can't think of anything to say? What if I run out of things to say after six minutes? What will I do for two minutes? I can't just stand there. It might help if I knew a little more about the topic. As it is, I know next to nothing about it. I suppose it's a little late to learn about the jury system of the United States anyway. It's four-fifteen and still no one has come. They have only fifteen minutes more.

The door is opening and someone is coming in. He looks a little old to be a debater. He's probably a judge, the one who'll have to decide the outcome. He's strolling across the back of the room like a skater gliding across a frozen lake. How can he be so calm! I wish my hands would stop shaking. My partner has almost run out of fingernails. It's four-twenty-five.

I can hear the doorknob rattling again. It's turning. The door is swinging open with a soft creaking noise. Two enemy debaters, each carrying four file boxes, come marching in. They're exactly as I imagined. I wish the one with the brown hair would put out his pipe. I wish my partner would stop staring at them. I wish the judge would smile at us the way he's smiling at them. I wish this whole thing were over. I think I'll crawl under my desk.

Tom Maurer

Is That Too Much To Ask?

I've been sixteen for two months now, but who cares. My life is all just a waste. I don't even know what I'm doing right now. I have no idea why I'm even thinking about this again, but I might just as well; it's something to do.

All that's ever happened to me has been bad. When I think back to my childhood all I can remember are bad times. I was always a loser or the dumb kid who tried hard.

When I was little I would go to Grammie's and play with Martha, my cousin. She would always break something or hurt herself and then go inside and tell Grammie I'd done it. Her favorite trick was to fall off her bike and say that I pushed her.

I always thought that things would change when we got older but they never did. The cold war between us only became more intense. Our disagreements grew worse, our rivalry for the same things increased, and our striving to be better than one another intensified.

When I look back at those times I say to myself, "Why didn't you fight back and really hit her once in a while?" I was always such a chicken, no guts, and I guess I still am. Even then I was a wishy-washy kid just like I am now.

Everyone treated me different. I'll never forget Christmas in the fifth grade. Gram and Gramp gave Cathy, my sister, a Barbie game. It was so pretty. She was in the second grade so I thought the game was a little advanced for her. But she loved it. I got a small junkie Brownie bracelet. I'd been a Junior Girl Scout for two years and I got a stupid Brownie bracelet. It wouldn't begin to fit my wrist. What a bummer that was.

It just goes to show that they really liked Cathy better anyway. I mean, she was cute, small, and always kept you laughing. I was chunky, ugly, and never very witty. But I still don't understand why people had to be so obvious about the fact that she was the favorite.

I never did understand people and I guess I never will. I don't even try anymore. There's no sense. I don't care if I live anyway. Life treats me so rotten I hate it. Maybe death is better than life.

Then there was the time in the second grade when I had to wear this dumb little sign all day that said "3X9=27." All the big kids laughed and thought it was a big joke. That really hurt.

It's funny. I guess I haven't changed much. All the feelings I had as a small child I still have as a teenager.

I don't want to think anymore about my terrible childhood right now. I want to mull over the latest tragedy in my life, for the millionth time.

I was in love, and I mean in love, with this guy named Charlie and we were going to be married the summer after I graduated from high school. I would only have one more year because I was going to take my junior and senior years in one. Everything was all planned and we were very happy.

Charlie was a terrific person but all of a sudden on July 28th he told me that it was all over. He just said that during the last week he had been seeing someone else. That was it; no explanation as to why or whether he still loved me or anything. I never saw him again.

Bill, his best friend, used to come to see me. He wasn't much help, though, because he didn't know why Charlie didn't love me either. After a while he must of got sick of listening to me crying on his shoulder because he stopped coming around.

He was someone to talk to, though. Now I have no one except myself and it's really getting me down as I go over all my thoughts about Charlie again and again. Now all I can do is keep repeating all the things that happened to us and cry. The good and happy times make me so sad because nothing like them will ever happen again. The arguments we had make me cry because I see now how trivial the things were that we fought about. I just wish I could have him back. If I could just talk with him for about an hour, or even a half-hour, I think I could persuade him to take me out again, even if it was just on a trial basis. I still love him so much.

I'm a failure. No one wants me. I'm a reject, ugly, twenty pounds overweight, and my face is one big mass of acne. My hair is brassy red and looks horrible; it's long and thick and never shines or looks pretty. I can understand why no guy wants to take me out.

Isn't there some guy out in the world who could love me? I'm not a total disaster. I have a lot of love to give and it's all going to waste. Why can't there be someone to love me?

I could be a good wife and mother to someone. I can cook and clean house. I love children and handle them very well. I wouldn't ask very much. All I want is for him to love me. I don't care if he's handsome or rich or anything special. I just want him to love me. Is that too much to ask?

I feel like a reject. I was used and thrown away. Like a small toy. Charlie played with me and when he was done he tossed me aside and picked up another new toy. He didn't even think about my feelings. He just kept me for a while, lying to me, and now he's found someone else.

I don't want to live anymore. There's not one thing to live for. No one wants me. I wish I had enough courage to kill myself. The only way I know to do it is to slit my wrists, but that would hurt too much. Sleeping pills! That's the answer. It's easy to take a bottle of pills. All I have to do is go to the kitchen and take a couple of bottles of Coke and then reach up in the medicine cabinet and take out the bottle of sleeping pills.

I wouldn't have to die if I had someone to care for and to love, who would love me in return. Maybe if I had a baby he would love me. But it's impossible for me to be pregnant since I'm a virgin. I wish I was pregnant by Charlie, though. If I was going to have his baby, I would have some part of him. But, as it is now, all I have are memories of our short life together. I wouldn't force him to marry me if I was going to have his baby. I wouldn't even want him to because he wouldn't be happy. He'll never be one to settle down and have a family.

I wonder what his reaction would be if I asked him to get me pregnant. He always wanted to make love to me, but I wouldn't let him. I wanted to be a virgin on our wedding night. All I want him to do is to make love to me so I can be pregnant. I wouldn't ask any more. I would go away and no one would ever hear from me again. I could go away and make a life for my baby and myself. I could change my name and no one could find me. It would all be simple. Well, not exactly simple, but I'm sure I could do it. It would be wonderful if I was going to have his baby.

But still, maybe I couldn't handle it. I'm so stupid, maybe I couldn't do it. I might not be good enough for my baby. What if I couldn't provide him with a place to sleep or something to eat? I wouldn't want to have him and allow him to grow up a reject like his mother.

Maybe having a baby by Charlie isn't such a good idea. The best part of it is that the baby would give me someone to give all my love to. As he grew up he could love me back.

That's all I want out of life, someone to love me and take care of me. Is that too much to ask?

Brenda Carroll

This Is My Living Room

My living room it ain't big but big enough for me and my family—my wife Rosie setting over there reading recipies in the Birmingham *News* and my two girls Ellen Jean and Martha Kay watching the TV. I am setting here holding *Life* magazine in my lap. I get *Life*, the *News*, and *Christian Living*. I read a lots, the newspaper everyday from cover to cover. I don't just look at the pictures in *Life*. I read what's under them and the stories. I consider myself a smart man and I ain't bragging. A man can learn a lots from just watching the TV, if he knows what to watch for and if he listens close. I do. There ain't many that can say that and be truthful. Maybe nobody else in this whole town, which is Pine Springs.

Yonder in the corner, to the other side of the Coca-Cola calendar, is my 12 gauge. When I go in to bed, I take it with me, set it against the wall, loaded, ready to use, so I can use it if I need to. I've used it before and maybe will again. The only one to protect you is yourself and if you don't you're a fool. I got me a pistol and a .22 locked up in the back room. I could use them too.

Rosie can shoot, I taught her how, but she's afraid. The noise scares her. She said, Don't make me shoot that thing one more time. We was in the forest. The girls was waiting for us in the car. Don't make me shoot that thing again, she said, and started to cry. I slapped her face and told her to shoot the rifle. She did. Then I took it and told her to go back to the car with the girls. She started to cry again, but I stayed a long time—till it was dark—and shot the rifle and pistol and shotgun.

You can't tell what people are going to do in a town like this. They want your money and they're jealous of you. They talk about you in front of the courthouse and plan up schemes. You can't trust the police or sheriff. You got to watch out for yourself.

My two girls are fourteen and sixteen year old. Both of them want to go on dates but I won't let them. I know what the boys will do, what they want to get out of a girl.

Ellen Jean, the oldest, is a right good-looking girl but sassy and you can't hardly do anything with her. She started to paint her face at school, so I took her out. I've got her working at my store.

I seen her passing notes to Elbert. I seen her get out of his car one night. She said she was going to the picture show by herself. She's a born liar and sassy. Like as not he's had her. Like as not she's got a baby starting in her belly right now. She's a sassy bitch-girl and don't take after her ma or me. Sometimes I wonder if she's mine.

Martha Kay is like her ma. She cries all the time, minds good. I let her stay in high school and will keep on letting her as long as she can act right. The first time I see lipstick, out she comes. She can work at the store too. I could use her to dust and sweep up. You can always use somebody to keep things clean.

I ask Martha Kay, Why're you late gettin' in from school? Where you been? Off in the woods with some boy? She starts to cry. She's like her ma.

Martha Kay helps at the store on Saturdays but can't add up figures good.

Ellen Jean is watching that man on TV make a fool of hisself and she's laughing. She'll end up a Birmingham whore. Her sister is laughing too and they look like a bunch of fools.

People in this town are like they are in any other town on earth. I was in the World War I and seen a good many places. Since then I've stayed here most of the time. What's the good of moving? People are as mean one place as they are another and they're always out to get you. They won't get me because I won't let them.

Take Sam Coates who owed me twenty dollars for that fencing. Sam wouldn't pay. I said to him pay up by first of the month or I'll make you pay. He says how will I make him. Sue him for twenty dollars? Won't no lawyer in town take it anyway, he says, because they're all looking out for election. You pay, I told him.

When first of the month come I got in my car and rode out in the country to his front door. Where is your husband? I said to his wife. Milking, she said, and I went around to the barn with my .22, stuck it in his face, and told him to pay me or I'd blow the hell out of him. Sam turned as white as that bucket of milk. Him and his wife counted me out the money.

There ain't a one on earth that wouldn't try to cheat you if they could.

I use to think that women was worse than men but now I think just the opposite. Women are easier to handle. About the worst they can do is talk and what does that matter?

Niggers are better than anybody because you can handle them. They don't hardly ever give you any trouble. Except that one time with Ezmo. I didn't have no trouble handling him.

My store is about the best thing I know of. It seems like a human being sometimes except a lots better because you can trust it.

I've got as much business as I need and make more profit than some people I know of. Maybe they've got better houses and ride in finer cars, but maybe they didn't make all their money like I did. Honest. I ain't earned a cent crooked. I didn't inherit my money. I worked for it.

Country folks and niggers is my customers. Saturday is my big day. Ellen Jean helps me all through the week and Martha Kay helps out on Saturday. They're not much help. Don't take the right kind of interest.

I like the smell of my store from the time I open it up at 7 in the morning till the time Ellen Jean throws oil sand on the floor when it's time to sweep up. I like everything about that store.

I sell canned goods, fresh meat, bread and crackers, flour, fencing, nails, hammers, guns. I sell all the things a body could need.

Not like at Admore's where it's just women's hats and dresses, or Taylor's where it's just for younguns.

I want to know what the world is coming to.

If Rosie ever dies and the girls go off I'll sell this house and sleep in my store. I'll put up a cot, take my guns and my clothes and that's all. Maybe the TV.

What do I care about this house?

This living room ain't no part of my body or my mind. The lace on the mantelpiece, what's it for? That nigger youngun setting on a commode with Mobile wrote on it, what's it for? Them pictures of movie stars in silver frames. This light-colored linoleum you can't step on without it leaving a mark from your heel. Them silky-lace curtains.

One time I took my hand across the mantel and knocked off Rosie's big clock and a vase full of flowers. Rosie set in here and cried half the night—till I got up and told her to get in bed with her husband where she belonged.

People, your own flesh and blood, will try to run over you, stomp you, steal from you, kill you if they can.

Take the law. A body would think—if he wasn't very smart—that a man of law was a good man. It ain't so. Ninety per cent of the time it ain't so. A body says then, if the law ain't good, who is? Nobody.

Sheriff Claine is a good example. He used to be always poking around my store, making hints. Standing outside the front window part of the time. One evening late I got in my car and followed Sheriff Claine down the highway towards Brushwood, then off down the country road towards Glory Church, and then he stopped. I stopped a good piece behind him and followed him through a pine thicket to a liquor still. A whole big wildcat setup. Sheriff Claine was the ringleader of the bunch.

Next time he come to my store, I said, Sheriff, finding much wildcat whisky? He grunted and pulled up his belt and let on like business was slow. Somebody said, and I eased it to him, they's a big still down towards Glory Church, off in a pine thicket.

Sheriff Claine couldn't talk for a minute and squinted his eyes. I'll have a look, he said.

Oh, probably ain't nothing to it, I told him. I ain't gonna mention it to nobody, nosir, not to a soul.

The police is just like him. They hide out at night and sleep when they're suppose to be patrolling. I've caught them at it.

Sheriff Claine didn't give me no trouble about Ezmo. He listened to what I said here at the house and that was that.

Old Ezmo was what you'd call a low class of nigger. He'd come into the store and say, Give me a pound of sugar and I'll pay you Saturday evening. I wouldn't do it. I'd say, You give me the money. I give you the best prices in town. You give me the money.

One time Ellen Jean let him have a loaf of bread on credit. I smacked her for it and told her she was a fool, which she is. On Saturday Ezmo come in and wanted some side meat for cooking greens. Pay me off, I told him, for that loaf of bread. What loaf? he wanted to know.

Ellen Jean, didn't you charge this nigger a loaf of bread? She said yes and he said she didn't. You ain't calling my girl a liar, are you? Naw, he said, but he didn't get no loaf of bread. Somebody's a liar, I told him, and it ain't my girl.

He said he wouldn't pay me. You're a crooked, low-down nigger, I told him, and they ain't nothing much worse than that. You ain't fit for making side meat out of. I told him if he had any younguns he better watch out. I didn't wants lots of black bastards like him growing up in my town. You get out of here right now.

That night I was setting in this chair where I am right now—this same chair. The girls was watching TV. Rosie was shelling peas.

I heard somebody outdoors and I knew right off who it was. I got better ears than most people. Any time somebody sets foot in this yard, I know it. Even if I'm alseep.

That's Ezmo, I said to myself. I got up, picked up my 12 gauge over in the corner and said I was gonna clean it, went through the house without turning any lights on, then eased out the back door.

There wasn't much moon but I spotted Ezmo right off, standing behind some hedge bushes over by my bedroom window. I got just this side of him without him hearing. EZMO! I hollered, and up he come with a knife about eight inches long. I was ready for him. I triggered my 12 gauge and got him square in the face.

Rosie and the girls come running to the back door. Get me a flashlight, I told them. I never seen such a blowed-up face. The girls started getting sick and Rosie started crying. I want you to take a good look, I told Rosie, and see what this world is coming to. You see that knife he had. I held Rosie's arm and made her stand there till Ellen Jean could get Sheriff Claine.

Rosie ain't exactly good-looking. She's got to be dried-up but once was on the fat side. She makes a good wife. I've been married to her for going on thirty years. Sometimes I get fed up with her and go to my woman in South

Town. I take her a couple of cans of beans and some hose or a pair of bloomers. There ain't nothing much a woman won't do for food or clothes.

Rosie knows about her, all about her. I talk about it sometimes when we're in bed. I wouldn't trade Rosie for her but Rosie don't know that.

Tomorrow's Saturday and I got to get some sleep.

"Turn off the TV, girls. Get in yonder to bed. Tomorrow's Saturday."

I stand in front of Rosie. "Go in yonder and get in bed." She starts to cry and that's all right. It wouldn't be a bit like her if she didn't.

Tom McAfee

Master of Ceremonies

Thank you, ladies and gentlemen, thank you, thank you, thank you. Really, though, ladies and gentlemen, I am very grateful to you all, every single solitary one of you. I don't mean that! Not every solitary one of you! When you come to the Night Mare, we don't want you to come here solitary. No, ma'am. Don't come solitary. The more the merrier, I always say, and let joy be unrefined. However, no matter how you come, we want you one and all to come here and have a good time, ladies and gentlemen. See the gorgeous beautiful girls in the stage show; yeah, man, gorgeous most beautiful girls you ever did see and I'm telling you. Boy, am I telling you! Floor show. And then we have a special all-star show and yours truly will introduce the acts as it comes their turn. But before I introduce the first number on our floor-show program, how about let's give a great big hand for Haps Gunderson and his Night Mare Collegians, the boys in the band that supply this beautiful music for you, come on, come on, lets give Haps and the boys a big hand! Wuddia say? A big hand for good old Haps Gunderson and his Night Mare Collegians. Haps, take a bow. . . .

Thank you, ladies and gentlemen, that was very nice. Glad to see you like Haps and the boys, because besides being associated with Haps here at the good old Night Mare, it also happens that Haps is one of my dearest friends. A swell guy, a real trouper, one of the best, ladies and gentlemen. I love that Haps. Anyhow, seriously, ladies and gentlemen, and all kidding aside, all kidding aside, I'm serious about it when I say to you it's my personal opinion that Haps Gunderson and his Night Mare Collegians have just about the best, the dancingest—if you'll pardon the word—the dancingest band in town. I mean it. I really do. Yeah, man. I've heard them all, too, from Paul Whitemen and Guy Lombardo to some of the best bands on the Pacific Coast, and I want to tell you I don't think there's a one of them that can touch Haps Gunderson and his Night Mare Collegians. So now for fifteen minutes, the next fifteen minutes, grab yourself somebody else's wife and dance to the music of Haps Gunderson and the boys, and no holds barred! . . .

Good work, boys. Nice going, Haps old boy. I notice the boys finished together on that one. Nice going, boys. And say, that's a swell number. Isn't that a swell number, ladies and gentlemen, that last number they just played? Or weren't you listening to it? Anyhow, I know two people that weren't listening to it and I want to introduce them to you. I want to introduce Mr. and Mrs.—Mr. and Mrs. Leonard Schoflinger, of York, P.A. Give 'em the blue lights, boy, and I hope it's a boy. Mr. and Mrs. Leonard Schoflinger of York, P.A., in the big town on their honeymoon! Let's give 'em a great big hand to start them off on the sea of wedded bliss. Wuddia say? . . . And now, and now, ladies and gentlemen, before we go any further I have an announcement, an announcement, ladies and gentlemen, of the greatest importance. Quiet, please! Little quiet there everybody! I have an announcement of greatest importance to make this evening. Ready for the announcement? Okay. Ladies and gentlemen, the management requests me to announce that Rudy Vallée will *not* sing here tonight! Must be a couple of Bing Crosby admirers in the house. Well, be that as it may, the next number which will be inflicted upon you, ladies and gentlemen, will be my own impression my own impression of Mawreece Shevaalyay singing "In the Park in the Spring," and I am goink to do it raht now. . . .

I only hope my good friend Irving Winslow was listening to that applause! I guess you all know Mr. Winslow takes more than a fatherly interest in the club, ladies and gentlemen, in fact I might as well break down and confess that my good friend Irving owns the Night Mare. And a sweeter guy I never worked for in all my life. I been round plenty, and I say it from the bottom of my heart, ladies and gentlemen, you won't find a sweeter guy in this business and I don't mean maybe. And now I take great pleasure in introducing Ila Burke cute little Ila Burke and I look for her to be a sensation. Ila Burke will dance for you and with her will be the Night Mare's pony chorus, and I want you all to give these kids a big hand, a beeg hand because they're swell kids every one of them. All ready, wuddia say? Ila Burke and the pony chorus. O-*kay*! Give it! . . .

Nice going, Ila, nice going, nice going, come here, darling. Come here and say hello to the nice people. . . . That's right. Folks, this is really one of the sweetest kids I ever saw. No kidding, I mean it. How about giving her a hand? . . . Well, Ila, wuddia say, do I get a little kiss? . . . How about that, men? Do you envy me or do you envy me? And I get paid for it. All right, Ila, you can go now. Ila will be back in just a few minutes, ladies and gentlemen, in another costume, consisting of a fan and a cigarette, and I hope she remembers to bring the cigarette. She forgot the fan the other night. But strangely enough, nobody missed it. And now, and now I want to introduce a few of my friends from the press, ladies and gentlemen. Over here we have my good friend Eddie Sullivan, from the *Daily News*. Wuddia say, lets give him a hand! . . . And Jimmie Cannon, of the *World-Telegram*, ladies and gentlemen. . . . And now Haps Gunderson and the boys will provide you with music for the next fifteen or twenty minutes and then we will resume the floor show. Give it, Haps!

John O'Hara

In a man's letters, you know, Madam, his soul lies naked, his letters are only the mirror of his heart: Whatever passes within him is shown undisguised in its natural process: nothing is inverted, nothing distorted: you see systems in their elements: you discover actions in their motives.

Samuel Johnson to Mrs. Thrale

SECTION 2 **Letters**

Letters are first cousins of diaries and journals in that they frequently contain our most intimate thoughts and feelings. This does not mean that they are always "confessional" but only that, as a rule, they are more personal and forthright than our other writing. It's as though we make a pact with our reader not to be tricky or deceitful or obscure. We sometimes break it, of course, and yet it is this basic expectation of honesty that helps to account for the peculiar energy and expressiveness of letters.

There are other reasons also. First, most of us write so many letters that they seem more a part of daily life than a specialized literary exercise. Consequently, we are more inclined to be chatty, digressive, and inventive because we feel less constrained by literary conventions. Furthermore, we usually write letters for specific reasons—to get a job, share an experience, give advice, express sympathy—which gives them a certain urgency and sharpness of focus that our other writing may lack. Finally, we write letters *to* someone, to a particular reader or audience, and not to the world at large. The repetition of "I" and "You" creates a humanizing push-pull with a reader that encourages us to speak our minds. One reason that form letters, particularly the "Dear Sir/Madam" variety, are so irritating is that they mock the kind of personal exchange that we expect in our correspondence.

> We take pride and pleasure in welcoming you to the community and we hope that your new home will be a source of great joy and happiness to you.
>
> You are cordially invited to take advantage of our many fine services and join our family of satisfied customers. You'll find our entire staff friendly and courteous, eager to be helpful to you in any way. Please feel free to call upon us at any time for any of your needs.
>
> Again, a warm welcome and our fond hope that you will number us among your new friends.

The fact that I received this same letter from an insurance agency, a furniture store, and a dry cleaning firm indicates how prefabricated its language and sentiments really are. It is a fine example of commercial treacle, all syrup and no substance.

In the monologue section we made a general distinction between writing style and talking style which, in rhetorical terms, might be a distinction between formal and informal voice. We can carry this idea a step further by discussing the relationship of voice to audience and subject matter. As Aristotle, and every rhetorician since, has noted, the first (voice or persona) is invariably a product of the other two. For example, you wouldn't begin a letter of condolence with a wisecrack or send your grandmother a note full of four-letter words. The occasion would preclude the first, the audience the second. Furthermore, the relationships among these three elements are such that a shift in one brings about a shift in the others. You might invite your classmates to supper in a breezy, informal manner: "Spaghettifest; Saturday, May 17. B. Y. O. B. and date. No setups of any kind provided by the management." If you were to invite the president of the university, however, you would probably be more formal: "You are cordially invited . . ." The difference in style wouldn't mean that the president was a stuffy bore but only that he was of a different age and social position from yourself. Or look at the two letters by Emily Dickinson in the readings (page 118). The one to T. H. Higginson, her literary mentor and patron, is polite but guarded, whereas the one addressed to her friend Abiah Root is chatty and charmingly unbuttoned. The circumstances are different, but so is the author's relationship to her correspondents. Generally speaking, the better we know a person the more relaxed and informal we are, in person and on paper.

The size of your audience also affects your voice. In *Shame of the Catholics, Shame of the English*, (page 123) which is a public rather than a personal letter, Graham Greene is appealing to the conscience of a nation, not to the sentiments of particular individuals or factions. Consequently his language is deliberate, measured, semi-formal, his illustrations typical, his suggestions basic. Were he writing to one person or to a select group he could have dealt with local issues or specific differences of opinion and perhaps employed a kind of verbal shorthand that only a few people would have fully understood.

No matter what you write, therefore, you must always adapt your voice, and therefore your style, to your subject and your audience. One advantage of writing letters is that it acquaints you with this dynamic relationship in such a simple, straightforward way.

SUMMARY

In letters we appeal to a reader more directly and personally than in other kinds of writing, which is why they make ideal texts for examining some basic relationships between style and audience. They are conversations at a distance in which what we say and how we say it depends on our estimations of the attitudes and probable reactions of our readers. We are usually more formal and guarded with strangers than with our families and close friends, and would certainly describe a weekend in Aspen differently to a fellow ski bum and a maiden aunt in Florida. Because letters establish a humanizing push-pull between *I* and *You* they invite us to be more ourselves; because they are appropriate for so many different subjects and situations they allow us to experiment with a wide range of voices and styles.

EXERCISES

1. We've all written notes to the mailman, the paperboy, and the landlord. Usually they are brief, styleless communications in which we give instructions or make demands in as few words as possible. Try your hand at several of the following:

   (a) Write a note asking for a loan of money, clothes, or a car. Specify what you want and why.

   (b) Write a note asking someone in the class for a date.

   (c) Get bolder and compose a marriage proposal. Make yourself as eligible as you can without becoming mawkish or melodramatic.

   (d) Enter a "Why I like such and such" contest, giving your reasons in the customary twenty-five words or less.

2. Most letters are prompted by specific emotions, events, or needs, which is why they are often so vigorous and urgent. Here are some "occasions" that might provoke you into writing a letter:

   (a) A close friend has recently lost a job, been jilted by his girlfriend, had his first novel rejected. Write a letter that would help him cope with his disappointment, but avoid cliché condolences like "Things always work out for the best." He needs help, not Hallmark.

   (b) A friend needs your advice in making an important personal decision. Write a letter giving your opinion about what he should do, drawing on your own experience whenever possible. You might also glance at a syndicated advice column like Dear Abby or Ann Landers to see what happens to the style and tone of a letter when correspondents are complete strangers.

   (c) Another friend needs a character reference for a job, a scholarship, or admission to some university organization. Write a letter that would be fair to your friend and helpful to the persons making the decision. Think carefully about what kinds of information would be relevant and what kinds would not.

   (d) You discover that you've been overcharged by the telephone company or a department store. Write a letter explaining the error and requesting an adjustment. Or, your new expensive camera (trail bike, tape deck) has broken because of faulty workmanship. Write a complaint letter to the manufacturer explaining what's happened and what you want done about it.

3. Want ads are usually dry, matter-of-fact requests for ordinary items like refrigerators and snow tires. But they can also be creative:

(a) Write a want ad for something whimsical and far-fetched like an astrolabe, a blimp, or a farthingale. Describe the item in detail.

(b) Write a want ad for the one thing that, if this were the best of all possible worlds, you would most like to own.

4. (a) Write a letter to an editor expressing your views on some controversial issue. Select a style and format that best suits your subject and your audience and be as emphatic about your views as you can. Graham Greene's letter to the *Times* on the civil war in Northern Ireland is one type of public letter.

(b) Talk back to a film critic or book reviewer whose opinions you disagree with strongly. Or write a letter to a critic who has changed your thinking about a book or film. Describe the change and how it came about.

5. Write letters to three persons of different ages and backgrounds whose views on some controversial subject are likely to differ from your own. Explain your views clearly to each person, making whatever adjustments in style and tone seem appropriate.

6. Write a letter to some historical or literary figure whose life or writings have influenced you (e.g., Shakespeare, Napoleon, Ghandi). Specify what the influence has been and why it is important to you.

READINGS

An Open Letter To Freshman Women

For the past several months I have thought about writing to you on the perhaps presumptuous belief that I can pass along some insights into the difficulties of being a woman, particularly a freshman woman, on this campus. I have not written before now because I foresee resistance to some of what I have to say.

You have chosen a school with a dangerous social environment. Unless you have some sensitivity to the intangible, coercive pressures of that social life you will make bad decisions. You will see other women suffer.

As a freshman it is difficult to get support for being serious about your academic work. In a situation where the social pressure to be successful with the right people, mostly male, is pervasive and powerful, and the support necessary to approach academic work with energy and curiosity seems far away, it is necessary to be very self-conscious about setting priorities and choosing friends.

The fraternities and sororities will be the principal initiators of social activity. Because the sororities lack the courage of the women who founded them, they now serve the social interests of the fraternities and have large control over social activities here. To decide to avoid them is to decide to have a difficult time meeting men and dating. I hope that you will be as horrified as I was at the tremendous pressure that women feel to date, to find some man to spend Friday or Saturday night with. If you decide to move in the fraternity-sorority world, which I decided not to do when I was there, beware of that pressure.

Digression: My objection to sororities is that they help perpetuate a social system that is bad for women. They do so in many ways: by their triviality, by their excessive concern with teas and fashion shows, and corollary inability to confront issues and ideas that are important, by their refusal to deal aggressively with their own racism, and by their tendency to provide women with an illusory, though temporarily comfortable, refuge from the struggle that women can't avoid, namely the struggle to find something substantive to do with their lives, which involves the creation of new roles, new institutions, and new notions about women. I'd like to see sororities disappear in order to force women to create groups that are meaningful.

In the university social setting, good looks, as defined by the cosmetics and clothing industries, assumes primary importance, far beyond what is reasonable and healthy. During my freshman year I remember being annoyed that what I wore and what I drank was more important in the date market that who I was. Body is objectified in the date market. There were occasions when this "objectification" was obscene enough to send me into a rage:

Fiji Olympics, which was, and I assume still is, a fraternity game day at which all of the women competitors have "fiji" painted across their butts, and in which one of the relays involves carrying a size 39D bra with a grapefruit in the cups.

Derby Day is another fraternity sponsored play day, part of which is a "beauty contest" in which the contestants are judged in swim suits with paper bags over their heads.

Pajama parties. In some cases the women wore the top half, the men the bottom. These speak for themselves.

There were many other less obvious but equally disgusting ways in which women were and are dehumanized by things that happen every day on this campus. If you think about them, and watch what happens, you will soon see that they are prototypes of other activities in which women are presented as one-dimensional.

The inevitable date pattern for freshmen is to start drinking as soon as you leave the dorm and end up drunk, all in the name of a good time. My objection to this practice is that it allows people to disclaim responsibility for their crude and obnoxious behavior. It also is a guarantee against having to talk with your date for too long. And, skeptic that I am, I wonder about the "candy is dandy but liquor is quicker" approach of upperclassmen.

Of the twenty-four women on my hall freshman year, three were either pregnant or married by the end of the year, and many more had suffered through pregnancy scares. A study done in a Research Methods class in 1973 indicated that nearly half the women on campus had suffered through pregnancy scares. This is at least partly the result of the pressure on women to keep their value on the date market high. When the pressure gets strong enough some women use sex as a draw. I don't think most of them are aware of how they are using sex, or more precisely how the pressure to be sexually active is using them. Sex is not something that suddenly overwhelms you in a fit of passion. There is no spontaneity in sex if a woman is worried about getting pregnant. For women who have good relationships with good men, sex and intercourse are often quite different issues.

It is not easy for us as women to learn to be responsible for our bodies. Four years ago it was very difficult to find a gynecologist and to get birth control information. A young woman had to go to Planned Parenthood because Texas law prohibited private physicians from giving contraceptives to a single woman under twenty-one without parental consent. The law has changed and now the university offers confidential, part-time gynecological care through the health center, including the prescription of birth control pills. For the women in your dorm who need help and don't want to go to the health center, the local Family Planning Center or Planned Parenthood is relatively inexpensive and confidential.

I have two more observations about women and social life. The first is that women, especially freshmen, have yet to learn to do things by themselves or with a group of women. During my freshman year I realized that I wasn't going to play the dating and drinking games, so I learned to entertain myself. I discovered that it's pleasant to attend a play, concert, or film on campus by yourself. I began going into town and to Austin on the bus. I ate out by myself, swam, bicycled and so forth. I met good people that year, male and female. I learned a lot about loneliness because I had not yet learned how to get other women to join me at the plays and concerts. Women need to do what they want, even if they have to do it alone sometimes.

My second observation is that women have a very difficult time initiating anything directly with a man. Whether it's a cup of coffee in the student center or an evening out, men carry the burden of initiating and women suffer from the inability to act directly. The best men I know are not at all bothered by women initiating things. They rather enjoy it, in fact, and feel relieved. I find that men who are bothered by assertiveness in women do not interest me. I learned to initiate simple things at first—a walk, a cup of coffee, pizza and beer. These were good things to start with because it was not too awkward for me to pay my own way. You may not feel it is important to pay your share of the expenses, but it is important to be sensitive to the pressures men feel to initiate and pay all the time.

My final words: Be critical of the social world you are going to be living in.

Kathy Kenyon

To His Students

Cambridge, Apr. 6, 1896.

Dear Young Ladies,   I am deeply touched by your remembrance. It is the first time anyone ever treated me so kindly, so you may well believe that the impression on the heart of the lonely sufferer will be even more durable than the impression on your minds of all the teachings of Philosophy 2A. I now perceive one immense omission in my Psychology,—the deepest principle of Human Nature is the *craving to be appreciated*, and I left it out altogether from the book, because I had never had it gratified till now. I fear you have let loose a demon in me, and that all my actions will now be for the sake of such rewards. However, I will try to be faithful to this one unique and beautiful azalea tree, the pride of my life and delight of my existence. Winter and summer will I tend and water it—even with my tears. Mrs. James shall never go near it or touch it. If it dies, I will die too; and if I die, it shall be planted on my grave.

Don't take all this too jocosely, but believe in the extreme pleasure you have caused me, and in the affectionate feelings with which I am and shall always be faithfully your friend,

William James

To a Gas and Electric Lighting Company in Hartford

Gentlemen:

There are but two places in our whole street where lights could be of any value, by any accident, and you have measured and appointed your intervals so ingeniously as to leave each of those places in the centre of a couple of hundred yards of solid darkness. When I noticed that you were setting one of your lights in such a way that I could almost see how to get into my gate at night, I suspected that it was a piece of carelessness on the part of the workmen, and would be corrected as soon as you should go around inspecting and find out. My judgment was right; it is always right, when you are concerned. For fifteen years, in spite of my prayers and fears, you persistently kept a gas lamp exactly half way between my gates, so that I couldn't find either of them after dark; and then furnished such execrable gas that I had to hang a danger signal on the lamp post to keep teams from running into it, nights. Now I suppose your present idea is to leave us a little more in the dark.

Don't mind us—out our way; we possess but one vote apiece, and no rights that you are in any way bound to respect. Please take your electric light and go to—but never mind, it is not for me to suggest; you will probably find the way; and anyway you can reasonably count on divine assistance if you lose your bearings.

S. L. Clemens

Emily Dickinson to Mr. Thomas W. Higginson
(Letter received April 26, 1862)

Mr. Higginson,—Your kindness claimed earlier gratitude, but I was ill, and write to-day from my pillow.

Thank you for the surgery; it was not so painful as I supposed. I bring you others, as you ask, though they might not differ. While my thought is undressed, I can make the distinction; but when I put them in the gown, they look alike and numb.

You asked how old I was? I made no verse, but one or two, until this winter, sir.

I had a terror since September, I could tell to none; and so I sing, as the boy does by the burying ground, because I am afraid.

You inquire my books. For poets, I have Keats, and Mr. and Mrs. Browning. For prose, Mr. Ruskin, Sir Thomas Browne, and the Revelations. I went to school, but in your manner of the phrase had no education. When a little girl, I had a friend who taught me Immortality; but venturing too near, himself, he never returned. Soon after my tutor died, and for several years my lexicon was my only companion. Then I found one more, but he was not contented I be his scholar, so he left the land.

You ask of my companions. Hills, sir, and the sundown, and a dog large as myself, that my father bought me. They are better than beings because they know, but do not tell; and the noise in the pool at noon excels my piano.

I have a brother and sister; my mother does not care for thought, and father, too busy with his briefs to notice what we do. He buys me many books, but begs me not to read them, because he fears they joggle the mind. They are religious, except me, and address an eclipse, every morning, whom they call their "Father."

But I fear my story fatigues you. I would like to learn. Could you tell me how to grow, or is it unconveyed, like melody or witchcraft?

You speak of Mr. Whitman. I never read his book, but was told that it was disgraceful.

I read Miss Prescott's "Circumstance," but it followed me in the dark, so I avoided her.

Two editors of journals came to my father's house this winter, and asked me for my mind, and when I asked them "why" they said I was penurious, and they would use it for the world.

I could not weigh myself, myself. My size felt small to me. I read your chapters in the "Atlantic," and experienced honor for you. I was sure you would not reject a confiding question.

Is this, sir, what you asked me to tell you? Your friend,

E. Dickinson

Emily Dickinson to Abiah Root

Amherst, Jan. 29, 1850

Very dear Abiah,—The folks have all gone away; they thought that they left me alone, and contrived things to amuse me should they stay long, and *I* be lonely. Lonely, indeed,—they didn't look, and they couldn't have seen if they had, who should bear me company. *Three* here, instead of *one*, wouldn't it scare them? A curious trio, part earthly and part spiritual two of us, the other, all heaven, and no earth. *God* is sitting here, looking into my very soul to see if I think right thoughts. Yet I am not afraid, for I try to be right and good; and He knows every one of my struggles. He looks very gloriously, and everything bright seems dull beside Him; and I don't dare to look directly at Him for fear I shall die. Then *you* are here, dressed in that quiet black gown and cap,—that funny little cap I used to laugh at you about,—and you don't appear to be thinking about anything in particular,—not in one of your *breaking-dish* moods, I take it. You seem aware that I'm writing you, and are amused, I should think, at any such friendly manifestation when you are already present. *Success*, however, even in making a fool of myself, isn't to be despised; so I shall persist in writing, and you may in laughing at me,—if you are fully aware of the value of time as regards your immortal spirit. I can't say that I advise you to laugh; but if you are punished, and I warned you, that can be no business of mine.

So I fold up my arms, and leave you to fate—may it deal very kindly with you! The trinity winds up with me, as you may have surmised, and I certainly wouldn't be at the fag-end but for civility to you. This self-sacrificing spirit will be the ruin of me!

I am occupied principally with a cold just now, and the dear creature *will* have so much attention that my time slips away amazingly. It has heard so much of New Englanders, of their kind attentions to strangers, that it's come all the way from the Alps to determine the truth of the tale. It says the half wasn't told it, and I begin to be afraid it wasn't. Only think—came all the way from that distant Switzerland to find what was the truth! Neither husband, protector, nor friend accompanied it, and so utter a state of loneliness gives friends if nothing else. You are dying of curiosity; let me arrange that pillow to make your exit easier. I stayed at home all Saturday afternoon, and treated some disagreeable people who insisted upon calling here as tolerably as I could; when evening shades began to fall, I turned upon my heel, and walked. Attracted by the gayety visible in the street, I still kept walking till a little creature pounced upon a thin shawl I wore, and commenced riding. I stopped, and begged the creature to alight, I was fatigued already, and quite unable to assist others. It wouldn't get down, and commenced talking to itself: "Can't be New England—must have made some mistake—disappointed in my reception—don't agree with accounts. Oh, what a world of deception and fraud! Marm, will you tell me the name of this country—it's Asia Minor, isn't it? I intended to stop in New England." By this time I was so completely exhausted that I made no further effort to rid me of my load, and travelled home at a moderate jog, paying no attention whatever to it, got into the house, threw off both bonnet and shawl, and out flew my tormentor, and putting both arms around my neck, began to kiss me immoderately, and express so much love it completely bewildered me. Since then it has slept in my bed, eaten from my plate, lived with me everywhere, and will tag me through life for all I know. I think I'll wake first, and get out of bed, and leave it; but early or late, it is dressed before me, and sits on the side of the bed looking right into my face with such a comical expression it almost makes me laugh in spite of myself. I can't call it interesting, but it certainly *is* curious, has two peculiarities which would quite win your heart,—a huge pocket-handkerchief and a very red nose. The first seems so very *abundant*, it gives you the idea of independence and prosperity in business. The last brings up the "jovial bowl, my boys," and such an association's worth the having. If it *ever* gets tired of *me*, I will forward it to *you*—you would love it for *my* sake, if not for its own; it will tell you some queer stories about me,—how I sneezed so loud one night that the family thought the last trump was sounding, and climbed into the currant-bushes to get out of the way; how the rest of the people, arrayed in long night-gowns, folded their arms, and were waiting; but this is a wicked story,—it can tell some better ones. Now, my dear friend, let me tell you that these last thoughts are fictions,—vain imaginations to lead astray foolish young women. They are flowers of speech; they both make and tell deliberate falsehoods; avoid them as the snake, and turn aside as from the rattle-snake, and I don't *think* you will be harmed. Honestly, though, a snakebite is a serious matter, and there can't be too much said or done about it. The big serpent bites the deepest; and we get so accustomed to its bites that we don't mind about them. "Verily I say unto you, fear *him*." Won't you read some work upon snakes?—I have a real anxiety for you. *I* love those little green ones that slide around by your shoes in the grass, and make it rustle with their elbows; they are rather my favorites on the whole; but I wouldn't influence *you* for the world. There is an air of misanthropy about the striped snake that will commend itself at once to your taste,—there is no monotony about it—but we will more of this again. Something besides severe colds and serpents, and we will try to find *that* something. It can't be a garden, can it? or a strawberry-bed, which rather belongs to a garden; nor it can't be a school-house, nor an attorney-at-law. Oh, dear! I don't know what it is. Love for the absent don't *sound* like it; but try it and see how it goes.

I miss you very much indeed; think of you at night when the world's nodding, nid, nid, nodding—think of you in the daytime when the cares of the world, and its continual vexations choke up the love for friends in some of our hearts; remember your warnings sometimes—try to do as you told me sometimes—and sometimes conclude it's no use to try; then my heart says it *is*, and new trial is followed by disappointment again. I wondered, when you had gone, why we didn't talk more,—it wasn't for want of a subject; it never *could be* for *that*. Too many, perhaps,—such a crowd of people that nobody heard the speaker, and all went away discontented. You astonished me in the outset, perplexed me in the continuance, and wound up in a grand snarl I shall be all my pilgrimage unravelling. Rather a dismal prospect certainly; but "it's always the darkest the hour before day," and this earlier sunset promises an earlier rise—a sun in splendor—and glory, flying out of its purple nest. Wouldn't you love to see God's bird, when it first tries its wings? If you were here I would tell you something—several somethings—which have happened since you went away; but time and space, as usual, oppose themselves, and I put my treasures away till "we two meet again." The hope that I shall continue in love towards you, and *vice versa*, will sustain me till then. If you are thinking soon to go away, and to show your face no more, just inform me, will you? I would have the "long, lingering look," which you cast behind,—it would be an invaluable addition to my treasures, and "keep your memory green." "Lord, keep all our memories green," and help on our affection, and tie the "link that doth us bind" in a tight bow-knot that will keep it from separation, and stop us from growing old; if that is impossible, make old age pleasant to us, put its arms around us kindly, and when we go home, let that home be called Heaven.

Your very sincere and *wicked* friend

Emily E. Dickinson

To a Young Friend

June 25, 1745.

My Dear Friend:

I know of no Medicine fit to diminish the violent natural inclination you mention; and if I did, I think I should not communicate it to you. Marriage is the proper Remedy. It is the most natural State of Man, and therefore the State in which you will find solid Happiness. Your Reason against entering into it at present appears to be not well founded. The Circumstantial Advantages you have in View by Postponing it, are not only uncertain, but they are small in comparison with the Thing itself, *the being married and settled*. It is the Man and Woman united that makes the complete human Being. Separate she wants his force of Body and Strength of Reason; he her Softness, Sensibility and acute Discernment. Together they are most likely to succeed in the World. A single Man has not nearly the Value he would have in that State of Union. He is an incomplete Animal. He resembles the odd Half of a Pair of Scissors.

If you get a prudent, healthy wife, your Industry in your Profession, with her good Economy, will be a Fortune sufficient.

But if you will not take this Counsel, and persist in thinking a Commerce with the Sex is inevitable, then I repeat my former Advice that in your Amours you should *prefer old Women to young ones*. This you call a Paradox, and demand my reasons. They are these:

1 Because they have more Knowledge of the world, and their Minds are better stored with Observations; their Conversation is more improving, and more lastingly agreeable.

2 Because when Women cease to be handsome, they study to be good. To maintain their Influence over Man, they supply the Diminution of Beauty by an Augmentation of Utility. They learn to do a thousand Services, small and great, and are the most tender and useful of all Friends when you are sick. Thus they continue amiable. And hence there is hardly such a thing to be found as an old Woman who is not a good Woman.

3 Because there is no hazard of children, which irregularly produced may be attended with much inconvenience.

4 Because through more Experience they are more prudent and discreet in conducting an Intrigue to prevent Suspicion. The Commerce with them is therefore safer with regard to your reputation; and regard to theirs, if the Affair should happen to be known, considerate People might be inclined to excuse an old Woman, who would kindly take care of a young Man, form his manners by her good Councils, and prevent his ruining his Health and Fortune among mercenary Prostitutes.

5 Because in every Animal that walks upright, the Deficiency of the Fluids that fill the Muscles appears first in the highest Part. The Face first grows lank and wrinkled; then the Neck; then the Breast and Arms; the lower parts continuing to the last as plump as ever; so that covering all above

with a Basket, and regarding only what is below the Girdle, it is impossible of two Women to know an old from a young one. And as in the Dark all Cats are grey, the Pleasure of Corporal Enjoyment with an old Woman is at least equal and frequently superior; every Knack being by Practice capable by improvement.

6 Because the sin is less. The Debauching of a Virgin may be her Ruin, and make her for Life unhappy.

7 Because the Compunction is less. The having made a young Girl *miserable* may give you frequent bitter Reflections; none of which can attend making an old Woman *happy*.

8th & lastly. They are so grateful!!!

Thus much for my Paradox. But still I advise you to marry immediately; being sincerely

Your Affectionate Friend,

Benj. Franklin

Shame of the Catholics,
Shame of the English*

To be at the same time a Catholic and an Englishman is today to be ashamed on both counts. As a Catholic one is ashamed that more than a thousand years of Christianity have not abated the brutality of those Catholic women who shaved a young girl's head and poured tar and red lead over her body because she intended to marry an English soldier. As an Englishman the shame is even greater.

"Deep interrogation"—a bureaucratic phrase which takes the place of the simpler word "torture" and is worthy of Orwell's *1984*—is on a different level of immorality than hysterical sadism or the indiscriminating bomb of urban guerrillas. It is something organized with imagination and a knowledge of psychology, calculated and cold-blooded, and it is only half condemned by the Compton probe.

Mr. Maudling, in his blithe jolly style, reminiscent of that used by defenders of corporal punishment when they remember their school days, suggests that no one has suffered permanent injury from this form of torture, by standing long hours pressed against a wall, hooded in darkness, isolated and deprived of hearing as well as sight by permanent noise, prevented in the intervals of the ordeal from sleep—these were the methods we condemned in the Slansky trial in Czechoslovakia and in the case of Cardinal Mindszenty in Hungary.

Slansky is dead; he cannot be asked by Mr. Maudling how permanent was the injury he suffered, but one would like to know the opinion of the

* This letter, written from Paris, was published by *The Times* of London on November 26, 1971, and by *The New York Times* on December 2, 1971.

Cardinal on methods which when applied by Communists or Fascists we call "torture" and when applied by the British become down-graded to "ill treatment." If I, as a Catholic, were living in Ulster today I confess I would have one savage and irrational ambition—to see Mr. Maudling pressed against a wall for hours on end, with a hood over his head, hearing nothing but the noise of a wind machine, deprived of sleep when the noise temporarily ceases by the bland voice of a politician telling him that his brain will suffer no irreparable damage.

The effect of these methods extends far beyond the borders of Ulster. How can any Englishman now protest against torture in Vietnam, in Greece, in Brazil, in the psychiatric wards of the U.S.S.R., without being told, "You have a double standard: one for others and another for your own country."

And after all the British tortures and Catholic outrages, what comes next? We all know the end of the story, however long the politicians keep up their parrot cry of "no talk until violence ends." When I was young it was the same cliché they repeated. Collins was "a gunman and a thug." "We will not talk to murderers." No one doubts that it was in our power then to hold Ireland by force. The Black and Tans matched the Republicans in terror. It was the English people who in the end forced the politicians to sit down at a table with "the gunman and the thug."

Now too, when the deaths and the tortures have gone on long enough to blacken us in the eyes of the world and to sicken even a Conservative of the right, there will inevitably be a temporary truce and a round-table conference—Mr. Maudling or his successor will sit down over the coffee and the sandwiches with representatives of Eire and Stormont, of the I.R.A. and the Provisional I.R.A. to discuss with no preordained conditions changes in the constitution and in the borders of Ulster. Why not now rather than later?

Graham Greene

The unexamined life is not worth living.

Socrates

SECTION 3   The Autobiographical Sketch
Part One: A Significant moment

Identifying a significant moment in your life, past or present, is a first step in writing an effective autobiographical sketch. Such a moment need not be catastrophic—in fact most of the essays in this section deal with quite ordinary events—but simply one that matters to you in some way, one that taught you something about yourself, perhaps, or about your family or your place in the community. Your task is twofold therefore: to tell what happened and what it meant to you. Whereas in description and narration you concentrated on capturing the qualities and configurations of objects and events, here you are more concerned with analyzing your responses to them. You are the principal subject, the dialogue between your mind and the external world the central focus.

Neither of the following essays is exceptional, but we would probably all agree that the first moves us while the second does not.

As a child I was shy, withdrawn, and easily embarrassed by any overtures of affection. I liked the warm feeling these gave me but I never knew quite how to respond to them. Subsequently I offered little love to the people I cared about.

One summer night Mama and I lay across her sofa, which was let out into a bed. The lights were turned off because the door and windows were open and anyone passing by could look in. The moon was full and bright and shone through the window and across the bed where we lay. The night was still, as nights usually are in a small town on a weeknight. Every now and then we'd feel a cool gush of air flutter across our bodies. I could hear the crickets making their cricket sounds and the leaves on the trees rustling when the wind suddenly filtered through.

The night was so calm and peaceful that I had a kind of breath-catching, aching feeling inside. Mama was telling me something about the old days. I'm not sure what it was since I was only half listening. I was staring out of the window at the big, comfortably warm moon set against the dark, diamond-studded sky. Mama finished what she was saying and we lay quietly, scarcely moving in the dark.

Suddenly, for no particular reason, I had an almost uncontrollable urge to reach over and hug Mama as hard as I could and tell her I loved her. Never having been an impulsive person, I resisted the urge, telling myself how foolish that would be. What if Mama asked me what she did to deserve a hug. I'd have no answer. If I tried to explain what I felt inside and she didn't understand, I'd be embarrassed. And how could I expect her to understand? She was my eighty-year-old grandmother. She didn't think like a child and couldn't know what I was feeling deep inside.

I kept staring at the moon. Several minutes passed. Somehow the night sounds were less striking, the moon's glow less vivid, the night less beautiful. I was saddened. I knew that no matter how many times I hugged Mama and told her I loved her I'd never be able to express what I felt at that moment. Somehow I knew I'd never feel exactly that way again because I'd never be quite the same innocent child I'd been before that lost moment.

Barbara Smith

During the span of nineteen years many things have happened to me that I will always remember. The two that had the greatest effect were my family and my friends.

As a child all I knew was the love and affection I received from my parents and family. Being the youngest, I was usually the center of attention, which gave me a sense of security. We were a closeknit family, and often went on picnics, played tennis, and attended church together.

Nine years ago a tragedy struck us—my father was killed in a plane crash. It was very hard on the entire family, especially my mother. She had to act as father and mother to us. My two sisters, who are four and six years older, were starting to mature and have a sense of independence. As a result, my mother and I became very close, and it got so that I couldn't bear to leave her alone. The thought of her being by herself made me sad and frightened.

Our family was "child-centered." My mom has always done everything she could for us. She even decided against working because she felt she would be neglecting us.

My older sister and I are unusually close, more like best friends than sisters. She would share all her experiences and advice with me, and tell me things you wouldn't normally tell a sister who was six years younger. From her experience and advice I have developed my own goals and ideas.

My friends have also had a great deal of influence on my development. Because I spend a great deal of time with them, I learned what their morals and values are, which have influenced mine. Having friends has made me more loyal and responsible. It has also made me appreciate what I have.

Perhaps the most striking difference between the two essays is that the first has a definite focus and the second does not. The first girl concentrates on a single incident, lying next to her grandmother on a summer evening, and connects it to a larger concern in her life, namely her inability to express affection. Even though her writing is occasionally flat and she fails to explore her responses in depth, she manages to establish the essential dialogue between self and other. We feel her sadness and guilt and understand how these feelings derive from, and in turn give meaning to, the event she describes.

The second essay, on the other hand, is simply a mechanical, direction-less autobiographical résumé. Each paragraph introduces a new topic—the father's death, the author's feelings about her mother, her relationship with her older sister—but none is examined critically. In place of analysis we get clichés ("My older sister and I are unusually close, more like best friends than sisters") and meaningless generalizations ("My friends have also had a great deal of influence on my development"). Even the father's death is presented in a detached, impersonal manner: "Nine years ago a tragedy struck us: my father was killed in a plane crash." It isn't that the girl is being evasive intentionally so much as that she has no idea what it means to speak personally and directly. Unlike the first writer, she does not discuss her feelings openly or probe an experience until it reveals something about herself. Consequently, we have no sense of her as a person or of the connections between the events she describes and larger issues in her life.

Neither essay is as sharply detailed as good autobiographical writing should be, not for the reader's benefit only but for the writer's as well. We don't remember abstractions, we remember objects, images, and sensations. The smell of fresh bread may suddenly remind you of Saturdays when you were a child or the sound of crashing waves may bring back an idyllic vacation on the coast of Maine. Whether you are writing about the remote or the recent past (e.g., yesterday, this morning) you need concrete details, and the emotions and impressions associated with them, to recapture it successfully. Note how meticulously Kazin records the noises and odors of his old neighborhood (page 23) or how James Agee uses familiar images and objects to recreate a moment in his childhood:

> But the men by now, one by one, have silenced their hoses and drained and coiled them. Now only two, and now only one, is left, and you see only ghostlike shirt with the sleeve garters and sober mystery of his mild face like the lifted face of large cattle enquiring of your presence in a pitchdark pool of meadow; and now he too is gone; and it has become that time of evening when people sit on their porches, rocking gently and talking gently and watching the street and the standing up into their sphere of possession of the trees, of birds hung havens, hangers. People go by; things go by. A horse, drawing a buggy, breaking his hollow iron music on the asphalt; a loud auto, a quiet auto, people in pairs, not in a hurry, scuffling, switching their weight of aestival body, talking casually, the taste hovering over them of vanilla, strawberry, pasteboard and starched milk, the image upon them of lovers and horsemen, squared with clowns in hueless amber. A street car raising its iron moan; stopping, belling and starting; stertorous; rousing and raising again its iron increasing moan and swimming its gold windows and straw seats on past and past and past, the bleak spark crackling and cursing above it like a small malignant spirit set to dog its tracks; the iron whine rises on rising speed; still risen, faints; halts; the faint stinging bell; rises again, still fainter; fainting, lifting, lifts, faints forgone: forgotten. Now is the night one blue dew.

Knoxville: Summer 1915

The point is not to try to imitate Agee's dreamy poetic prose but merely to recognize the importance of sensory detail in unlocking a past experience. You live in space and time; bring your narrative and descriptive skills to bear on your private experience in order to make it public.

The Agee passage also illustrates an interesting stylistic strategy. Although essentially a memory piece, it is written in what might be called a "presentational" style, meaning that besides its highly tactile language, which is appropriate for a child's point of view, it contains numerous present participles, independent active verbs, and run-on sentences that immerse a reader in the experience being described. For a moment we are back in Knoxville, lying on the grass, watching and listening to night coming on. There is a marked absence of any interpretative commentary that would break the spell, although it is present subtly in phrases like "aestival body" and "their sphere of possession of the trees." Agee is attempting to recreate a past experience rather than analyze it. Conroy (page 133) and Ginsberg (page 138), although much less poetic than Agee, are also presenters.

For contrast, study this passage from Max Beerbohm's essay *A Relic*:

> I did once see her, and in Normandy, and by moonlight, and her name was Angelique. She was graceful, she was even more beautiful. I was but nineteen years old. Yet even so I cannot say that she impressed me favorably. I was seated at a table of a cafe on the terrace of a casino. I sat facing the sea, with my back to the casino. I sat listening to the quiet sea, which I had crossed that morning. The hour was late, there were few people about. I heard the swing door behind me flap open, and was aware of a sharp snapping and crackling sound as a lady in white passed quickly by me. I stared at her erect, thin back and her agitated elbows. A short fat man passed in pursuit of her, an elderly man in a black alpaca jacket that billowed. I saw that she had left a trail of little white things on the asphalt. I watched the efforts of the agonized short fat man to overtake her as she swept wraithlike away to the distant end of the terrace. What was the matter? What had made her so spectacularly angry with him? The three or four waiters of the cafe were exchanging cynical smiles and shrugs, as waiters will. I tried to feel cynical, but was thrilled with excitement, with wonder and curiosity.

This too is concrete and detailed, yet we are more conscious of a reflective, analytical voice than in the preceding passage. Beerbohm summarizes and generalizes freely, and is much more explicitly interpretative than Agee. (See the last two sentences for example.) The original incident has clearly become an occasion for an adult's reflection, and in fact throughout the essay Beerbohm asks us to compare the boy's perspective with the man's. This opposition in points of view is one source of the essay's appeal, but it also makes us, as readers, stand farther back. We are more observers than participants.

As you do some of the exercises in this section, therefore, experiment with both strategies to see which suits your purposes better.

SUMMARY

In this section you are asked to recount a single important experience in your life, perhaps one that gave you a fresh insight into yourself or into your relationships with people and institutions. It may have occurred yesterday, last month, ten years ago; it may have been dramatic or extremely ordinary. In any case, memory, supplemented by narrative and descriptive details, is the principal means for bringing it alive for your reader and yourself. You may decide to compare your past and present impressions of the experience in order to show a change in attitude, or you may attempt to recreate it as it actually happened and allow the reader to draw his own conclusions. One approach is essentially analytical, the other essentially dramatic. Both demand a willingness to examine a personal experience closely and an ability to describe it honestly and straightforwardly for a reader.

EXERCISES

1. (a) Make a list of the ten words that describe you best. Write an extended definition of one of them as it applies to your life.

   (b) In one paragraph give a reader a single "telling fact" about yourself.

2. We often retain sharp memories of those moments in which we discovered an important truth about ourselves, our families and friends, our relationship to society in general. Here are several kinds of first experiences that may generate an autobiographical essay. Be detailed, concrete, and extremely wary of wispy generalizations like "It was the most thrilling spectacle I'd ever seen" or "It was the most meaningful experience of my life." Unless you can somehow show the thrills and the meaning your reader will ignore the superlatives.

   (a) The first time you realized that you had some skill, insight, or ambition that made you different from other people.

   (b) The first time you became aware of a prejudice, lie, or misconception that was influencing your actions and attitudes.

   (c) The first time you discovered that someone you loved or admired was imperfect.

   (d) Your first encounter with an institution or agency that taught you something about your place in society.

   (e) Your first experience with a book, film, or work of art that significantly changed your way of looking at yourself and your world.

3. In his autobiography, *A Sort of Life*, Graham Greene mentions coming across an old grade school questionnaire on which he had listed his favorite books, songs, foods, hobbies and so forth. From this simple document he was able to reconstruct a small yet significant portion of his childhood. Fill out a similar questionnaire for your own grade school years and see what kind of self-image it projects. Discuss how your habits and tastes have changed and how they have remained the same.

4. Recall a time in your childhood or early adolescence when you felt extremely lonely, fearful, embarrassed, or wronged. As precisely as you can, describe the feeling, the circumstances that aroused it, and how you tried to cope with both.

5. Write a brief essay (500 words) about a childhood experience that at the time seemed momentous but which, as you reflect upon it now, seems inconsequential. Here you are trying not only to recapture a moment in

your past but to describe a shift in perception as well. You might find Max Beerbohm's essay *A Relic* (page 144) helpful.

6. Describe an incident, past or present, which involved a dramatic reversal of your expectations. For example, a time when you expected to be praised and were criticized, or a time when you were convinced that you were going to succeed and you failed. Describe your feelings before and after the reversal.

READINGS

Russell

I was standing at the stove trying to look as domestic as possible for someone who hates to cook when I felt a hand on my shoulder. I turned around as Russell began to lead me out of the kitchen. He looked serious, but all he said was, "I want to show you something." I protested as we got in the car, not wanting to leave Maggie to cook breakfast by herself, but I could see that what he was about to show me was important to him. I took a chance and asked him where we were going, but as I expected I didn't get an answer.

We rode in silence most of the way, commenting only on the weather and the beauty of the mountains around us. It was a fairly short drive, winding around the river and through the trees. "I want to show you something Mark and Jim and I worked really hard on," Russell finally said. Before I had time to puzzle on what it could be we rounded a curve and stopped in front of a rusty gate. I looked up to see a sign that said "Con-Can Cemetery." "How could I have forgotten about Larry being buried up here?" I wondered as we pulled onto a dirt road leading into the cemetery.

I was not sure at all that I wanted to see Larry's grave. I had heard so much about the murder of Russell's brother, but it was different somehow to stand and look at the tombstone. "Free men are never equal, equal men are never free. I am free." Larry's favorite saying sounded like the independent guy I'd heard so much about. Tears came to my eyes as I remembered some of Larry's poems that Russell had let me read. I thought of all the unopened journals full of his poetry and ideas stored up in the attic. How sad it seemed that he had kept so much of himself from others! But I could understand why Russell and his parents preferred not to read what Larry had chosen to keep quiet.

It suddenly occurred to me that I should be strong so I blinked away my tears and turned to Russell where he stood watering the wild jasmine planted next to the grave. "Isn't this place beautiful?" he asked for the third time. I decided that he was trying to cover up his feelings by chattering nervously so I said, "Yes," without adding "if you like cemeteries."

He talked on and on about the different plants that the deer had eaten the flowers off until I wanted to ask him to quit covering up his feelings for me. It would have been easier, I thought, if he had simply been quiet or started crying instead of the constant empty chatter.

He continued to water the jasmine and other flowers while I contemplated what it must have been like for an eighteen-year-old boy to lose a big brother. I remembered he had told me that he was forced to be the strong one, comforting his parents and Grandma. I thought about the way that Larry's death had affected Russell's father coming within a month after the death of his own mother. I thought about the way Russell's mother writes to him every day and how she had told me that he was trying to get everything into his lifetime that Larry had missed. And I tried to realize what it must have been like to no longer have an older brother in whose footsteps he could follow.

I turned to look at Russell as he soaked the flowers with the hose and marveled at the strength it must have taken for him to stand up to a decision to go to school in the city where his only brother had been killed. I walked over to him hoping that he would get rid of all the stored up emotion and forced strength long enough to cry on my shoulder. Instead he picked three flowers off the yellow jasmine, gave them to me and said, "I don't know why the deer don't eat the jasmine."

Donna Morris

From *Stop-Time*

A perpendicular column of blue light descended from the sky to the parking field, striking the earth behind a screen of silhouetted automobiles, spreading a pool of white radiance, a vague open-topped dome of light in the air above us. Insects drifted through like snowflakes, disappearing at the perimeter.

"Now make sure you know where the car is," Mrs. Rawlings said. "We'll meet here at midnight." She saw Sean rushing off. "Sean! Did you mind me?" He was gone before she could stop him. "That boy," she said sadly.

The old man took out his change purse. "How much money have you got?"

"Sixty cents," Tobey answered.

"Frankie?"

"Seventy-three cents, sir."

He counted some change and held it out to us. "That makes a dollar and a half each. And don't spend it all in one place."

"Thank you!" we yelled together.

Pat gave us each a quarter, and just before we took off, Tobey's mother held out two silver coins. "That's eating money," she said. "And you ain't getting any more so don't spend it on those bumper cars like last time."

"We won't, Momma. Thanks."

"Thank you, ma'am."

"All right, boys. Have a good time and stay out of trouble. We'll see you later." She moved off on her husband's arm, smiling, one hand unnecessarily holding down her hat (as if he were sweeping her away in a waltz or a polka, as if only now, at the last moment, could she control her appearance before giving up to the madcap whirl of the evening), her buttocks rolling like ships at sea.

On the fairway Tobey and I darted through the crowd like needles through a tapestry, turning, pausing, deftly insinuating ourselves across the slow movement of the parade.

The bumper cars! Waiting in line we draped ourselves over the wooden railing and surveyed the scene. On the steel floor small cars raced into the distance, took a curve, and raced back, each with a long pole to the shiny roof trailing sparks of power. Most of the drivers were children, but here and there an adult could be seen, or a young couple crammed in together, giggling, trying to avoid collisions. WHOMP! We laughed as a kid in overalls caught a teen-aged girl broadside and spun away before she could retaliate. WHOMP! Someone else hit her. This time she straightened out and gave it some speed, accelerating nicely.

"That one looks good," I said. "Number Ten. I hope she gets out." There were small but critical differences in the power of the cars. It was important to get the faster ones.

"Thirty-eight," Tobey said. "And that blue one, Ninety-nine."

When the boy came around we each bought a ribbon of tickets. The air was full of ozone, a thin, sharp, white smell in the back of one's nose. A whistle blew and the power was cut. All over the floor cars rolled to a stop.

"She's getting out," I yelled as the crowd pushed up behind us. "Number Ten! I've got Number Ten."

"Ninety-nine! In the back."

As the floor cleared the boy swung open the barrier and stepped to the side. With a tremendous roar fifty kids rushed out onto the steel track, fanning out from the narrow gate in all directions like water from a split hose. Someone was at my side, racing me to Number Ten, but at the last moment (when he was slowing down) I leaped into the air and landed with both feet in the cockpit, my hands grabbing the pole for support. Laughing, I slithered down into position and watched him run off for another car.

The controls were simple. An accelerator and a steering wheel. I spun the wheel, testing the amount of play. It was fairly tight. Waiting, I tried to find Tobey, but the view was obscured.

At last every kid had a car. The barrier was closed and a whistle sounded. I pressed the accelerator to the floor as somewhere out of sight the power was turned on. My car began to move. The sound in that vast room filled with cars was not unlike the powerful noise of a subway train as it pulls away from the platform. Dozens of cars moved at top speed around the track, dodging in and out as the drivers attempted to get the feel of their vehicles. I bent back my head, sighting up the pole to watch the metal tongue sliding across the roof, sucking power.

Confident, after a few experiments, that my car was one of the best on the floor, I took off to look for Tobey, sideswiping a few kids along the way just for the hell of it. "One Way Only!" said a sign on the wall, "No Head On Collisions." Tobey was waiting for me at the edge of the curve. He'd got the car he wanted, the blue one. I pulled up beside him.

"Okay?"

"Okay!"

"Who do we get?"

"Watch it!" Tobey was struck by a giggling girl who made no attempt to control her vehicle. She'd been pushed into Tobey by a fat boy in a Tom Mix T-shirt. "Him!" Tobey yelled. "Tom Mix!"

Our strategy had been worked out the previous year. The only question was who went first. Tobey took off, and after skirting the helpless girl, I counted to ten under my breath and followed. Elbows out, back curved over the wheel, Tobey pursued the fat boy, slowly closing the gap. We went an entire lap before Tom Mix made his move. He went to the outside, figuring to cut across and catch the giggling girl from behind. Tobey anticipated this and raced down the rail, turning at the last moment to cross paths with plenty of speed. At exactly the same time I aimed for the spot where it seemed to me Tom Mix would end up, collecting maximum speed on the long straight run.

It worked perfectly. Tobey closed in, his head bent down. At the last instant Tom Mix saw him coming and tried to turn away, but it was too late. FA-BOOM! Tobey caught him solidly on the left fender, spinning the car a quarter turn, reversing his wheels, and bringing him to a halt. Tom Mix spun the steering wheel frantically, trying to straighten himself out and get started again. He'd been prepared for Tobey, but as I barreled in, teeth clenched, straight-armed, I could see he didn't expect me. His body was loose. Innocent. FA-BAM! A marvelous, straight-on hit, jolting him in his seat, shaking his fat like Jello.

We were invincible! Gasping, choking with laughter too wild and sweet to come out, our brains bursting with excitement, we drove off to new conquests.

It was getting late. The crowds had thinned out and along the fairway most of the stalls were closing down for the night. Tobey and I sat on the guard rail of a darkened carousel eating hot dogs, automatically waving away the flies.

"How much have you got left?"

"Thirty-five cents," I said.

"I've got a quarter."

"I guess it's almost midnight."

Tobey jumped down from the fence and ran to ask someone what time it was. Tired, I walked after him.

"Ten of," he said when I reached him.

"Well, let's mosey on down."

We ambled along the littered promenade in the general direction of the parking field, checking the sandy ground for dropped coins. Tobey bent over and picked up a small felt pennant on a stick. DANIA-FLA. on a background of orange blossoms. "For the tree house."

We stopped in front of a freak show to look at the posters. The alligator man. The duck woman. The armless wonder. Special attraction! The man without a face.

"I saw it last year," Tobey said. "It's a fake."

"They say he's got alligator skin."

"He's painted up. He lies around in a pit full of sawdust with these big hunks of raw meat. But he doesn't touch the meat or anything. It's a fake."

"You mean he's just like us only painted up?"

"Well, no," Tobey said, pausing. "He don't have no arms. His hands sort of grow out of his shoulders."

"What?"

"Like little baby hands. But they're dead. He can't move them."

"Didn't it make you feel funny to look at him?"

"I didn't like it. He just lay there in the sawdust, real still, like he was dead, with his head turned away. And we all walked by. If he'd really been an alligator man, well then okay, but it was a fake and I didn't want to look." He turned away from the poster. "Let's go."

At the edge of the fair a small booth is still open, its lights shining out into the empty air. A big man in a purple jacket sits on a stool behind the counter drinking a container of coffee. As we approach he pauses momentarily, looks at us over the rim of the container, and then continues drinking as if he hadn't seen us.

We stop twenty feet away to examine the game. It's a ring toss. Ten cents a throw and the prizes are on the walls. Pennants, funny hats, candy boxes, two live canaries, china dolls, stuffed animals, canned hams, ukuleles, toasters, radios, silverware. Tobey nudges me. "Look there, on the back wall." I whistle softly. Mounted on a wooden plaque, with a belt and holster hanging next to it, is the grand prize, a silver revolver.

"Wow," Tobey whispers as we move forward.

"It's beautiful. Look at the carving on the handle."

"With a holster and everything."

The big man hasn't looked at us, or moved a muscle.

"How do you win the gun?" Tobey asks.

"Two out of three tosses on the red peg," he says expressionlessly.

We look at the back wall. Recessed into a lighted chamber under the pistol is a red peg, angled backwards under a sloping roof. I give Tobey a nickel. "We can both try."

"Okay. Give me three, please."

It's as if the man is blind. He stares fixedly out into the darkness. Bright lights shine behind his head. He leans forward slightly, collects the change with one hand, and brings up three rings from under the counter with the other, all in one smooth movement, without looking down or changing position on the stool.

Tobey takes aim and throws a ring. It strikes the wall and falls onto a shelf below. "Too high," he says, and throws again. The second ring is too low. "Shucks," Tobey says. "Well, for one I get a radio." He throws the last ring. It strikes the recessed enclosure straight on, but doesn't fit and falls away. "Did you see that?" he asks me.

"It won't go that way. You have to lob it in at an angle so it'll fit."

"I'm going to ask Momma for another thirty cents. I'll be right back." He runs off into the darkness.

I stand for a moment, studying the red peg. My heart beats quickly because of the discovery of throwing at an angle. It'll still be difficult, the ring must enter the enclosure at exactly the right tilt. Once inside, it must fall on the peg by its own weight. I remind myself to throw softly so it won't bounce off the back wall.

"I'll take three."

Once again he leans forward in the smooth gesture, slapping the rings on the counter near my hands. Behind me, far away, I can hear cars starting up on the parking field.

The edge of the counter presses against my stomach. I toss the first ring, giving a faint flick of the wrist at the last instant to keep it from turning over in the air. It sails into the enclosure as if guided by an invisible hand. I can hardly believe my eyes. It falls slowly toward the peg, strikes, and leans. I duck down my head and shield my eyes from the bright lights. Yes! It covers the top of the peg! Another good toss could knock it over.

Three feet away the man sits absolutely without movement. I can hear his breathing. He hasn't looked up, or back at the red peg. It's as if I'm not there.

Picking up the second ring I know I'm going to win. Nothing can stop it, as if it's already happened, as if time were runing backward. A peculiar, giddy feeling comes over me. A lightheadedness, strangely familiar. I throw the second ring. It misses and falls away. I shrug, blinking, as if something annoying had happened around me, some minor irritation interrupting my concentration. I feel like asking for the ring back even though I know it makes no difference. The third ring is in my hands. I lean forward, aim, and throw. It goes into the enclosure, as I had known it would, falls onto the peg, and knocks the other loose underneath itself. I've won. Two rings over the red peg. I look at them for a moment. An immense calmness lies over my soul. Then I look up at the revolver.

"I've won."

The man doesn't move.

"I've won. Look."

He turns around and looks at the peg. Then he gets off the stool and walks back and takes the rings off the peg and drops them with the others on the shelf. He comes back and stands in front of me, gazing out over my head. "You missed."

"What?"

He says nothing.

For a moment I don't know what to do. I stand there looking up at him. His face is white and hard.

"But I won," I say.

Slowly he lowers his head and looks at me. His eyes are dark under thick black eyebrows. He lifts his arm from behind the counter and extends it to me. As if in a dream I reach out to shake hands.

Gently but firmly he takes my wrist, bends, and spreads his knees a fraction of an inch, and slowly rubs my palm under his balls.

Frank Conroy

From *Allen Ginsberg in America*

Ginsberg finished Columbia at the end of 1948, under somewhat unusual circumstances.

"Huncke got out of jail again," Ginsberg recalls. "I had told him, like, 'Never darken my door again,' but that kind of thing wasn't part of Huncke's vocabulary, so he found out where I was living and just kind of arrived. It was snowing outside, and his shoes were so bad that his feet were bleeding. He'd been up wandering for four days—the cops had chased him off Times Square—and he was in a funny, almost suicidal state, in a very high state of awareness of things around him, very neurasthenically sensitive and at the same time in a kind of total, somnolent depression. He didn't know where else to go, and I couldn't put him out again, so he got on the couch and stayed there, sleeping, for about three weeks. Then one day he finally went out, to my relief, and came back with some money. He'd robbed a car. I was overjoyed! He'd come back to life. Like he was back operating again, which meant that he wasn't going to die. It was really a very funny, paradoxical situation, because at the time there was all this talk at Columbia about what is right, what is wrong, what's ethics, what's morality, what's social good, what's social bad, what's utilitarianism, what's justifiable, what's unjustifiable—all of it from people who were fighting and scrambling to get ahead and making atom bombs. So I began to notice that Huncke was like a victim of a monstrosity of laws and attitudes. He was a twenty-year addict and in any decent system he would have been pensioned off and supplied with drugs—and how was I in a position to judge whether he was right or wrong in stealing or if he was right or wrong in being an addict? It was beyond that at this point. So with Huncke around, I found my social views altering increasingly through experience. And I began to get that alienated view of the actual structure of society which everybody then thought was disgraceful, but now they call it 'elite alienation' and things like that. Well, Huncke became more and more prosperous. I didn't quite disapprove. I didn't quite approve. I just sort of asked him about it from time to time. I was busy with my own work, writing poems and psalms. Glad that Huncke was alive. But then he began bringing people over to the house. First, there was this chick I already knew, who had first turned Kerouac and me on to Benzedrine inhalers. A tall red-headed chick. She had been mainly a whore, actually, with very expensive johns who would pay her a hundred dollars a shot. And she was a very lively chick, who took a lot of pot. Really a remark-able, beautiful, goodhearted, tender girl. I had a special regard for her from years before, because she had really put herself out to straighten me out, and here she was like a big, expensive whore. It had seemed like an extraordi-nary gesture. So I wasn't in any position to kick her out of the house now. She came with her boy friend, a guy named Little Jack Melody, who was a sort of subdivision cousin of the Mafia. He was an interesting guy—like he had this Italian background and a big happy Italian family out on Long Island—and he was in love with the girl. They were going to have a child. So it was like a whole *Beggar's Opera* scene at my house. The three of them were going out on burglary expeditions together, and bringing back all the loot. They even robbed a detective's house in Harlem. I remonstrated in vain. There wasn't really much I could do, and anyway, every time I'd put Huncke down he'd say, 'What do you want me to do? What am I *supposed* to do?' So meanwhile my house was filling up with chests of silver, silver sets, all sorts of dreck like radios, phonograph machines. It was getting crowded, actu-ally. I didn't know what to do, and I began thinking, 'I've got to kick them out or I've got to leave myself.' Well, it was too difficult to kick *them* out, and I really wanted to get away anyway, so I made plans to go down to Mexico and visit Burroughs. I saved up a little money, and packed all my stuff in one big set of cardboard boxes. Manuscripts. Letters from Burroughs. Letters from Kerouac. Letters from Cassady. Everything. Little Jack had a car, and the plan was that we were going to drive out to Long Island, where Little Jack would drop off some of his things at his mother's. Then we'd take all my uptown stuff to store with my brother, who was at law school at NYU. So we piled everything in the car—Little Jack, me, and the girl; Huncke stayed home—and started out toward Long Island, and then, on Utopia Parkway, Little Jack took the wrong turn down a one-way street at the end of which was a police car. Now it so happened that the car we were in was a stolen car. And, in addition to having my papers in it, it had Little Jack's things, which were like a great pile of stolen suits and clothes from the detective's house. So Little Jack, being like a slightly flipped-out Mafia gangster, immediately panicked. And like put his foot down on the gas and instead of just stopping and getting a ticket, tried to outrun the police car. And in the process almost ran over one of the policemen, who were out on the street by now, trying to wave him down. So the police thought Melody was trying to hit them, and *they* immediately panicked, too, and got in *their* car and began chasing us. The next thing I knew, there I was in a car speeding down Utopia Parkway at ninety miles per hour, chased by the police with drawn guns. With Little Jack getting more and more frantic, driving faster and faster and then sud-denly swerving the car around, trying to get into a side street, and smashing into a telephone pole. Turning the car over and over and over. And with me having the very distinct sensation, slightly mystical, that all my mistakes of the past year—my moral indecisions and my slight acquisitive interest in some of the loot that was coming into the house—had led in a chain to this one retribution moment where now I was going to have to pay for it. And facing it. Singing as we rolled over in the car, 'Lord God of Israel, Isaac, and Abraham,' from the *Messiah*, like evoking the Hebraic father-figure authority divinity to come and get me, which was a very weird thing. When everything settled down, finally, the car was upside down. My manuscript and all those letters—love letters, incriminating letters about pot from Texas—were swimming around all over the place. And I couldn't find my glasses. I started searching for them, and then I realized that if I didn't beat it I was going to get caught. And I didn't want to get caught yet. Like I might have been able to get out of it then and there—it wasn't my car and it wasn't my stealing—but my house was full of stolen objects, and the address was in the car all over everything. So—quick thinking—I said, 'I'd better get home immediately. Clean out the house. Phone Huncke.' We had all escaped from the car, actually—the police had overshot the side street and were on their way back—and so we ran off in different directions. The girl got to a friend's house—I don't know how. Little Jack was captured, on the parkway, and beaten up by the police—black and blue. I just sort of wandered off without my eyeglasses down the side street and into a candy store and said, 'How do you get to New York?' They said, 'Are you in a car or what?' So I said, 'I'm a naturalist. And I'm taking a walk with nature.' I only had seven cents in my pocket, and I bummed I think twelve cents more and was able to phone and get a message through to Huncke. And then, somehow or other, I got back to New York—hitchhiking and then the subway, when I had bummed another ten cents—and I walked into the apartment and there was Huncke, looking miserable, like just sort of slowly sweeping the floor. I said, 'What are you doing, Herbert? The police will be here any minute,' but he just said, 'Oh, it's hopeless now. I've been through this so many times. There's nothing you can do.' 'Hunke, for the love of God!' I said, and then bang-bang-bang on the door, and like six big policemen charge in, and some detectives. 'Does Allen Ginsberg live here?' So the next day the New York *Daily News* had a big front-page picture of me and Huncke and the girl coming out of a police car, and the whole situation was transformed from the hermetic, cosmic, nebulous Dostoevskian thing that it was, with like *real* people involved, into this total stereotype of a giant robbery operation—six-foot, marijuana-smoking redhead, three-time-loser pariah criminal, boy-wonder mastermind. Yeah, I was advertised as the brilliant student genius who was like plotting out big criminal scenes. Another newspaper had it that I was addicted to drugs, and this gang kept me supplied and forced me to mastermind robberies. It was all a bunch of awful misinterpretations. By this time my father had come in from New Jersey, weeping, and of course everybody around Columbia was aghast. Like, 'You've made scandals before, Ginsberg, but *this*! And on top of everything, a Columbia student right on the front page of the *Daily News*!' It was really an archetypal scandal. Van Doren felt bad, but like he couldn't really understand it. 'What were you doing with those people?' he said. 'What were you doing with simple common criminals?' And he gave me like a big lecture. He said, 'A lot of us around here have been thinking maybe you'd better hear the clank of iron, Ginsberg. You don't seem to realize what you're doing. If you want my help, you've got to promise never to break the law again.' Which I suppose was very kind of sensible—like work within the society, within the normal structure of society. He posed the problem really very clearly, but at the same time he didn't have the right answer, because I was like saying that if you really felt that people like Huncke were saintly in some way or other, then you should be prepared to suffer for them and go to jail, or *something*. One professor who was really swinging on this, though, was Meyer Schapiro. He said, 'Oh, yeah, so you've been busted. That reminds me of the time *I* went to jail in Europe.' Like he had a completely humane attitude and understood the vicissitudes of poetic life. Lionel Trilling was *horrified* but friendly, helpful, and he took me up to see Professor Herbert Wechsler, at the Law School, to get some advice. The thing Wechsler said was that what I had to do was put myself into a bughouse. Plead insanity and go to a bughouse and get out of all this. So my father got me a lawyer who was an old friend of the family and who was like a real middle-class cat. And it was again like an archetypal situation where a kid gets busted and a lot of middle-class values are offended and the whole family gets excited and says, 'Why does it have to be *our* son? Why does he *do* these things?' And where the lawyer is paternal and helpful but is like saying, 'Abandon everybody! Abandon these terrible people!' And where the youthful offender, like me, becomes very confused and unsure of himself and doesn't know what he's doing and feels like he must have made some terrific cosmic *error*. And so I was thinking all this time, 'What am I doing? What am I going through, having visions and ending up in jail? What *is* reality? Is it my visions, or Huncke's void, or what's actually going on? Why can't I be like everybody else?' I saw righteousness and sensitivity being persecuted in every direction. And I was feeling guilty and ashamed because I didn't even go to court, or *anything*, like the others did, and because they were going to have to go to jail whereas the charges against me were dropped and all I had to do was tell some psychiatrist that I heard voices and had visions and *I* got to go to the Columbia Psychiatric Institute . . . Everything changed the minute I got to the bughouse. I was sitting in the reception room with my valises, waiting to be shown a bed, and like all of a sudden I began feeling very rueful and mad at Huncke, because he was always getting me into scrapes and he should have known better and protected me. He shouldn't have put me in this kind of terrible situation. *He* didn't mind going to jail, but he didn't have to continue the operation to the point where it actually involved *me*. I didn't want to be locked up in a bughouse for months and maybe years! So *I* was like sitting there and brooding. About how Huncke was doing bad things like robbing people's cars, inconveniencing people terribly. And about the cruelty of the law, and the ignorance involved. And about the excessive cruelty of the mass-media people, who were like vultures and harpies. And about the cruelty of the family apparatus and the cruelty of the criminal apparatus and my *own* cruelty, making everybody unhappy. And about the cruelty of the police who had like confiscated my Bhagavad Gita back at my house, saying, 'We don't allow anything but religious books in the can,' and about how I kept explaining about the Bhagavad Gita all the way down to the station. Like it was my main preoccupation. So I was brooding, when all of a sudden this guy Carl Solomon—Carl comes up out of the depths of the hospital from a shock streak and waddles over to me. He's in this giant bathrobe, looking very fat because of I think insulin and metrosol. And he looks at me and says, 'Who are *you*?' So I say, 'I'm Myshkin.' 'I'm Kirilov,' he says."

Jane Kramer

From *Father and Son*

Several things tended at this time to alienate my conscience from the line which my Father had so rigidly traced for it. The question of the efficacy of prayer, which has puzzled wiser heads than mine was, began to trouble me. It was insisted on in our household that if anything was desired, you should not, as my Mother said, "lose any time in seeking for it, but ask God to guide you to it." In many junctures of life this is precisely what, in sober fact, they did. I will not dwell here on their theories, which my Mother put forth, with unflinching directness, in her published writings. But I found that a difference was made between my privileges in this matter and theirs, and this led to many discussions. My parents said: "Whatever you need, tell Him and He will grant it, if it is His will." Very well; I had need of a large painted humming-top which I had seen in a shop-window in the Caledonian Road. Accordingly, I introduced a supplication for this object into my evening prayer, carefully adding the words: "If it is Thy will." This, I recollect, placed my Mother in a dilemma, and she consulted my Father. Taken, I suppose, at a disadvantage, my Father told me I must not pray for "things like that." To which I answered by another query, "Why?" And I added that he said we ought to pray for things we needed, and that I needed the humming-top a great deal more than I did the conversion of the heathen or the restitution of Jerusalem to the Jews, two objects of my nightly supplication which left me very cold.

I have reason to believe, looking back upon this scene, conducted by candle-light in the front parlour, that my Mother was much baffled by the logic of my argument. She had gone so far as to say publicly that no "things or circumstances are too insignificant to bring before the God of the whole earth." I persisted that this covered the case of the humming-top, which was extremely significant to me. I noticed that she held aloof from the discussion, which was carried on with some show of annoyance by my Father. He had never gone quite so far as she did in regard to this question of praying for material things. I am not sure that she was convinced that I ought to have been checked; but he could not help seeing that it reduced their favourite theory to an absurdity for a small child to exercise the privilege. He ceased to argue, and told me peremptorily that it was not right for me to pray for things like humming-tops, and that I must do it no more. His authority, of course, was paramount, and I yielded; but my faith in the efficacy of prayer was a good deal shaken. The fatal suspicion had crossed my mind that the reason why I was not to pray for the top was because it was too expensive for my parents to buy, that being the usual excuse for not getting things I wished for.

It was about the date of my sixth birthday that I did something very naughty, some act of direct disobedience, for which my Father, after a solemn sermon, chastised me, sacrificially, by giving me several cuts with a cane. This action was justified, as everything he did was justified, by reference to Scripture — "Spare the rod and spoil the child." I suppose that there are some children, of a sullen and lymphatic temperament, who are smartened up and made more wide-awake by a whipping. It is largely a matter of convention, the exercise being endured (I am told) with pride by the infants of our aristocracy, but not tolerated by the lower classes. I am afraid that I proved my inherent vulgarity by being made, not contrite or humble, but furiously angry by this caning. I cannot account for the flame of rage which it awakened in my bosom. My dear, excellent Father had beaten me, not very severely, without ill-temper, and with the most genuine desire to improve me. But he was not well-advised especially so far as the "dedication to the Lord's service" was concerned. This same "dedication" had ministered to my vanity, and there are some natures which are not improved by being humiliated. I have to confess with shame that I went about the house for some days with a murderous hatred of my Father locked within my bosom. He did not suspect that the chastisement had not been wholly efficacious, and he bore me no malice; so that after a while, I forgot and thus forgave him. But I do not regard physical punishment as a wise element in the education of proud and sensitive children.

My theological misdeeds culminated, however, in an act so puerile and preposterous that I should not venture to record it if it did not throw some glimmering of light on the subject which I have proposed to myself in writing these pages. My mind continued to dwell on the mysterious question of prayer. It puzzled me greatly to know why, if we were God's children, and if he was watching over us by night and day, we might not supplicate for toys and sweets and smart clothes as well as for the conversion of the heathen. Just at this juncture, we had a special service at the Room, at which our attention was particularly called to what we always spoke of as "the field of missionary labour." The East was represented among "the saints" by an excellent Irish peer, who had, in his early youth, converted and married a lady of colour; this Asiatic shared in our Sunday morning meetings, and was an object of helpless terror to me; I shrank from her amiable caresses, and vaguely identified her with a personage much spoken of in our family circle, the "Personal Devil."

All these matters drew my thoughts to the subject of idolatry, which was severely censured at the missionary meeting. I cross-examined my Father very closely as to the nature of this sin, and pinned him down to the categorical statement that idolatry consisted in praying to any one or anything but God himself. Wood and stone, in the words of the hymn, were peculiarly liable to be bowed down to by the heathen in their blindness. I pressed my Father further on this subject, and he assured me that God would be very angry, and would signify His anger, if any one, in a Christian country, bowed down to wood and stone. I cannot recall why I was so pertinacious on this subject, but I remember that my Father became a little restive under my cross-examination. I determined, however, to test the matter for myself, and one morning, when both my parents were safely out of the house, I prepared for the great act of heresy. I was in the morning-room on the ground-floor, where, with much labour, I hoisted a small chair on to the table close to the window. My heart was now beating as if it would leap out of my side, but I pursued my experiment. I knelt down on the carpet in front of the table and looking up I said my daily prayer in a loud voice, only substituting the address "O Chair!" for the habitual one.

Having carried this act of idolatry safely through, I waited to see what would happen. It was a fine day, and I gazed up at the slip of white sky above the houses opposite, and expected something to appear in it. God would certainly exhibit his anger in some terrible form, and would chastise my impious and wilful action. I was very much alarmed, but still more excited; I breathed the high, sharp air of defiance. But nothing happened; there was not a cloud in the sky, not an unusual sound in the street. Presently I was quite sure that nothing would happen. I had committed idolatry, flagrantly and deliberately, and God did not care.

The result of this ridiculous act was not to make me question the existence and power of God; those were forces which I did not dream of ignoring. But what it did was to lessen still further my confidence in my Father's knowledge of the Divine mind. My Father had said, positively, that if I worshipped a thing made of wood, God would manifest his anger. I had then worshipped a chair, made (or partly made) of wood, and God had made no sign whatever. My Father, therefore, was not really acquainted with the Divine practice in cases of idolatry. And with that, dismissing the subject, I dived again into the unplumbed depths of the *Penny Cyclopaedia*.

Edmund Gosse

A Relic

Yesterday I found in a cupboard an old, small, battered portmanteau which, by the initials on it, I recognized as my own property. The lock appeared to have been forced. I dimly remembered having forced it myself, with a poker, in my hot youth, after some journey in which I had lost the key; and this act of violence was probably the reason why the trunk had so long ago ceased to travel. I unstrapped it, not without dust; it exhaled the faint scent of its long closure; it contained a tweed suit of Late Victorian pattern, some bills, some letters, a collar-stud, and—something which, after I had wondered for a moment or two what on earth it was, caused me suddenly to murmur, "Down below, the sea rustled to and fro over the shingle."

Strange that these words had, year after long year, been existing in some obscure cell at the back of my brain!—forgotten but all the while existing, like the trunk in that cupboard. What released them, what threw open the cell door, was nothing but the fragment of a fan; just the butt-end of an inexpensive fan. The sticks are of white bone, clipped together with a semicircular ring that is not silver. They are neatly oval at the base, but variously jagged at the other end. The longest of them measures perhaps two inches. Ring and all, they have no market value; for a farthing is the least coin in our currency. And yet, though I had so long forgotten them, for me they are not worthless. They touch a chord . . . Lest this confession raise false hopes in the reader, I add that I did not know their owner.

I did once see her, and in Normandy, and by moonlight, and her name was Angélique. She was graceful, she was even beautiful. I was but nineteen years old. Yet even so I cannot say that she impressed me favorably. I was seated at a table of a café on the terrace of a casino. I sat facing the sea, with my back to the casino. I sat listening to the quiet sea, which I had crossed that morning. The hour was late, there were few people about. I heard the swing-door behind me flap open, and was aware of a sharp snapping and crackling sound as a lady in white passed quickly by me. I stared at her erect thin back and her agitated elbows. A short fat man passed in pursuit of her—an elderly man in a black alpaca jacket that billowed. I saw that she had left a trail of little white things on the asphalt. I watched the efforts of the agonized short fat man to overtake her as she swept wraithlike away to the distant end of the terrace. What was the matter? What had made her so spectacularly angry with him? The three or four waiters of the café were exchanging cynical smiles and shrugs, as waiters will. I tried to feel cynical, but was thrilled with excitement, with wonder and curiosity. The woman out yonder had doubled on her tracks. She had not slackened her furious speed, but the man waddlingly contrived to keep pace with her now. With every moment they became more distinct, and the prospect that they would presently pass by me, back into the casino, gave me that physical tension which one feels on a wayside platform at the imminent passing of an express. In the rushingly enlarged vision I had of them, the wrath on the woman's face was even more saliently the main thing than I had supposed it would be. That very hard Parisian face must have been as white as the powder that coated it. "Écoute, Angélique," gasped the perspiring bourgeois, "écoute, je te supplie—" The swing-door received them and was left swinging to and fro. I wanted to follow, but had not paid for my bock. I beckoned my waiter. On his way to me he stooped down and picked up something which, with a smile and a shrug, he laid on my table: "Il semble que Mademoiselle ne s'en servira plus." This is the thing I now write of, and at sight of it I understood why there had been that snapping and crackling, and what the white fragments on the ground were.

I hurried through the rooms, hoping to see a continuation of that drama—a scene of appeasement, perhaps, or of fury still implacable. But the two oddly assorted players were not performing there. My waiter had told me he had not seen either of them before. I suppose they had arrived that day. But I was not destined to see either of them again. They went away, I suppose, next morning; jointly or singly; singly, I imagine.

They made, however, a prolonged stay in my young memory, and would have done so even had I not had that tangible memento of them. Who were they, those two of whom that one strange glimpse had befallen me? What, I wondered, was the previous history of each? What, in particular, had all that tragic pother been about? Mlle. Angélique I guessed to be thirty years old, her friend perhaps fifty-five. Each of their faces was as clear to me as in the moment of actual vision—the man's fat shiny bewildered face; the taut white face of the woman, the hard red line of her mouth, the eyes that were not flashing, but positively dull, with rage. I presumed that the fan had been a present from him, and a recent present—bought perhaps that very day, after their arrival in the town. But what, *what* had he done that she should break it between her hands, scattering the splinters as who should sow dragon's teeth? I could not believe he had done anything much amiss. I imagined her grievance a trivial one. But this did not make the case less engrossing. Again and again I would take the fan-stump from my pocket, examining it on the palm of my hand, or between finger and thumb, hoping to read the mystery it had been mixed up in, so that I might reveal that mystery to the world. To the world, yes; nothing less than that. I was determined to make a story of what I had seen—a *conte* in the manner of great Guy de Maupassant. Now and again, in the course of the past year or so, it had occurred to me that I might be a writer. But I had not felt the impulse to sit down and write something. I did feel that impulse now. It would indeed have been an irresistible impulse if I had known just what to write.

I felt I might know at any moment, and had but to give my mind to it. Maupassant was an impeccable artist, but I think the secret of the hold he had on the young men of my day was not so much that we discerned his cunning as that we delighted in the simplicity which his cunning achieved. I had read a great number of his short stories, but none that had made me feel as though I, if I were a writer, mightn't have written it myself. Maupassant had an European reputation. It was pleasing, it was soothing and gratifying, to feel that one could at any time win an equal fame if one chose to set pen to paper. And now, suddenly, the spring had been touched in me, the time was come. I was grateful for the fluke by which I had witnessed on the terrace that evocative scene. I looked forward to reading the MS. of "The Fan"—tomorrow, at latest. I was not wildly ambitious. I was not inordi-

nately vain. I knew I couldn't ever, with the best will in the world, write like
Mr. George Meredith. Those wondrous works of his, seething with wit,
with poetry and philosophy and what not, never had beguiled me with the
sense that I might do something similar. I had full consciousness of not being
a philosopher, of not being a poet, and of not being a wit. Well, Maupassant
was none of these things. He was just an observer like me. Of course he was
a good deal older than I, and had observed a good deal more. But it seemed
to me that he was not my superior in knowledge of life. I knew all about life
through *him*.

Dimly, the initial paragraph of my tale floated in my mind. I—not exactly
I myself, but rather that impersonal *je* familiar to me through
Maupassant—was to be sitting at that table, with a book before me, just as I
had sat. Four or five short sentences would give the whole scene. One of
these I had quite definitely composed. You have already heard it. "Down
below, the sea rustled to and fro over the shingle."

These words, which pleased me much, were to do double duty. They
were to recur. They were to be, by a fine stroke, the very last words of my
tale, their tranquillity striking a sharp ironic contrast with the stress of what
had just been narrated. I had, you see, advanced further in the form of my
tale than in the substance. But even the form was as yet vague. What,
exactly, was to happen after Mlle. Angélique and M. Joumand (as I provi-
sionally called him) had rushed back past me into the casino? It was clear that
I must hear the whole inner history from the lips of one or the other of them.
Which? Should M. Joumand stagger out on to the terrace, sit down heavily
at the table next to mine, bury his head in his hands, and presently, in broken words, blurt out to me all that might be of interest? . . .

" 'And I tell you I gave up everything for her—everything.' He stared at
me with his old hopeless eyes. 'She is more than the fiend I have described to
you. Yet I swear to you, monsieur, that if I had anything left to give, it should
be hers.'

"Down below, the sea rustled to and fro over the shingle."

Or should the lady herself be my informant? For a while, I rather leaned
to this alternative. It was more exciting, it seemed to make the writer more
signally a man of the world. On the other hand, it was less simple to manage.
Wronged persons might be ever so communicative, but I surmised that persons in the wrong were reticent. Mlle. Angélique, therefore, would have to
be modified by me in appearance and behavior, toned down, touched up;
and poor M. Joumand must look like a man of whom one could believe anything. . . .

"She ceased speaking. She gazed down at the fragments of her fan, and
then, as though finding in them an image of her own life, whispered, 'To
think what I once was, monsieur!—what, but for him, I might be, even now!'
She buried her face in her hands, then stared out into the night. Suddenly
she uttered a short, harsh laugh.

"Down below, the sea rustled to and fro over the shingle."

I decided that I must choose the first of these two ways. It was the less chivalrous as well as the less lurid way, but clearly it was the more artistic as well as the easier. The "chose vue," the "tranche de la vie"—this was the thing to aim at. Honesty was the best policy. I must be nothing if not merciless. Maupassant was nothing if not merciless. He would not have spared Mlle. Angélique. Besides, why should I libel M. Joumand? Poor—no, not *poor* M. Joumand! I warned myself against pitying him. One touch of "sentimentality," and I should be lost. M. Joumand was ridiculous. I must keep him so. But—what was his position in life? Was he a lawyer perhaps?—or the proprietor of a shop in the Rue de Rivoli? I toyed with the possibility that he kept a fan shop—that the business had once been a prosperous one, but had gone down, down, because of his infatuation for this woman to whom he was always giving fans—which she *always* smashed. . . . " 'Ah monsieur, cruel and ungrateful to me though she is, I swear to you that if I had anything left to give, it should be hers; but,' he stared at me with his old hopeless eyes, 'the fan she broke tonight was the last—the last, monsieur— of my stock.' Down below,"—but I pulled myself together, and asked pardon of my Muse.

It may be that I had offended her by my fooling. Or it may be that she had a sisterly desire to shield Mlle. Angélique from my mordant art. Or it may be that she was bent on saving M. de Maupassant from a dangerous rivalry. Anyway, she withheld from me the inspiration I had so confidently solicited. I *could not* think what had led up to that scene on the terrace. I tried hard and soberly. I turned the "chose vue" over and over in my mind, day by day, and the fan-stump over and over in my hand. But the "chose à figurer"—what, oh what, was that? Nightly I revisited the café, and sat there with an open mind—a mind wide open to catch the idea that should drop into it like a ripe golden plum. The plum did not ripen. The mind remained wide open for a week or more, but nothing except that phrase about the sea rustled to and fro in it.

A full quarter of a century has gone by. M. Joumand's death, so far too fat was he all those years ago, may be presumed. A temper so violent as Mlle. Angélique's must surely have brought its owner to the grave, long since. But here, all unchanged, the stump of her fan is; and once more I turn it over and over in my hand, not learning its secret—no, nor even trying to, now. The chord this relic strikes in me is not one of curiosity as to that old quarrel, but (if you will forgive me) one of tenderness for my first effort to write, and for my first hopes of excellence.

Max Beerbohm

*For some time now–I think since I was a child–I have been
possessed of the desire to put down the stuff of my life. That is
a commonplace impulse, apparently, among persons of massive self-interest; sooner or later we all do it. And, I am quite
certain, there is only one internal quarrel: how much of the
truth to tell? How much, how much, how much! It is brutal,
in sober, uncompromising moments, to reflect on the comedy
of concern we all enact when it comes to our precious images.*

Lorraine Hansberry

SECTION 4   The Autobiographical Sketch
Part Two: A Coherent Self-Portrait

In the preceding section you wrote about a single important moment
in your life; in this section you are asked to combine a number of such moments into a coherent self-portrait that will give a reader a clear idea of who
you are. Your first task, therefore, is to distinguish between essential and
accidental autobiographical details, between those which just happen to be
true and those which reveal some basic truth about you. What are your
strengths as a person? What matters most to you at this moment? What are
your outstanding accomplishments? What would you like to be doing in five
years? An autobiographical sketch is more than a series of questions and
answers, of course, and yet without this kind of preliminary inventory you
are likely to compile a list of incidental and perhaps irrelevant personal details. Before telling your reader about your putting technique and your passion for sour cream enchiladas ask yourself if such information really says
anything about you. An autobiographical sketch must be not only compact
but selective.

Which raises a second crucial point, namely that you have to decide
what image(s) of yourself you are going to project to your reader. On Madison Avenue the word "image" usually implies something bogus and mis-
leading, a surface glitter that conceals underlying defects. As used here,
however, it means simply the dominant or controlling impression in your
sketch. Do you see yourself as glamorous, sexy, talented, witty? Convince
your reader with appropriate details. E.B. White, for example, writes (page
158) as a beleaguered average man wracked by statistics and bureaucratic
red tape; Jan Carroll, a student, presents herself (page 152) in terms of a
single amusing disability—clumsiness. An image is always a partial, sim-
plified picture of the total person but, to mix a metaphor, it is also the literary
glue that holds everything in place.

Finally, you must decide on the most effective method of organizing
your material. Because he wants to emphasize both the persistence and the

development of his desire to write poetry, Archibald MacLeish (page 153) proceeds chronologically. He avoids a mechanical résumé, however, by commenting on important events as he goes, thereby creating a continuous dialogue between facts and character. Francis Bacon (page 155) focuses on his one great passion, the study of truth, whereas the French essayist François de la Rochefoucauld (page 155) conducts a meticulous self-examination that starts at his forehead and concludes with his reflections on the "beautiful passions." What begins as a physical profile becomes a psychological one as well.

The readings throughout this chapter illustrate various other methods of organizing autobiographical materials. Which one you choose is less important than the fact that you do choose one and adhere to it.

SUMMARY

An autobiographical profile is an epitome, constructed from memories and observations, of the principal facts of your life. It may be organized chronologically, topically, or thematically, and include everything from passages of physical description to accounts of your dreams and travels. Individual details are less important in themselves, however, than for the image or images of you that they project collectively. In the preceding section you concentrated on single events, in this section you are trying to combine single events into a coherent self-portrait which, if necessarily partial, is at least authentic.

EXERCISES

1. (a) Make a list of the principal facts of your life. Include intellectual interests, honors, hobbies, travels, prejudices, in short whatever you think makes you an individual. Next, arrange this material in different ways in order to create different self-portraits: the "artistic" you, the "academic" you, the "radical" you. The point is not to see how many "you's" there are but rather to see how different self-images can be created from the same body of information.

   (b) What would happen if you substituted *he* or *she* for *I* in the preceding exercise? How would using third person change the style and tone of the original portrait?

2. (a) Prepare autobiographical résumés for three different audiences; for example, a prospective employer, a scholarship committee, and the membership of a student organization. Consider what each audience would want to know about you and adapt the style and content of your résumé to suit their respective interests.

   (b) Describe yourself through the eyes of another person—your mother, a teacher, a close friend. How do their images of you compare with your own? E. B. White's essay *About Myself* (page 158) is an ingenious variation on this type of exercise.

3. (a) Draw a portrait of yourself as you would like to be.

   (b) Imagine that you are in an art museum. As you walk into one of the rooms you notice a statue. You move closer and, to your astonishment, you see that the statue is of you. It may be large or small, abstract or realistic, yet it somehow expresses the essential you. Describe what you see as you look at this statue. Move around so that you can observe all of its features. After observing the statue from the outside, *become* the statue. Describe what you feel and think and what your life is like. Speak as the statue. Does anything change?

4. We are known by our deeds, our words, the company we keep, and, to a certain extent, by our possessions. What could a person tell about you from the objects on your desk, for example, or from the clothes in your closet? Draw a self-portrait in terms of the things you own and value.

READINGS

Amazingly Graceless

I'll always have a warm spot in my heart for the guiding geniuses behind platform shoes and negative-heel "earth" shoes because they've managed to do the impossible.

They've evened out the clumsiness quotient between me and the rest of the world.

Now, all those people wearing the latest in shoedom fall and stumble, careen and trip, zig-zag and wobble the same way I've been doing in my crepe soled desert boots for years.

Being graceful is one thing I've never been accused of. My mother used to threaten that she was going to send me to dancing school so I could learn to walk across a room without falling over.

But, unfortunately for me, good old Mom never came through on her threat, so I went through my childhood knowing that klutziness was going to be a way of life from then on out.

How many other people do you know who can break a leg while playing a friendly game of doctor in a cousin's basement? I did. The part of the patient fell to me, and as I sat waiting to be "examined" by Dr. Gale and her assistant, Norie, the examining table collapsed. On my leg. Break. Crunch.

Days went by. A lot of them. The cast was removed, and without wasting any time, I proceeded to take one too many steps backward and fell down a flight of stairs.

No injuries. Just Mom standing at the doorway at the top of the stairs, shaking her head, wondering where the genes had fouled up.

Let's not forget the time old sure-foot tripped over a ladder that was lying on the ground. Casualty report: one broken arm.

Later, there was a short-lived trip down a gravel road on the back of a bicycle. See Klutz hanging on the bicycle for dear life. See Klutz picking the gravel out of her legs after "sliding" off the passenger seat of the bike.

Most of the trauma from those incidents of clumsiness tend to fade from memory, unless you make a point to dredge them out of the nether depths. It's hard to remember the pain, and most of the scars have disappeared, except for one reminder of a harrowing chase down a cinder road: three black notches on the inside of my right knee.

All that was before I had reached the ripe old age of five. The 5-year, 50,000-mile warranty was pretty well shot.

Then came the days at Catholic school, when even a St. Christopher medal couldn't undo the damage my genes had done.

Sister Juanita should have saved her breath when she warned us not to run on the playground after the rain. Chalk up one mangled leg after a losing round with the St. Rita blacktop.

That particular incident marked the beginning of my long and enduring love affair with mercurochrome. Scraped knees became an identifying mark. The nuns had taken to warning the rest of the class to clear their schoolbags from the aisles. There was no sense tempting fate.

Through it all, Mom crossed her fingers and hoped that clumsiness, like biting your fingernails, is something you outgrow, in time. Sorry to report I haven't outgrown either.

Show me a patch of ice, I'll slip on it. Give me a wire, I'll get caught in it. Put a waste basket in sight, I'll trip over it. And roller skates, well, let's not talk about them.

In a brief attempt to master the graceful art of snow skiing, predictably, I failed. The ski lift monitor stifled uproarious laughter when, time after time, skis would cross, feet would begin to slip, and down Klutz would fall into a snowdrift.

Then I'd casually dust off the powder and stare at him superciliously, and ask, "Whatsa matter? Haven't you ever seen hiney skiing before?"

When you're born into clumsiness, you learn early not to put a very high premium on pride. The secret to keeping even a modicum of your self-respect is the snappy rejoinder, a nervous laugh and a quick eye. "Hey, look at that purple elephant over there."

It tends to distract attention.

So I don't even flinch when someone falls off their platforms, or when someone topples over backwards in their healthy, posture improving "earth shoes" or even when a waitress dumps a glass of ice water in my lap.

I understand.

Jan Carroll

Self-Portrait

Born May 7, 1892, in a wooden house with two round towers overlooking, from a clay bluff and a grove of oak trees, the waters of Lake Michigan.

Father a Scot, a Glasgow man, born a Presbyterian, ultimately a Baptist, always a devout Protestant; one of the early settlers of Chicago; fifty-four when I was born; a merchant: a cold, tall, rigorous man of very beautiful speech.

Mother a Connecticut woman, daughter of a Congregational minister, herself a graduate of Vassar and a teacher there; her family a seafaring family from the Connecticut Coast about Norwich; very passionate people with some insanity among them; a very strong family resemblance from one generation to the next—small dark eyes and high cheek bones and similar voices; she was my father's third wife; intelligent and energetic and entirely self-less and beloved.

Four of us grew up—one to be killed flying over Belgium in the last weeks of the war. Public schools. Lake beach. Oak thickets.

Went to a fashionable Connecticut preparatory school for four years and hated it. Went to Yale. Regular undergraduate life: football team—swimming team—chairman of the literary magazine—Phi Beta Kappa—senior society. Began writing, but learned little about it and had little life of my own. Went to Harvard Law School to avoid going to work; led my class in the last year; worked terribly hard because of the competition, but was never really good. Married Ada Hitchcock, who is a singer. This while I was in the Law School. Son born early in 1917. War; went abroad in a hospital unit so as to do the right thing but not be hurt. In France got shifted to the Field Artillery out of shame; few weeks at the front north of Meaux in June, July, 1918; sent home to take battery in new regiment of 155 G.P.F.s: ended up a captain of F.A. at Camp Mead with no distinction but fact that my brother Kenneth had been a grand flier and had been killed. Taught for a year at Harvard to avoid (again) going to work. Wrote a little all the time, but it wasn't any good. One book of undergraduate verses published by the Yale Press while I was in France. Practiced law for three years in the office of Charles F. Choate, Jr., in Boston—trying cases mostly—and did pretty well, but couldn't write. Only one desire—to write the poems I wanted to write and not the poems I was writing. Winter of 1923, decided to go to France anyway on what we had. Date the beginning of my more or less adult life from that year. Went in the fall of 1923 with two children. Lived in the Boulevard Saint-Michel and at Saint Cloud and later in the rue du Bac. One summer in Normandy. After that on the Mediterranean—cruising a great deal. Went one spring for five months to Persia going down through the central cities to Bushire and west along the Persian Gulf to Mohamara and back through Shiraz and Ispahan to Teheran. All this time reading—mostly French poetry and chiefly La Forgue, Rimbaud, Léon Paul Fargue, St. J. Perse, Valéry. Also Eliot and Pound. Began writing in 1923. Houghton Mifflin Company published "The Happy Marriage," "The Pot of Earth," "Streets in the Moon."

Came home in 1928 and lived on a farm. Published "Hamlet of A. MacLeish," which was written in France, and "New Found Land," part of which was written in this country. Started work on a poem about the Spanish conquistadores in Mexico, and spent some time in 1929 traveling alone through the *monte* and up from the coast over the route of Cortez to the Valley of Mexico. Met the depression head on in the winter of 1929-30, and started to support myself writing for *Fortune*. Traveled a good bit as a journalist—England and France, and Japan, and the American West. In the intervals of this kind of work wrote and published "Conquistador," a series of American scenes called "Frescoes for Mr. Rockefeller's City," a ballet of the building of the Union Pacific Railroad for the Monte Carlo Ballet Russe, a verse play of the bank panic of 1933, which succeeded or not in running for three nights, and a volume of short poems called "Public Speech."

Archibald MacLeish

From *The Works of Francis Bacon*

Believing that I was born for the service of mankind, and regarding the care of the Commonwealth as a kind of common property which, like the air and water, belongs to everybody, I set myself to consider in what way mankind might be best served, and what service I was myself best fitted by nature to perform.

Now, among all the benefits that could be conferred upon mankind, I found none so great as the discovery of new arts for the bettering of human life. For I saw that among the rude people of early times, inventors and discoverers were reckoned as gods. It was seen that the works of founders of States, lawgivers, tyrant-destroyers, and heroes cover but narrow spaces and endure but for a time; while the work of the inventor, though of less pomp, is felt everywhere and lasts forever. But above all, if a man could, I do not say devise some invention, however useful, but kindle a light in nature—a light which, even in rising, should touch and illuminate the borders of existing knowledge, and spreading further on should bring to light all that is most secret—that man, in my view, would be indeed the benefactor of mankind, the extender of man's empire over nature, the champion of freedom, the conqueror of fate.

For myself, I found that I was fitted for nothing so well as for the study of Truth: as having a mind nimble and versatile enough to discern resemblances in things (the main point), and yet steady enough to distinguish the subtle differences in them; as being endowed with zeal to seek, patience to doubt, love of meditation, slowness of assertion, readiness to reconsider, carefulness to arrange and set in order; and as being a man that affects not the new nor admires the old, but hates all imposture. So I thought my nature had a certain familiarity and kindred with Truth.

Francis Bacon

From *Mémoires du Duc de la Rochefoucauld*

DESCRIBES HIMSELF

I am of medium stature, supple and well proportioned. I have a tanned complexion but quite smooth; a high forehead, of reasonable size; black eyes, small and deep-set; the eyebrows black and thick, but well turned. I would hesitate to say what kind of a nose I have; because it is neither blunt, nor acquiline, nor broad, nor pointed, at least so far as I believe; all that I know is that it is rather large than small and that it points a little downwards. I have a large mouth and ordinarily quite red lips, which are neither well nor badly shaped. I have white teeth and passably regular. I have been told that I have a little too much chin: I have just looked in the mirror and I cannot decide about that. As for the shape of the face, it is either square or oval; which of the two it is would be very difficult for me to say. My hair is black and naturally curly, and withal quite thick and quite long enough for me to be able to claim a good-looking head.

I have something fretful and haughty in my countenance: this leads many people to believe that I am scornful, although I am not really at all. I gesticulate freely, perhaps too much so, to the point of making too many gestures while speaking. This is the way I think, perhaps naïvely, that I am fashioned; and it will be found, I believe, that what I think of myself in this matter is not far removed from reality. I will employ the same fidelity for the rest of my portrait; for I have studied myself sufficiently to know myself well, and I shall lack neither the assurance to speak freely of my good qualities, nor the sincerity to admit frankly my faults.

First, as to my disposition, I am melancholy, and I am so to a point that in the course of three or four years I have laughed hardly three or four times. It seems to me that this melancholy would be quite bearable and quite easy if it derived only from my temperament; but so much comes from elsewhere and so fills my imagination and occupies my mind that most of the time I either dream without saying a word, or I have an air of abstraction in my speech. I am very reserved with those whom I do not know. That is a fault, I realize, and I shall neglect nothing to correct it: but since a certain somber air which I have in my face contributes to make me appear even more withdrawn than I am, and since it is not in our power to change a bad expression which comes from one's innate disposition, I think that after having corrected myself from within I will not always remain with this undesirable expression outside.

I have intelligence and I do not hesitate to say it. For why pretend otherwise? To lower or to mitigate one's advantages, it seems to me, is to hide a little vanity under an apparent modesty and to employ a very shrewd manner in making believe that one is much better than one really is. As for me, I am content that one should consider me neither more handsome than I am, nor of a better temper than I have depicted myself, nor more intellectual or more rational than I am. To repeat, I have intelligence but it is impaired by melancholy; for, even though I have a fair command of language, a fortunate memory and I do not think too confusedly, I am nevertheless so strongly subject to my fretfulness that often I express very badly what I wish to say.

The conversation of virtuous men is one of the pleasures that moves me most. I like it to be serious and that it be mostly of a moral nature. Still I can also enjoy it when it is playful; and if I do not utter many amusing trifles, it is not that I do not appreciate the value of well-expressed bagatelles or that I do not find this kind of banter very diverting, where there are certain quick wits who do it well. I write prose well and I make good verse; and if I were sensible of the glory which comes from that, I believe that with a little effort I could acquire quite a reputation.

I like reading in general: the kind where one can find something which instructs the mind and fortifies the soul is what I like most. Above all, I have an extreme satisfaction in reading with a person of intelligence; because in this way one reflects every moment on what one reads, and the reflections which one makes form a conversation that is most agreeable and most useful.

I am quite a good judge of works of poetry and prose; but I express my opinions in these matters perhaps too freely. But what is still a fault with me is that sometimes I have too scrupulous a delicacy and am too severe a critic. I do not hate listening to arguments, and often also I quite voluntarily join in a dispute, but ordinarily I maintain my opinions with too much heat; and when sometimes somebody takes an unfair position, I, moved by a passion for reason, myself become very unreasonable.

My sensibilities are on the side of virtue, my inclinations are fine, and I have so strong a desire to be an altogether upright man that my friends could not give me greater pleasure than candidly to point out my faults to me. Those who know me fairly well, and who have the kindness occasionally to do so, are aware that I have always received criticism with pleasure and all possible humility.

All my passions are quite mild and controlled. Hardly anyone has seen me angry and I have never hated anybody. Nevertheless, I am not incapable of avenging myself if I have been offended and if my honor has been injured. On the contrary, I am certain that, instead of hate, a sense of duty in me would make me pursue my vengeance with more vigor than anybody else.

Ambition moves me in no way. I dread but few things, and death not at all. I am hardly sensitive to pity and I wish I had none. Still, there is nothing I would not do for the relief of an afflicted person, and I believe truly that one ought to do everything, even up to the point of showing much compassion, for the wretched are so sottish that this does them the greatest good in the world. But I hold also that one should content oneself with merely showing it, and to keep oneself carefully from having it. Pity is a passion which is good for nothing in a well-integrated person; it weakens the spirit and it should be left only to people who, never executing anything through reason, need passion to make them do things.

I love my friends; and I love them in a way that I would not hesitate a moment to sacrifice my interests to theirs. I yield to them, and I suffer patiently their bad moods; but I am neither very affectionate in their presence nor greatly anxious about them in their absence.

I have naturally very little curiosity about most things that interest other people. I am very secretive, and I have less difficulty than others in keeping silent about what has been told to me in confidence. I am extremely exact in keeping my word; I never fail in it, no matter what the consequences of my promise might be; and I have made that an indispensable law all my life. Among women my courtesy is extremely correct; and I do not believe I have ever said anything in their presence that might have caused them pain. When they are intelligent, I prefer their conversation to that of men: one finds in it a certain gentleness that is lacking in us; and it seems to me, besides that, that they express themselves with more clarity and that they give a more pleasant turn to their speech. As for gallantry, I had a little bit of it formerly; now I no longer have it, even though I am young. I have given up saying pretty things, and I am only surprised that there are still so many decent men who occupy themselves with such things.

I very much approve of the beautiful passions; they show greatness of soul; and though the anxieties which they cause are contrary to stern wisdom, they nevertheless so accommodate themselves to the most austere virtue that I do not believe they could be condemned with justice. As for me, who had known all that was delicate and strong in the great feelings of love, if ever I should love again, it will assuredly be of that kind; but, constituted as I am, I do not believe that such knowledge as I have will ever proceed from my mind to my heart.

François de la Rochefoucauld

From *The Second Tree from the Corner*

ABOUT MYSELF

I am a man of medium height. I keep my records in a Weis Folder Re-order Number 8003. The unpaid balance of my estimated tax for the year 1945 is item 3 less the sum of items 4 and 5. My eyes are gray. My Selective Service order number is 10789. The serial number is T1654. I am in Class IV-A, and have been variously in Class 3-A, Class I-A(H), and Class 4-H. My social security number is 067-01-9841. I am married to U.S. Woman Number 067-01-9807. Her eyes are gray. This is not a joint declaration, nor is it made by an agent; therefore it need be signed only by me—and, as I said, I am a man of medium height.

I am the holder of a quit-claim deed recorded in Book 682, Page 501, in the country where I live. I hold Fire Insurance Policy Number 424747, continuing until the 23 day of October in the year nineteen hundred forty-five, at noon, and it is important that the written portions of all policies covering the same property read exactly alike. My cervical spine shows relatively good alignment with evidence of proliferative changes about the bodies consistent with early arthritis. (Essential clinical data: pain in neck radiating to mastoids and occipito-temporal region, not constant, moderately severe; patient in good general health and working.) My operator's license is Number 16200. It expired December 31, 1943, more than a year ago, but I am still carrying it and it appears to be serving the purpose. I shall renew it when I get time. I have made, published, and declared my last will and testament, and it thereby revokes all other wills and codicils at any time heretofore made by me. I hold Basic A Mileage Ration 108950, O.P.A. Form R-525-C. The number of my car is 18-388. Tickets A-14 are valid through March 21st.

I was born in District Number 5903, New York State. My birth is registered in Volume 3/58 of the Department of Health. My father was a man of medium height. His telephone number was 484. My mother was a housewife. Her eyes were blue. Neither parent had a social security number and neither was secure socially. They drove to the depot behind an unnumbered horse.

I hold Individual Certificate Number 4320-209 with the Equitable Life Assurance Society, in which a corporation hereinafter called the employer has contracted to insure my life for the sum of two thousand dollars. My left front tire is Number 48KE8846, my right front tire is Number 63T6895. My rear tires are, from left to right, Number 6N4M5384 and Number A26E5806D. I brush my hair with Whiting-Adams Brush Number 010 and comb my hair with Pro-Phy-Lac-Tic Comb Number 1201. My shaving brush is sterilized. I take Pill Number 43934 after each meal and I can get more of them by calling ELdorado 5-6770. I spray my nose with De Vilbiss Atomizer Number 14. Sometimes I stop the pain with Squibb Pill, Control Number 3K49979 (aspirin). My wife (Number 067-01-9807) takes Pill Number 49345.

I hold War Ration Book 40289EW, from which have been torn Airplane Stamps Numbers 1, 2, and 3. I also hold Book 159378CD, from which have been torn Spare Number 2, Spare Number 37, and certain other coupons. My wife holds Book 40288EW and Book 159374CD. In accepting them, she recognized that they remained the property of the United States Government.

I have a black dog with cheeks of tan. Her number is 11032. It is an old number. I shall renew it when I get time. The analysis of her prepared food is guaranteed and is Case Number 1312. The ingredients are: Cereal Flaked feeds (from Corn, Rice, Bran, and Wheat), Meat Meal, Fish Liver and Glandular Meal, Soybean Oil Meal, Wheat Bran, Corn Germ Meal, 5% Kel-Centrate [containing Dried Skim Milk, Dehydrated Cheese, Vitamin B$_1$ (Thiamin), Flavin Concentrate, Carotene, Yeast, Vitamin A and D Feeding Oil (containing 3,000 U.S.P. units Vitamin A and 400 U.S.P. units Vitamin D per gram), Diastase (Enzyme), Wheat Germ Meal, Rice Polish Extract], 1½% Calcium Carbonate, .00037% Potassium Iodide, and ¼% Salt. She prefers offal.

When I finish what I am now writing it will be late in the day. It will be about half past five. I will then take up Purchase Order Number 245-9077-B-Final, which I received this morning from the Office of War Information and which covers the use of certain material they want to translate into a foreign language. Attached to the order are Standard Form Number 1034 (white) and three copies of Standard Form Number 1034a (yellow), also "Instructions for Preparation of Voucher by Vendor and Example of Prepared Voucher." The Appropriation Symbol of the Purchase Order is 1153700.001-501. The requisition number is B-827. The allotment is X5-207.1-R2-11. Voucher shall be prepared in ink, indelible pencil, or type-writer. For a while I will be vendor preparing voucher. Later on, when my head gets bad and the pain radiates, I will be voucher preparing vendor. I see that there is a list of twenty-one instructions which I will be following. Number One on the list is: "Name of payor agency as shown in the block 'appropriation symbol and title' in the upper left-hand corner of the Purchase Order." Number Five on the list is: "Vendor's personal account or invoice number," but whether that means Order Number 245-9077-B-Final, or Requisition B-827, or Allotment X5-207.1-R2-11, or Appropriation Symbol 1153700.001-501, I do not know, nor will I know later on in the evening after several hours of meditation, nor will I be able to find out by consulting Woman 067-01-9807, who is no better at filling out forms than I am, nor after taking Pill Number 43934, which tends merely to make me drowsy.

I owe a letter to Corporal 32413654, Hq and Hq Sq., VII AAF S.C., APO 953, c/o PM San Francisco, Calif., thanking him for the necktie he sent me at Christmas. In 1918 I was a private in the Army. My number was 4,345,016. I was a boy of medium height. I had light hair. I had no absences from duty under G.O. 31, 1912, or G.O. 45, 1914. The number of that war was Number One.

E. B. White

6 | Biography

When I was a young man, and frequented the Pre-Raphaelites, I used to notice that Rossetti had a very curious way of tilting a glass or cup out of which he was drinking, and gulping down the last drops in a great hurry. I have never heard or seen this trick noticed by anyone else, and it is so trivial that I have never thought of recording it myself. But here it is, in my memory; the feverish, swarthy face turned upward in profile, and the large lips eagerly supping down the stream of liquid. I don't know why, but in that trifle I see Rossetti again after all these years; there is something, to me, characteristic, personal, unique, in the habitual gesture.

Edmund Gosse

SECTION 1 Profiles and Characters

Like portrait painters writers look constantly for expressive, individualizing human details in order to make their subjects live in our memories and imaginations. Just as we picture Napoleon with one hand thrust inside his jacket and John Kennedy with a wave of hair slanting across his forehead, so we associate Captain Ahab with a wooden leg, Falstaff with a flagon of sack and a great belly, and Mr. Micawber with serenely optimistic pronouncements about the future. I remember one history professor because he introduced nearly every sentence in his lectures with the phrase "In the question of"; another, a distinguished medievalist, always wore a pork-pie hat crushed over his right ear, thereby creating the startling impression that his head was going one way and his body another. Such details may not be extraordinary but they are, like Rossetti's eager swallowing, the kind that bring a person to life. They provoke the memory.

Your first job in writing a character sketch, therefore, is to observe how people stand, sit, smile, dress, talk, and hold their hands. Describe these mannerisms clearly and precisely, using figurative language whenever appropriate: "He's as relaxed as a strand of cooked spaghetti," "She bobs her head like a chicken pecking at gravel." Remember that general words like "amusing," "glamorous," and "sexy" are usually meaningless unless anchored to concrete particulars. And yet, as this student sample illustrates, facts alone can't make a sketch interesting.

> My roommate Jack is about 5'8" with long brown hair that comes about three inches past his shoulders. He has a black beard that he's been growing for about seven months. He also has a Long Island accent because he comes from Oyster Bay, New York. He plays the tuba in the band and likes to listen to all kinds of good music, particularly hard rock and jazz. Jogging and karate are two of his favorite pastimes.

The first problem is that the details are all so obvious and colorless. Although we might be able to distinguish Jack from Garry and Fred if all three were standing in front of us, we wouldn't remember him five minutes after he left. Instead of looking for distinctive details, which, by the way, needn't be grotesque, the writer has recorded whatever ordinary facts come to mind, as though he were filling out an insurance form.

The second problem is that this sketch lacks coherence and consequently fails to present an image of Jack. What connections exist between his being 5'8", having a Long Island accent, and playing the tuba in the band? None that we can see. We are given a list of random biographical details that tell little about Jack as a person. In other words, we get information but no insight.

As an example of a character sketch that does present a coherent image, here is Dickens's description of Mrs. Joe Gargary in *Great Expectations*:

> My sister, Mrs. Joe, with black hair and eyes, had such a prevailing redness of skin that I sometimes used to wonder whether it was possible she washed herself with a nutmeg-grater instead of soap. She was tall and bony, and almost always wore a coarse apron, fastened over her figure behind with two loops, and having a square, impregnable bib in front that was stuck full of pins and needles. She made it a powerful merit in herself, and a strong reproach against Joe, that she wore this apron so much. Though I really see no reason why she should have worn it at all; or why, if she did wear it at all, she should not have taken it off, every day of her life. . . .
>
> My sister had a trenchant way of cutting our bread-and-butter for us, that never varied. First, with her left hand, she jammed the loaf hard and fast against her bib—where it sometimes got a pin in it, and sometimes a needle, which we afterwards got into our mouths. Then, she took some butter (not too much) on a knife, and spread it on the loaf, in an apothecary kind of way, as if she were making a plaister—using both sides of the knife with a slapping dexterity, and trimming and moulding the butter off round with the crust. Then, she gave the

knife a final smart wipe on the edge of the plaister, and sawed a very thick round off the loaf, which she finally, before separating from the loaf, hewed into two halves, of which Joe got one and I got the other.

Instead of establishing a tiny precinct of its own, each detail contributes to an impression of Mrs. Joe as a stern, demanding, censorious woman who asserts her will over Joe and Pip as methodically and impassively as she cuts and butters a slice of bread. Her tall, bony frame, red skin, and notably heavy hand make her seem forbidding, while her apron, with its impregnable bib stuck full of pins and needles, is at once the badge of her oppression and a prickly defense against intimacy. We know how Dickens intends that we view her.

"Characters" provide somewhat different opportunities for biographical writing. As defined by Sir Thomas Overbury, a seventeenth-century essayist, a Character "is an impress or short emblem: in little comprehending much. To square out a Character by our English level, it is a picture (real or personal) quaintly drawn, in various colours, all of them heightened by one shadowing." In modern English, it is a sketch of a human type—doctor, lawyer, student, teacher—fashioned from representative rather than unique personal details. In writing a sketch of your philosophy professor, for example, you would certainly focus on those qualities that make him an individual: his thick Bavarian accent, his day-glo meerschaum pipe and noxious cherry tobacco, his habit of removing his glasses whenever he wants to emphasize a point. In a Character of a philosophy professor, however, you would focus on the qualities possessed generally by the group. Perhaps you feel that they are all drunk on fanciful utopian schemes or obsessed by polysyllabic Latin gibberish. You would not omit concrete particulars—the words "picture," "colours," and "shadowing" are essential parts of Overbury's definition—but you would select them for the purpose of describing a group of people rather than a single individual. The Arndt Brothers necktie, Mercury shoes, and Plymouth 6 in Kenneth Fearing's poem "Portrait" (page 174) are really appropriate for a whole group. Writing sketches and Characters together gives you practice in using both kinds of detail.

SUMMARY

A profile is an arrangement of specific personal details (physical features, speech, dress, mannerisms, gestures) into a coherent, expressive image. It is not a list of random facts, therefore, but a description that truly distinguishes one person from another. The difference between a profile and a Character is that the latter focuses on representative rather than distinctive details and describes a group or a type, not a single individual. Nevertheless, both are convincing insofar as they show as well as tell.

EXERCISES

1. (a) Write a profile of someone you know very well, then a profile of some-
    one you know only slightly. Be personal and subjective in the first, de-
    tached and objective in the second. Compare the two. Was one more
    difficult to write than the other? What special problems did each pre-
    sent?

   (b) Write a sketch of a person engaged in some expressive physical activ-
    ity such as kneading bread, playing the piano, or running a hundred
    yard dash. Describe both the activity itself and the feelings of the per-
    son doing it. In other words, try to combine objective and subjective
    details in one sketch. Review the discussion of description in Chapter
    2, Section 1.

   (c) Tell an anecdote that reveals a single important truth about another
    person. Limit yourself to 150 words.

   (d) Write a character sketch of the most amusing person you've ever met.
    The most obnoxious. The most depressing. Make clear why the per-
    son deserves this distinction.

   (e) In Exercise 4, Chapter 5, Section 4, you were asked to write an
    autobiographical sketch in terms of your possessions. Now do a
    sketch of someone else in terms of his.

   (f) Write a group profile of people at a football game, parade, concert, or
    other public event. Try to characterize the entire group as well as some
    of the individuals in it. Find a theme or a point of view that enables you
    to relate parts to a whole.

2. (a) Write several brief sketches (200-300 words) of persons you see on the
    street, at the supermarket, or around your campus. Pay close attention
    to physical features, dress, speech, mannerisms, in short, to anything
    that expresses character and that might make a person stand out in a
    reader's mind. Here is a student sketch:

> Standing in front of Neiman-Marcus was a petite black girl. Her skin was
> the color of milk chocolate and she was obviously pregnant.
>   Her hair was straightened, the ends were bleached orange-yellow, and the
> top part was pulled into a ponytail and fastened with white yarn. She was wear-
> ing a white smock, pink pants, white boys' tennis shoes, and a dirty blue and red
> school jacket. Wide silver loops hung from her ears and several tarnished silver
> and gold rings were on her fingers. Her nails were long and painted with glossy
> black polish.
>   She stood with her weight on her left foot and clutched her book in front of
> her as if to hide her stomach.

Her small eyes looked straight ahead, defiantly. She seemed accustomed to being stared at and whispered about.

Cathy Landin

(b) Compile a class portfolio of the eight best sketches from the preceding exercise. Consider not only the most striking individual pieces but those that make the most interesting combinations as well.

3. Do a character sketch of another student in your class, making notes on the kinds of details mentioned in 2. (a) and organizing them into a clear, coherent description that the rest of the class could recognize without being told the person's name. Look for details that truly express character, however, instead of recording what is merely superficial and obvious (e.g., "This person has light brown hair and is wearing a Budweiser T-shirt with a torn sleeve.").

4. Write a Character of at least one of the following: used car salesmen, librarians, cab drivers, stewardesses, football coaches, English teachers. Even though you are focusing on a group, and therefore on common characteristics, don't neglect concrete details. A Character is more than a list of abstract qualities.

5. Expand an obituary, personal, or wedding announcement into a character sketch, using the information contained in the original as the basis for a longer piece. Let your imagination run by creating a past, a career, and a group of friends for your subject. Turn quotes into monologues, anecdotes into brief dramatic scenes. Magazines like *Time* and *Newsweek* have sections entitled "People" and "Newsmakers" that might also be useful.

READINGS

As Close To Death

Far away from this Hilltop is a small town zippered between the Black Hills of South Dakota. During the winter months, Deadwood would be just another western ghost town if not for the mechanized gold mining which strips the mountain sides raw and turns the streams black.

But for three months out of the year Deadwood thrives on a large tourist population. The visitors arrive in their Winnebagos and station wagons. Most of them flock to the main center of attraction—the Old Style Saloon—which sits wedged in the middle of the main street.

It is the same bar where the aging Wild Bill Hickok took a bullet in his back while holding two pair in his poker hand. His death chair is still displayed in a place of honor above the entrance.

Once through the swinging doors and past the bartender who occasionally checks I.D.'s, the Old Style is a mausoleum of memories from the Old West—an era captured now only by those John Wayne movies on the late show.

One cold Saturday night in August the free riders of the open country came to Deadwood to once again reclaim the town.

Days before Saturday, the motorcyclists had wound their way through the Black Hills to get to the annual Sturgis rallies. Eight died on this Exodus—unable to control their monstrous Harley-Davidsons on the curves of the mountain passes.

For the cyclists, the pilgrimage to Sturgis is a yearly ritual. There are the "boulevard putters" who hold down their nine-to-five jobs during the week but spend their Saturdays and Sundays on the road. Then there are the lifers who settle down only long enough to earn enough money to go back on their machines.

They wear the black leather jackets with their gang names emblazoned on their backs—the Highway Pacers, the Gooses, El Foresteros, the Empties. And with them they carry the frightening legends born of the Hell's Angels.

There are a few lifers who will admit quietly that the tales of rape, murder and gang wars have been distorted in the telling. But it is these horrifying images in the minds of the naive which the cyclists know they can prey upon.

With the ability to frighten, the cycle games are played. Although in actuality the violence is presently restricted to only a few isolated incidents, the riders can still manipulate police and townspeople into a panic with their coarse but confident style.

By nightfall, Saturday's rain had broken in Deadwood and the riders roared into the small town. The huge Harleys, individualized with chrome and extenders, covered both sides of the street for almost five blocks. As they dismounted and entered the bars, the games had begun for the evening.

About nine o'clock, Easy limps into the Old Style, a can of Budweiser in one hand and a homemade cane in the other.

The bad leg came from hitting a semi-truck broadside a couple of years back, but Easy explains he only really uses the cane to prop himself up in front of a toilet.

Easy clutches his beer. He has been drinking steadily since the morning. The only leather he wears is a wide-brimmed hat trimmed with a feather band. On each shoulder of his flannel-lined jean jacket are patches: "Just Passin' Through" and "Somebody Up There Likes Me."

The nickname came to him before Peter Fonda rode to fame on his red, white and blue chopper and Easy quickly denies that his last name is Rider.

His voice is low and slurred from the booze or maybe just from too many years on the road. He sticks a Marlboro in his mouth and lights it.

"I was working at the North Star Steel Mill up in St. Paul. And it gets kinda boring sometimes. So I filled up a thermos with two quarts of 7-UP and two quarts of Seagrams. By the time I got through with it, I was passed out on the floor. This guy came up to me and said, 'hey, you're easy,' and it just stuck."

Now, when Easy is home he goes to work in his leather jacket with "I'm Easy If You Can Be Had" inscribed on the back.

Easy loves his name because "it just fits me. I'm easy going. Just a take-it-as-it-comes kinda guy. I don't mean to hurt anybody. I'm just out for good times. I don't get into fights. That is, unless somebody deserves it. Then I'll get in on it."

Easy's 1973 Harley is in the three patriotic colors. ("I have to keep up the image," he explains.) And he brags that he can get up to 170 miles an hour before the front wheel begins to shake.

For Easy, there is nothing better than getting on the road with a good "chicken" holding on behind him. "You don't have to stop for anything. You ride, maybe smoke a little dope and that just makes it better."

But Easy doesn't have his good chicken. His wife, a beautician in St. Paul, hates his motorcycle. Their marriage didn't work out and divorce will soon be final.

In fact, except for his bike, nothing has really worked for Easy. Right out of high school, he was pulled into the Army. He was stationed in Missouri and Virginia before he was shipped overseas.

Easy talks hesitantly when mentioning his life off the road. Talking about his bike, though, relaxes him and he begins to ramble.

"The Black Hills are the best for riding. Going up the mountains you can feel the wind on your face when it changes temperatures. You always have to have control, though. Those eight people that got themselves killed were stupid. They just couldn't handle it. You can't do that. But the danger is part of it. You gotta live life to the fullest—and you gotta be as close to death as possible to do that."

Easy was in a gang once but his accident took him away from that. "I travel light now—by myself. But what I'd really like to have is a good chicken to ride behind me. Just travel and have a few parties."

Easy says that he'll be riding ten years from now. And he probably will be since he's been riding for the past 14 of his 27 years.

He slept in his wet sleeping bag that night before he went back to St. Paul the next day. Sturgis was the last leg of a three-month trek.

Before returning to the North Star Steel Mill, Easy put on his leather work jacket and perhaps took a thermos full of Seagrams with him. Working in a steel mill probably doesn't offer too much excitement without it.

With the cycle, Easy can play his part well. But as one boulevard putter explains, lifers are losers in life. Once they get on their cycles they're winners. For Easy and others like him, those are the games that really matter.

Nancy Kruh

From *The History of Pendennis*

General, or Captain Costigan—for the latter was the rank which he preferred to assume—was seated in the window with the newspaper held before him at arm's length. The Captain's eyes were somewhat dim; and he was spelling the paper, with the help of his lips, as well as of those bloodshot eyes of his, as you see gentlemen do to whom reading is a rare and difficult occupation. His hat was cocked very much on one ear; and as one of his feet lay up in the window seat, the observer of such matters might remark, by the size and shabbiness of the boots which the Captain wore, that times did not go very well with him. Poverty seems as if it were disposed, before it takes possession of a man entirely, to attack his extremities first: the coverings of his head, feet, and hands, are its first prey. All these parts of the Captain's person were particularly rakish and shabby. As soon as he saw Pen he descended from the window seat and saluted the new-comer, first in a military manner, by conveying a couple of his fingers (covered with a broken black glove) to his hat, and then removing that ornament altogether. The Captain was inclined to be bald, but he brought a quantity of lank iron-grey hair over his pate, and had a couple of wisps of the same falling down on each side of his face. Much whisky had spoiled what complexion Mr. Costigan may have possessed in his youth. His once handsome face had now a copper tinge. He wore a very high stock, scarred and stained in many places; and a dress-coat tightly buttoned up in those parts where the buttons had not parted company from the garment.

"The young gentleman to whom I had the honour to be introduced yesterday in the Cathedral Yard," said the Captain, with a splendid bow and wave of his hat. "I hope I see you well, sir. I marked ye in the thayater last night during me daughter's perfawrumance; and missed ye on my return. I did but conduct her home, sir, for Jack Costigan, though poor, is a gentleman; and when I reintered the house to pay me respects to me joyous young friend, Mr. Foker—ye were gone. We had a jolly night of ut, sir—Mr. Foker, the three gallant young dragoons, and your 'umble servant. Gad, sir, it put me in mind of one of our old nights when I bore Her Majesty's commission in the Foighting Hundtherd and Third." And he pulled out an old snuff-box, which he presented with a stately air to his new acquaintance.

William Makepeace Thackeray

From *Hard Times*

SLEARY'S HORSEMANSHIP

Meanwhile, the various members of Sleary's company gradually gathered together from the upper regions, where they were quartered, and, from standing about, talking in low voices to one another and to Mr Childers, gradually insinuated themselves and him into the room. There were two or three handsome young women among them, with their two or three husbands, and their two or three mothers, and their eight or nine little children, who did the fairy business when required. The father of one of the families was in the habit of balancing the father of another of the families on the top of a great pole; the father of a third family often made a pyramid of both those fathers, with Master Kidderminster for the apex, and himself for the base; all the fathers could dance upon rolling casks, stand upon bottles, catch knives and balls, twirl hand-basins, ride upon anything, jump over everything, and stick at nothing. All the mothers could (and did) dance, upon the slack wire and the tight rope, and perform rapid acts on barebacked steeds; none of them were at all particular in respect of showing their legs; and one of them, alone in a Greek chariot, drove six in hand into every town they came to. They all assumed to be mighty rakish and knowing, they were not very tidy in their private dresses, they were not at all orderly in their domestic arrangements, and the combined literature of the whole company would have produced but a poor letter on any subject. Yet there was a remarkable gentleness and childishness about these people, a special inaptitude for any kind of sharp practice, and an untiring readiness to help and pity one another, deserving, often of as much respect, and always of as much generous construction, as the everyday virtues of any class of people in the world.

Last of all appeared Mr Sleary: a stout man as already mentioned, with one fixed eye and one loose eye, a voice (if it can be called so) like the efforts of a broken old pair of bellows, a flabby surface, and a muddled head which was never sober and never drunk.

"Thquire!" said Mr Sleary, who was troubled with asthma, and whose breath came far too thick and heavy for the letter s, "Your thervant! Thith ith a bad piethe of bithnith, thith ith. You've heard of my Clown and hith dog being thuppothed to have morrithed?"

He addressed Mr Gradgrind, who answered "Yes."

"Well Thquire," he returned, taking off his hat, and rubbing the lining with his pocket-handkerchief, which he kept inside it for the purpose. "Ith it your intenthion to do anything for the poor girl, Thquire?"

"I shall have something to propose to her when she comes back," said Mr Gradgrind.

"Glad to hear it, Thquire. Not that I want to get rid of the child, any more than I want to thtand in her way. I'm willing to take her prentith, though at her age ith late. My voithe ith a little huthky, Thquire, and not eathy heard by them ath don't know me; but if you'd been chilled and heated, heated and chilled, chilled and heated in the ring when you wath young, ath often ath I have been, *your* voithe wouldn't have lathted out, Thquire, no more then mine."

"I dare say not," said Mr Gradgrind.

"What thall it be, Thquire, while you wait? Thall it be Therry? Give it a name, Thquire!" said Mr Sleary, with hospitable ease.

"Nothing for me, I thank you," said Mr Gradgrind.

"Don't thay nothing, Thquire. What doth your friend thay? If you haven't took your feed yet, have a glath of bitterth."

Here his daughter Josephine—a pretty fair-haired girl of eighteen, who had been tied on a horse at two years old, and had made a will at twelve, which she always carried about with her, expressive of her dying desire to be drawn to the grave by the two piebald ponies—cried "Father, hush! she has come back!" Then came Sissy Jupe, running into the room as she had run out of it. And when she saw them all assembled, and saw their looks, and saw no father there, she broke into a most deplorable cry, and took refuge on the bosom of the most accomplished tight-rope lady (herself in the family way), who knelt down on the floor to nurse her, and to weep over her.

"Ith an infernal thame, upon my thoul it ith," said Sleary.

Charles Dickens

From *Dombey and Son*

The lady thus specially presented was a long lean figure, wearing such a faded air that she seemed not to have been made in what linen-drapers call "fast colours" originally, and to have, by little and little, washed out. But for this, she might have been described as the very pink of general propitiation and politeness. From a long habit of listening admirably to everything that was said in her presence, and looking at the speakers as if she were mentally engaged in taking off impressions of their images upon her soul, never to part with the same but with life, her head had quite settled on one side. Her hands had contracted a spasmodic habit of raising themselves of their own accord as an involuntary admiration. Her eyes were liable to a similar affection. She had the softest voice that ever was heard; and her nose, stupendously aquiline, had a little knob in the very centre or keystone of the bridge, whence it tended downwards toward her face, as in an invincible determination never to turn up at anything.

Miss Tox's dress, though perfectly genteel and good, had a certain character of angularity and scantiness. She was accustomed to wear odd weedy little flowers in her bonnets and caps. Strange grasses were sometimes perceived in her hair; and it was observed by the curious, of all her collars, frills, tuckers, wristbands, and other gossamer articles—indeed of everything she wore which had two ends to it intended to unite—that the two ends were never on good terms, and wouldn't quite meet without a struggle. She had furry articles for winter wear, as tippets, boas, and muffs, which stood up on end in a rampant manner, and were not at all sleek. She was much given to the carrying about of small bags with snaps to them, that went off like little pistols when they were shut up; and when full-dressed, she wore round her neck the barrenest of lockets, representing a fishy old eye, with no approach to speculation in it. These and other appearances of a similar nature had served to propagate the opinion that Miss Tox was a lady of what is called a limited independence, which she turned to the best account. Possibly her mincing gait encouraged the belief, and suggested that her clipping a step of ordinary compass into two or three originated in her habit of making the most of everything.

"I am sure," said Miss Tox, with a prodigious curtsy, "that to have the honour of being presented to Mr. Dombey is a distinction which I have long sought, but very little expected at the present moment. My dear Mrs. Chick—may I say Louisa!"

Mrs. Chick took Miss Tox's hand in hers, rested the foot of her wine-glass upon it, repressed a tear, and said in a low voice, "Bless you!"

"My dear Louisa then," said Miss Tox, "my sweet friend, how are you now?"

"Better," Mrs. Chick returned. "Take some wine. You have been almost as anxious as I have been, and must want it, I am sure."

Mr. Dombey of course officiated.

"Miss Tox, Paul," pursued Mrs. Chick, still retaining her hand, "knowing how much I have been interested in the anticipation of the event of to-day, has been working at a little gift for Fanny, which I promised to present. It is only a pincushion for the toilette table, Paul, but I do say, and will say, and must say, that Miss Tox has very prettily adapted the sentiment to the occasion. I call 'Welcome little Dombey' poetry, myself!"

"Is that the device?" inquired her brother.

"That is the device," returned Louisa.

"But do me the justice to remember, my dear Louisa," said Miss Tox in a tone of low and earnest entreaty, "that nothing but the—I have some difficulty in expressing myself—the dubiousness of the result would have induced me to take so great a liberty: 'Welcome, Master Dombey,' would have been much more congenial to my feelings, as I am sure you know. But the uncertainty attendant on angelic strangers will, I hope, excuse what must otherwise appear an unwarrantable familiarity." Miss Tox made a graceful bend as she spoke, in favour of Mr. Dombey, which that gentleman graciously acknowledged. Even the sort of recognition of Dombey and Son conveyed in the foregoing conversation was so palatable to him that his sister, Mrs. Chick—though he affected to consider her a weak good-natured person—had perhaps more influence over him than anybody else.

Charles Dickens

The Patented Gate and the Mean Hamburger

You have seen him a thousand times. You have seen him standing on the street corner on Saturday afternoon, in the little county-seat towns. He wears blue jean pants, or overalls washed to a pale pastel blue like the color of sky after a shower in spring, but because it is Saturday he has on a wool coat, an old one, perhaps the coat left from the suit he got married in a long time back. His long wrist bones hang out from the sleeves of the coat, the tendons showing along the bone like the dry twist of grapevine still corded on the stove-length of a hickory sapling you would find in his wood box beside his cookstove among the split chunks of gum and red oak. The big hands, with the knotted, cracked joints and the square, horn-thick nails, hang loose off the wrist bone like clumsy, home-made tools hung on the wall of a shed after work. If it is summer, he wears a straw hat with a wide brim, the straw fraying loose around the edge. If it is winter, he wears a felt hat, black once, but now weathered with streaks of dark gray and dull purple in the sunlight. His face is long and bony, the jawbone long under the drawn-in cheeks. The flesh along the jawbone is nicked in a couple of places where the unaccustomed razor has been drawn over the leather-coarse skin. A tiny bit of blood crusts brown where the nick is. The color of the face is red, a dull red like the red clay mud or clay dust which clings to the bottom of his pants and to the cast-iron-looking brogans on his feet, or a red like the color of a piece of hewed cedar which has been left in the weather. The face does not look alive. It seems to be molded from the clay or hewed from the cedar. When the jaw moves, once, with its deliberate, massive motion on the quid of tobacco, you are still not convinced. That motion is but the cunning triumph of a mechanism concealed within.

But you see the eyes. You see that the eyes are alive. They are pale blue or gray, set back under the deep brows and thorny eyebrows. They are not wide, but are squinched up like eyes accustomed to wind or sun or to measuring the stroke of the ax or to fixing the object over the rifle sights. When you pass, you see that the eyes are alive and are warily and dispassionately estimating you from the ambush of the thorny brows. Then you pass on, and he stands there in that stillness which is his gift.

Robert Penn Warren

From *Microcosmography: or, A Piece of the World
Discovered in Essays & Characters*

A YOUNG GENTLEMAN OF THE UNIVERSITY

Is one that comes there to wear a gown, and to say hereafter, he had been at the university. His father sent him thither because he heard there were the best fencing and dancing schools; from these he has his education, from his tutor the oversight. The first element of his knowledge is to be shown the colleges, and initiated in a tavern by the way, which hereafter he will learn of himself. The two marks of his seniority is the bare velvet of his gown, and his proficiency at tennis, where when he can once play a set, he is a freshman no more. His study has commonly handsome shelves, his books neat silk strings, which he shows to his father's man, and is loth to untie or take down for fear of misplacing. Upon foul days for recreation he retires thither, and looks over the pretty book his tutor reads to him, which is commonly some short history, or a piece of Euphormio for which his tutor gives him money to spend next day. His main loitering is at the library, where he studies arms and books of honor, and turns a gentleman critic in pedigrees. Of all things he endures not to be mistaken for a scholar, and hates a black suit though it be made of satin. His companion is ordinarily some stale fellow, that has been notorious for an ingle to gold hatbands, whom he admires at first, afterwards scorns. If he have spirit or wit he may light of better company, and may learn some flashes of wit, which may do him knight's service in the country hereafter. But he is now gone to the inns-of-court, where he studies to forget what he learned before, his acquaintance and the fashion.

A MERE ALDERMAN

He is venerable in his gown, more in his beard, wherewith he sets not forth so much his own, as the face of a city. You must look on him as one of the town gates, and consider him not as a body, but a corporation. His eminency above others hath made him a man of worship, for he had never been preferred, but that he was worth thousands. He oversees the commonwealth as his shop, and it is an argument of his policy, that he has thriven by his craft. He is a rigorous magistrate in his ward; yet his scale of justice is suspected, lest it be like the balances in his warehouse. A ponderous man he is, and substantial, for his weight is commonly extraordinary, and in his preferment nothing rises so much as his belly. His head is of no great depth, yet well furnished; and when it is in conjunction with his brethren, may bring forth a city apothegm, or some such sage matter. He is one that will not hastily run into error, for he treads with great deliberation, and his judgment consists much in his pace. His discourse is commonly the annals of his mayoralty, and what good government there was in the days of his gold chain; though the door-posts were the only things that suffered reformation. He seems most sincerely religious, especially on solemn days; for he comes often to church to make a show and is a part of the choir hangings. He is the highest stair of his profession, and an example to his trade, what in time they may come to. He makes very much of his authority, but more of his satin doublet, which, though of good years, bears its age very well, and looks fresh every Sunday: but his scarlet gown is a monument, and lasts from generation to generation.

John Earle

Portrait

The clear brown eyes, kindly and alert, with 12-20 vision, give confident regard to the passing world through R. K. Lampert & Company lenses
framed in gold:
His soul, however, is all his own;
Arndt Brothers necktie and hat (with feather) supply a touch of youth.

With his soul his own, he drives, drives, chats and drives,
The first and second bicuspids, lower right, replaced by bridgework, while
two incisors have porcelain crowns;

(Render unto Federal, state, and city Caesar, but not unto time;
Render nothing unto time until Amalgamated Death serves final notice, in
proper form;

The vault is ready;
The will has been drawn by Clagget, Clagget, Clagget & Brown;
The policies are adequate, Confidential's best, reimbursing for disability,
partial or complete, with double indemnity should the end be a pure and
simple accident)

Nothing unto time,
Nothing unto change, nothing unto fate,
Nothing unto you, and nothing unto me, or to any other known or unknown
party or parties, living or deceased;

But Mercury shoes, with special arch supports, take much of the wear and
tear;
On the course, a custombuilt driver corrects a tendency to slice;
Love's ravages have been repaired (it was a textbook case) by Drs. Schultz,
Lightner, Mannheim, and Goode,
While all of it is enclosed in excellent tweed, with Mr. Baumer's personal
attention to the shoulders and the waist;

And all of it now roving, chatting amiably through space in a Plymouth 6,
With his soul (his own) at peace, soothed by Walter Lippmann, and sustained by Haig & Haig.

Kenneth Fearing

Speech is what characters do to each other.

Elizabeth Bowen

SECTION 2 **Dialogues**

Speech is at once the most characteristic human gesture and, because it crystallizes so many social, ethnic, and regional differences, the most revealing one as well. The expressions a person uses habitually, the way he pronounces his *a's* and *r's*, usually tell us whether he's a college professor or a longshoreman, an Okie or a proper Bostonian. No novelist or short story writer can get along without dialogue, and most essayists find direct quotation one of the most effective devices for illustrating and explaining new ideas. Speech humanizes discourse by putting a reader in touch with a person instead of an abstraction. To say that your uncle is "very opinionated" about politics is to say nothing dully; to quote him, however ("Damn that reactionary, bourgeois legislature anyhow," my uncle shouted) is to bring his opinions to life on the page and in the imagination. One of the greatest biographies in English, Boswell's *Life of Samuel Johnson*, is built around sparkling conversation:

> To such a degree of unrestrained frankness had he now accustomed me, that in the course of this evening I talked of the numerous reflections which had been thrown out against him on account of his having accepted a pension from his present Majesty. "Why sir, (said he, with a hearty laugh,) it is a mighty foolish noise that they make. I have accepted of a pension as a reward which has been thought due to my literary merit; and now that I have this pension, I am the same man in every respect that I have ever been; I retain the same principles. It is true, that I cannot now curse the House of Hanover; nor would it be decent for me to drink King James health in the wine that King George gives me money to pay for. But, Sir, I think that the pleasure of cursing the House of Hanover, and drinking King James health, are amply overbalanced by three hundred pounds a year."
>
> . . .
>
> Mr. Arthur Lee mentioned some Scotch who had taken possession of a barren part of America, and wondered why they should choose it. JOHNSON. "Why, Sir, all barrenness is comparative. The Scotch would not know it to be barren." BOSWELL: "Come, come, he is flattering the English. You have now been in Scotland, Sir, and say if you did not see meat and drink enough there." JOHNSON. "Why yes, Sir; meat and drink enough to give the inhabitants sufficient strength to run away from home."

These passages illustrate another benefit of dialogue—economy. By allowing Dr. Johnson to speak for himself Boswell can show in one paragraph what it would take him several pages to explain. Color and brevity are combined.

But there are also some crucial differences between dialogue, or written speech, and ordinary conversation. Unlike talk, which can go on for hours about nothing in particular, a dialogue must always go somewhere. Every statement must reveal character or clarify an idea or forward the action. Furthermore, all the pauses, digressions, and redundancies that clog real speech must be edited out, leaving a condensed, polished imitation that must appear natural and spontaneous even though it is highly artificial. In fact, the closer a dialogue is to a verbatim transcript of a conversation the duller it is to read.

Here is a "quickie" student dialogue with some typical strengths and weaknesses:

> "You've got no sense of responsibility," his sister shouted, "none at all."
>
> "You've got a point there."
>
> "You're a slob and, what's worse, you're inconsiderate."
>
> "I may be a slob, but I'm not inconsiderate."
>
> "Well, I think you are. You don't give a damn about my feelings or about mom's or dad's either. It always looks like a bomb went off in here. How can you live in such filth?"
>
> "Easy. Takes hardly any work at all."
>
> "You're getting to be a smartass also. Just remember, there's going to be trouble around here if you don't start sharing the responsibilities. Dad's going to tell you to shape up or ship out."
>
> "As a matter of fact, I've been thinking a lot about shipping out lately. . . . By the way, what's for dinner tonight?"

The dialogue has a certain colloquial vigor. It moves briskly towards an amusing ending. We always know who's speaking. At the same time, the speakers tend to repeat one another too often, as though both are slightly hard of hearing. They also volley words like "inconsiderate" and "responsibility" back and forth without indicating what they mean. Whatever else is behind this quarrel is unclear. We assume, without really knowing, that the argument takes place in the brother's room. A short narrative bridge or some internal reference ("Why do you always drape your jeans over the dresser?") would clear up the confusion and also allow us to visualize the scene better.

No two people talk alike any more than they think or act alike, which is what makes writing dialogue exciting and challenging. Your job is to help a reader to *hear* speech differences. Here are some general guidelines:

1. Listen attentively to conversation and ask yourself questions about it: Is this person's vocabulary formal, colloquial, jargonized? Does he speak with an accent? Is it regional or ethnic? What expressions does he use habitually? Is he anecdotal or businesslike? Is his tone of voice

detached, humorous, gentle, sarcastic? These are the things that distinguish one person's speech from the next.

2. Remember that dialogue is a dramatic action between people, not a succession of monologues or a vehicle for ideas only. Make something happen by having speakers question, challenge, and interrupt one another.

3. Read your dialogues aloud.

4. Speech is always more compressed and elliptical than writing. If you saw a person about to be hit by a rock you wouldn't say, "Pardon me, but unless you move approximately three feet to the left you will be struck by a large piece of feldspar." You'd shout "Duck!" or "Heads Up!" and hope for the best. In monologues and dialogues you can use imperatives, sentence fragments, slang, and other devices of informality in order to make speech sound authentic. Add to your stylistic reserves.

5. Resist the temptation to use elegant tags like "she chimed" and "he chortled." You'll have a hard time making conversation chime and chortle and you'll also annoy your reader by seeming to ask for more response than your writing deserves.

6. Avoid long paragraphs in a dialogue. They're difficult to read and inevitably contain a lot of deadwood. Cut and summarize to sustain forward momentum.

7. Read your dialogues aloud.

SUMMARY

Dialogue is a *dramatic* action involving two or more persons, not a series of alternating monologues and lectures. It is also an edited, stylized imitation of real speech, meaning that it contains few of the *ahs* and *umms*, the redundancies and ambiguities that clutter our everyday conversation. We attempt instead to emphasize those words, intonations, and speech patterns that actually reveal attitude and character. As a literary device dialogue advances action, makes writing more colorful, and reduces the amount of explanatory commentary. It is a source of both vividness and economy.

EXERCISES

1. (a) Eavesdrop in a public place such as a restaurant, theater lobby, or bus station, taking notes on what you overhear. Later, develop these notes into brief sketches (250–350 words) in which you introduce the speakers and what is between them through dialogue alone.

   (b) Write several pages of dialogue without using any narrative bridges ("John smiled seductively and inched closer to Janice.") or descriptive tags ("He bellowed," "She snarled"). Make conversation the only vehicle for conveying information about the speakers. Later, rewrite the dialogue *with* bridges and tags. What is gained and lost by the additions?

   (c) Tape a class discussion or a conversation at a party and then transcribe and edit it into a coherent reading script that captures both the flavor of the occasion and the attitudes of the speakers. What changes are necessary to make real conversation readable?

2. The following exercises are designed to acquaint you with a few basic speech patterns, not to produce authentic, convincing dialogue. In this instance form comes before content.

   (a) Write several brief dialogues in which each speaker is restricted to a single type of statement. For example, a dialogue in which one person makes only "I" statements and the other only "We" statements; or, a dialogue in which the first speaker makes declarative statements and the second responds only with questions. Experiment with other patterns ("I-You," "Why-Because," imperatives) in order to get a feel for their function in dialogues.

   (b) Write a parody, that is a broad, comic imitation, of the speech of someone you know well like your father or your roommate. Deliberately exaggerate any grammatical and stylistic peculiarities in order to make the person's speech unique.

   (c) Write a dialogue in the jargon of a particular trade, profession, or discipline (e. g., carpentry, auto racing, sociology), making as many statements in this private language as you can without becoming completely incoherent.

   (d) Dialect is a regional or ethnic species of a language that differs from the standard version in grammar, syntax, vocabulary, and punctuation. Here is a passage in an Appalachian Mountain dialect:

   > Poppy had a awful hard time, an' his daddy died a way' fore he was born so he had a hard time t'begin with. Well, atter he's married he had a worse time I'll say, with all 'at sickness'n ever'thing on 'im. Mommy did love wheat bread, an'

he worked for a peck a'corn a day so he could get Mommy bread t'eat. Why, he'uz as good t'Mommy as a baby. Now Ulysses didn't believe this, an' I didn't care whether he did'r not—you know, if I tell anybody anything an' they believe it, it's all right; an' if they don't believe it, I don't care whether they do'r not—I never heard Poppy give Mommy a ill word in my life. Now we had some hogs, and one of our hogs got in a neighbor's corn patch an' eat some of his corn. And he come after Poppy an' told him t'come get his hog, an' he charged Poppy two dollars fer what it eat. Poppy's s'mad he didn't know what to' do. That uz the maddest I ever seed Poppy in my life. An' Mommy—he called her Dink, that was her nickname—she said somethin' t'Poppy. "Now," he says, "Dink, don't you say a *word* to me while I'm mad." An' that was ever'thing's ever said about that. She hushed, of course. An' he never said nary another word. That was the' illest word I ever heerd Poppy tell Mommy in my life.

Eliot Wigginton, *The Foxfire Book*

Using this passage as a general model, write either a monologue or a dialogue in a dialect you're familiar with, deviating from standard English whenever necessary in order to capture its distinctive qualities.

3. Compose a dialogue between your present self and a younger self on a subject about which your views have changed significantly. Make these selves talk to one another rather than simply exchange statements.

4. Here are some "occasions" that might generate dialogues:
Two guys discover they've been dating the same girl, or vice versa.
Two friends discover that they've applied for the same job or scholarship.
A student asks a teacher to explain a failing grade on an examination.
A father tries to discuss sex, careers, or colleges with his son. A mother tries to do the same thing with her daughter.

READINGS

From *Conversations and Things Overheard*

"For God's sake," Lew groaned, "I don't want to meet any people. I know some people."

"Look me up in the Social Register."

"You hate people, don't you?"
"Yes, and you do, too."
"I hate them like hell."
"What are you going to do about it?"
"I don't know. But not that anyhow. If I'm cold I'm not always going to use it to learn their secrets by finding them off guard and vulnerable. And I'm not going around saying I'm fond of people when I mean I'm so damned used to their reactions to my personal charm that I can't do without it. Getting emptier and emptier. Love is shy. I thought from the first that no one who thought about it like you did ever had it."

"Oh, have you got an engagement with your drug-taking friend in Monte Carlo?"

He sat down and began putting on his shoes.

"I shouldn't have told you that. I suppose you think he'll convert me to the habit."

"I certainly don't think it's a very profitable association."

"Oh, yes it is. It's not everybody who can get the dope habit from a prominent moving picture director. In fact, it's begun already. At this very moment I'm full of dope. He started me on cocaine, and we're working slowly up to heroin."

"That isn't really funny, Francis."

"Excuse me. I was trying to be funny and I know you don't like my way of being funny."

She countered his growing bitterness by adopting a tone of calm patience.

In Virginia the Italian children say:
"Lincoln threw blacks out; now they're back."
"The white people fit the Yankees."
"Yankees *are* white people."
"Not I ever hear tell of."

I really loved him, but of course it wore out like a love affair. The fairies have spoiled all that.

"Just a couple of old drunks, just a couple of ol-l-ld circus clowns."

"I'm in a hurry.
"I'm in a hurry—I'm in a hurry."

"What are you in a hurry about?"
"I can't explain—I'm in a hurry."

"This is a tough girl and I'm taking her to a tough place."

Three hundred a day die in auto accidents in the U.S.A.

Man looking at aeroplane: "That's one of them new gyropractors."

Bijou, regarding her cigarette fingers: "Oh, Trevah! Get me the pumice stone."

His life was a sort of dream, as are most lives with the mainspring left out.

Suddenly her face resumed that expression which can only come from studying moving picture magazines over and over, and only be described as one long blond wish toward something—a wish that you'd have a wedlock with the youth of Shirley Temple, the earning power of Clark Gable; the love of Clark Gable and the talent of Charles Laughton—and with a bright smile the girl was gone.

Feel wide awake—no, but at least I feel born, which is more than I did the first time I woke up.

The cartoon cat licked the cartoon kitten and a girl behind me said, "Isn't that sweet?"

We can't just let our worlds crash around us like a lot of dropped trays.

Q. What did he die of? A. He died of jus' dieability.

"Hello, Sam." When you were a good guest, you knew the names of the servants, the smallest babies, and the oldest aunts. "Is Bonny in?"

"I like writers. If you speak to a writer, you often get an answer."

Woman says about husband that he keeps bringing whole great masses of dogs back from the pound.

"We haven't got any more gin," he said. "Will you have a bromide?" he added hopefully.

Long engagement: nothing to do but to marry or quarrel, so I decided to quarrel.

"*I* didn't do it," he said, using the scented "I."

"Remember you're physically repulsive to me."

"Learn young about hard work and good manners—and you'll be through the whole dirty mess and nicely dead again before you know it."

Now it's all as useless as repeating a dream.

"I'm going to break that stubborn stupid part of you that thinks that any

American woman who has met Brancusi is automatically a genius and entitled ever after to leave the dishes and walk around with her head in the clouds."

"You look to me like a very ordinary three-piece suit."

Man to Woman: "You look as if you wanted excitement—is that true?"

F. Scott Fitzgerald

Aunt Em

"Frank! Frank!" came a querulous voice.
A small, shy, self-effacing man came into the parlour at once in response to his invalid wife's call.
"Yes, dear" he replied, meekly awaiting his orders.
"This pillow needs to be a little higher at my back."
Frank gently rearranged the pillows on the overstuffed arm chair on which Emma was sitting, her body oozing out over the sides. Her swollen legs lay flopped out on a fancy ottoman. Her puffy, piglike eyes peered through a frizzled mop of graying hair. Her mouth was drooping and petulant.
"It seems so hot. Bring my black slippers. A change will cool my feet," she whined, in a kind of listless sing song.
Frank whisked away like a shadow. The whine continued, following him out into the bedroom and then back into the parlour.
"Make some lemonade, Frank. I think you can fan me now too. I have such a sinking feeling."
"Yes, dear." Frank lifted the plump feet from the ottoman and carefully changed the slippers. Then he began waving a palm leaf back and forth methodically to create a stir of cool air.
"I don't think there are any lemons, dear," he said timidly.
Emma sat bolt upright. "What do you mean, no lemons. When you shopped yesterday you knew very well it was going to be hot today."
She sat back limply in her chair.
"No wonder I'm so poorly, putting up with your neglect all the time. You are such a trial." She dabbed at her little pig eyes with a fat, beringed hand. "Ah, well, call that little Jones girl. She'll run to the store. Mind you, don't give her any money for the errand. We can't afford to waste money like that."
Emma paused for a moment, then went on in a pleasanter voice. "Tell the child to come talk with me. I must find out where her aunt went all gussied up this morning."
Frank went outside and yoo-hooed to the little girl, who trotted off willingly on the errand.
For fifteen minutes he fanned Emma's face and plumped her pillows and

listened to her complaints. He had learned early in marriage to remain silent. The girl returned and went into the dim parlour.

"How are you today, Aunt Em? Feeling well, I hope." She handed Frank the lemons.

"No dear, I'm feeling poorly. Heat takes ahold of me somethin' awful. I seen your aunt go out this morning, dolled up fit to kill. Where's she go?" The child scuffed the rug with her bare toes.

"Cat got yer tongue? Speak up. Frank, stop gaping. Go make the lemonade. Mind you pump the water till it's cold. Well child, answer me."

"My father says you're an old snoop," she blurted out.

Emma let out a piercing, pained shriek. The child fled to the kitchen and started out the back door. Frank grabbed her gently and pressed a five-cent piece into her damp hand.

"Don't never tell I gave it to you."

Then he hurried back to the parlour.

Millicent Ball

From *Listening to America*

ON THE ROAD IN EAST TEXAS

It was late and dark and I wanted one more cup of coffee for the last hour on the road. Somewhere past Center before you get to Carthage—I think it was around Tencha—I stopped at a roadside café. It was about eleven o'clock and the place was full of young couples having hamburgers and Cokes before they headed for the piny woods and the back seats. Several truckers were there. The waitress was harassed but friendly, and between orders she stood behind the counter and talked with me. I noticed through a square open window in the wall behind the counter at least four Negro men drinking coffee in a small back room that appeared to be part of the kitchen.

"They ever come up here?" I asked.

"Naw. That's their place back there."

I said, quite casually: "Did you know that's against the law?"

"Against the law?"

"Yep, the Public Accommodations Act of 1964 says you can't do that."

"You're pullin' my leg."

"No, no, I'm not. It's right there in the law. You have to open the same facilities to everyone if you run a business that caters to the public."

"That a state law?"

"Nope, federal law. Passed in 1964."

"I'll be damned."

"Course it's the owner that's liable. I don't think the fault would be on you."

She turned to her left and said in a very loud Shelby County voice:

"Hey, Charlie, c'm here." And there arose from the table in the corner a vast square block of a man with his shirt collar open down to the hair on his chest and thick hard arms protruding out of the short sleeves of his sport shirt.

"Yeah?"

"This feller says it's against the law for us to serve them nigras back there."

Without changing his expression he said: "No shit."

"That's what he said. Said it was a fed'r'l law passed five years ago. Is that what you said? Five years ago?"

"Yes."

"Who says?"

"The government—the Congress—the Public Accommodations Act of 1964."

"Never heard of it."

"Well, it's there. It's there on the books."

He turned toward the square window in the wall, stabbed two fingers of his left hand into the corners of his mouth, and let out a loud throaty whistle like a hunter calling back his bird dogs.

The Negro men in the small back room looked up startled and glanced at each other apprehensively, and when Charlie motioned to them with a jerk of his head they got up and came through the door from the kitchen. They were nervous. Each appeared to be in his mid-forties, except for one, a much older man. I took them to be farm hands.

Charlie jerked his head toward me and said: "Feller here says it's against the law to serve you folks back there."

They were silent. I could not tell if they were more frightened than I was.

"Says it's something—what'd you say they call it, Mister?"

"The Public Accommodations Act of 1964."

"You ever hear of that?"

"Naw sir, never did." The older man was answering.

"You think it's against the law for you to have a nice place back there to eat so's you can talk among yourselves?"

"Naw sir, naw sir."

He turned to me and said: "They don't think it's against the law. And I don't think it's against the law. And nobody's told me it's against the law but you. Now what are you going to do?"

I said, "I'm going to hit the road." And I put down a quarter, which included a fifteen-cent tip for his lady friend, the waitress, walked out of the diner, got into my car, locked the doors, and sped away.

Bill Moyers

But it is a work of very great labour and difficulty to keep a journal of life, occupied in various pursuits, mingled with concomitant speculations and reflections, in so much, that I do not think it possible to do it unless one has a peculiar talent for abridging. I have tried it in that way, when it has been my good fortune to live in a multiplicity of instructive and entertaining scenes, and I have thought my notes like portable soup, of which a little bit by being dissolved in water will make a large good dish.

James Boswell

SECTION 3   The Biographical Capsule

This section is both an extension of Section 1, "Profiles and Characters," and a companion to the "Autobiographical Sketch" sections in Chapter 5. Although different in focus, all three demand what Boswell calls "a peculiar talent for abridging." Since it is impossible to tell everything about yourself or someone else, it is necessary to focus on essential, telling facts in order to say more with less. Apply "abridging" principles rigorously:

1. Look for habitual gestures, expressions, and actions that might serve as abstracts for a whole life, and organize them into a coherent image. Note, for example, how all of Landor's eccentricities (page 188) seem to confirm the observation that he was "the sanest madman and the maddest reasonable man in the world," or how in his portrait of Robert LaFollette (page 194) John Dos Passos repeats the critical phrase "He bucked the machine " at strategic intervals. In examining your own piece ask yourself what detail *A* has to do with detail *B* and detail *C*. If the answer is "Nothing at all," start revising.

2. Always support generalizations with concrete details (physical description, anecdotes, direct quotes) but beware of bloating your piece with redundant illustrations. If you recall a dozen examples of your father's narrow-mindedness mention the most amusing or the most irritating and make it proxy for the other eleven. E.E. Cummings's sketch of his father (page 189) and Meyer Berger's portrait of Rachel MacDowell (page 189) are two models of solid yet spare biographical writing.

3. Establish clear priorities among the different sections of your essay so that the most important details receive appropriate emphasis. If your aunt spent most of her life fighting for civil rights and other minority legislation don't equate this, spatially, with her interest in Italian cooking

and contract bridge. Avoid entombing crucial details in the middles of paragraphs or saving your most suggestive observation for the last sentence. Be clear about what's important.

4. Experiment with different methods of organizing your materials instead of accepting the first one that comes to mind. Straight chronology, for example, is easy to use but unless you are careful it can lead to a boring recitation of facts. Note how Archibald MacLeish avoids this problem in his *Self-Portrait* (page 153). Consider various forms of topical and thematic organization as well. If there is a metaphor implicit in your material, develop it; if you think of an apt analogy, see if you can make it an armature for the entire essay. The idea is to be systematic in your presentation without drying and mounting your subject like a laboratory specimen.

SUMMARY

In a biographical capsule you attempt to recount a person's entire life in terms of a few carefully chosen details. These may be arranged topically, thematically, dramatically, or chronologically; the important thing is that they present a coherent image of your subject instead of remaining discrete observations. Like an autobiographical sketch, a capsule demands what Boswell refers to as "a peculiar talent for abridging," that is, a talent for reducing information to essentials and thereby saying more with less.

EXERCISES

1. (a) Compose a short biographical sketch (150–250 words) of a close friend
   that would be suitable for the dust jacket of a novel or the program for
   a concert. Include details that characterize as well as simply identify
   the person.

   (b) Write a sketch of one of your classmates based on information contained in a school yearbook. Bring all those dull, characterless facts to
   life.

   (c) Write a capsule (250–300 words) biography of a literary character,
   perhaps a minor one, based entirely on information gathered from the
   work in which he or she appears. Include distinctive physical details,
   actions, and remarks.

2. Compose a capsule biography of a celebrity (writer, actress, politician,
   artist) whose life and work you know well. Since this assignment will involve some research you might consult such standard reference works as
   *The Dictionary of National Biography, The Dictionary of American Biography,
   Who's Who*, and the *Encyclopedia Britannica*. Remember, however, that
   you are not merely collecting data but trying to communicate a point of
   view about this person to a reader. It should be clear from the details you
   include whether you admire, envy, distrust, or despise him. Essays like
   Fighting Bob (page 194) and *Lady Bishop* (page 189) should be helpful for
   this assignment.

3. Write a capsule biography of a parent, relative, or close friend. Think
   carefully about the kinds of detail you will include (physical description,
   anecdotes, direct quotes, comments from other people) and also about
   how they might be organized (topically, thematically, chronologically).
   Experiment with different combinations until you find the most appropriate one for your material. If possible, talk with the person about his
   experiences, goals, expectations and so forth. And be precise in your
   questioning. If he speaks in generalities ask for specific examples, if he
   talks only about ideas ask about feelings, if he concentrates on the past
   ask about the present, if he mentions only isolated incidents ask about
   relationships (1500 words).

READINGS

From *The Story of My Life*

Once a week at least I used to go into Bath itself, to dine with my father's old friend Walter Savage Landor, who had been driven away from his Florentine home by his wife's violent temper. Mr. Landor's rooms . . . were entirely covered with pictures, the frames fitting close to one another, leaving not the smallest space of wall visible. One or two of these pictures were real works of art, but as a rule he had bought them at Bath, quite willing to imagine that the little shops of the Bath dealers could be storehouses of Titians, Giorgiones, and Vandycks. The Bath picture-dealers never had such a time; for some years almost all their wares made their way to Mr. Landor's walls. Mr. Landor lived alone with his beautiful white Spitz dog Pomero, which he allowed to do whatever it liked, and frequently to sit in the oddest way on the bald top of his head. He would talk to Pomero by the hour together, poetry, philosophy, whatever he was thinking of, all of it imbued with his own powerful personality, and would often roar with laughter till the whole house seemed to shake. I have never heard a laugh like that of Mr. Landor—"deep-mouthed Boeotian Savage Landor," as Byron called him—such a regular cannonade. He was "the sanest madman and the maddest reasonable man in the world," as Cervantes says of Don Quixote. In the evenings he would sit for hours in impassioned contemplation; in the mornings he wrote incessantly, to fling off sheet after sheet for the *Examiner,* seldom looking them over afterwards. He scarcely ever read, for he only possessed one shelf of books. If any one gave him a volume he mastered it and gave it away, and this he did because he believed that if he knew he was to keep the book and be able to refer to it, he should not be able to absorb its contents so as to retain them. When he left Florence, he had made over all he possessed to his wife, retaining only £200 a year— afterwards increased to £400—for himself, and this sufficed for his simple needs. He never bought any new clothes, and a chimney-sweep would have been ashamed to wear his coat, which was always the same as long as I knew him; though it in no way detracted from his majestic and lion-like appearance. But he was very particular about his little dinners, and it was about these that his violent explosions of passion usually took place. I have seen him take a pheasant up by the legs when it was brought to table and throw it into the back of the fire over the head of the servant in attendance. This was always a failing, and, in later days, I have heard Mr. Browning describe how in his fury at being kept waiting for dinner at Siena, he shouted: "I will not eat it now, I will not eat it if it comes," and when it came, threw it all out of the window.

Augustus Hare

My Father

By way of describing my father, let me quote a letter and tell you a story. The letter was written by me to my good friend Paul Rosenfeld; who used it in an essay which graced the fifth number of that ambiguously entitled periodical The Harvard Wake: I wot not how to answer your query about my father. He was a New Hampshire man, 6 foot 2, a crack shot & a famous fly-fisherman & a firstrate sailor (his sloop was named The Actress) & a woodsman who could find his way through forests primeval without a compass & a canoeist who'd stillpaddle you up to a deer without ruffling the surface of a pond & an ornithologist & taxidermist & (when he gave up hunting) an expert photographer (the best I've ever seen) & an actor who portrayed Julius Caesar in Sanders Theatre & a painter (both in oils & watercolours) & a better carpenter than any professional & an architect who designed his own houses before building them & (when he liked) a plumber who just for the fun of it installed all his own waterworks & (while at Harvard) a teacher with small use for professors—by whom (Royce, Lanman, Taussig, etc.) we were literally surrounded (but not defeated)—& later (at Doctor Hale's socalled South Congregational really Unitarian church) a preacher who announced, during the last war, that the Gott Mit Uns boys were in error since the only thing which mattered was for man to be on God's side (& one beautiful Sunday in Spring remarked from the pulpit that he couldn't understand why anyone had come to hear him on such a day) & horribly shocked his pewholders by crying "the Kingdom of Heaven is no spiritual roofgarden: it's inside you" & my father had the first telephone in Cambridge & (long before any Model T Ford) he piloted an Orient Buckboard with Friction Drive produced by the Waltham watch company & my father sent me to a certain public school because its principal was a gentle immense coalblack negress & when he became a diplomat (for World Peace) he gave me & my friends a tremendous party up in a tree at Sceaux Robinson & my father was a servant of the people who fought Boston's biggest & crookedest politician fiercely all day & a few evenings later sat down with him cheerfully at the Rotary Club & my father's voice was so magnificent that he was called on to impersonate God speaking from Beacon Hill (he was heard all over the common) & my father gave me Plato's metaphor of the cave with my mother's milk.

E. E. Cummings

Lady Bishop

Two events stand out sharply in Rachel Kollock McDowell's memories of 40 years on New York newspapers. She cannot forget how she was accidentally entombed one day many years ago in Princess Anastasia's mausoleum in Woodlawn Cemetery while working on an exclusive story for The Times. Neither can she forget the virginal embarrassment that overwhelmed her when a Times doctor removed her shoe and stocking in her remote corner in the city room and set her left leg after she had broken it on a church assignment.

Within these two events lie the keys to Miss McDowell's character, and journalistic career. The tomb incident points up the fact that she would go anywhere, any time, to get an exclusive for the paper. The other stresses her fear and distrust of laymen, which decades of newspaper work could not overcome. She won her unofficial title, the Lady Bishop, by unchallenged pre-eminence as a religious news editor, and secretly delighted in it. When she retired in 1949, ill, but with her journalistic fires still briskly burning, she remained the first, and only, religious news editor The Times had had in the 100 years since the newspaper was founded. Giving up the job and title all but broke her heart. Her eyes spilled over when she contemplated an existence shorn of them.

The Lady Bishop's childhood and ancestry show why she was so extraordinarily equipped for her work. Her forebears were grim church folk. Two early 19th-century McDowells were moderators of the Presbyterian General Assembly. The ink that runs in her veins traces back to Shepard Kollock who got out the first New York City directory in 1786 from his little print shop at Water and Wall, and who published The New York Gazeteer and Country Journal around the same time.

Miss McDowell's own father, Dr. William O. McDowell, was a businessman in lower Broadway when she was born in Newark in 1880. Of his seven offspring she was the only one who did not marry. "I was dark-haired, blue-eyed and vivacious as a girl," she remembers, "and I had many beaux and many honest-to-goodness propositions, but I wanted to be an entity, not just a Mrs. Somebody." She thinks the many wedding stories she hammered out early in her journalistic career may have had something to do with it, too. To this day she has not forgiven a young gentleman who persuaded her to skip a night sermon at a Bible Conference at Winona Lake, Ind., so he could take her rowing in the moonlight. She got something into the sermon that the preacher never said, because she took the material from an advance script. Even that was a factor in her deciding to forsake romance for a lifetime of tracking down ecclesiastical items for The Times and other papers.

The Newark McDowells went to church three times on Sundays. The children also went to Sunday School and belonged to Christian Endeavor. They were not allowed to read on the Sabbath the more or less worldly books they read on weekdays. "Sometimes," Miss McDowell recalls, "Mamma would let us have an Elsie Dinsmore book on Sunday, because you found nothing wicked in the Elsie books." Miss McDowell cannot remember a time when she did not delight in a thumping good sermon. Though sermons are no longer her professional concern, she spends all Sunday listening to them on the radio in her 14th-floor room in the Hotel Times Square. She is puzzled by Christians who prefer Jack Benny or Fred Allen.

Miss McDowell's first symptoms of literary itch broke out not as church items, but as verse. Her first published effort was a sonnet she dashed off when Queen Victoria died. It ran in The New York Jounal in severe black type under a two-column head with black border—and the editors sent her five dollars for it. She was 15 years old at the time. Later she won a $10 prize in a poetry contest run by The Newark Daily Advertiser. When she was 20, and working for the Prudential Life Insurance Company, she got a black silk umbrella with silver handle and black tassels, for a promotional poem. All she remembers of that one is that each verse ended with the line, "We're out to win, and win we will." Prudential executives thought it was brilliant.

Miss McDowell did not like insurance work. She appealed audibly to Heaven every working day to give her something different to do. It took a little time, but eventually The Newark Evening News took her on as society reporter at $10 a week, and carfare. One day, in the rush of handling 12 weddings, she hitched—as she puts it—the bride to the best man. She is still contrite about this error, for the Lady Bishop was bearish on accuracy to the hour of her retirement.

Mr. James Gordon Bennett's New York Herald started a New Jersey Sunday page while Miss McDowell was panting after social items in Newark and in 1908 she went on The Herald. Her parents were a little worried about this. Her mother still regarded New York City as wicked and didn't relish the idea of Rachel associating with profane journalists. Before this, incidentally, Miss McDowell had spent her vacations at Winona Lake and at Summer Bible Conferences at the Dwight Moody School in East Northfield, Mass. Working as a free lance during these periods she made herself some extra money, and put both places on the map. Gentlemen of the cloth were astonished, but pleased, at the sizable chunks of publicity she got for them, when no one else bothered.

Miss McDowell had to break out of bed before sun-up, sometimes, to cover early morning church assignments in New York, because "mamma," as she explains it, "felt that a woman couldn't stay in New York City overnight, and keep her character." These parental restrictions did not keep Miss McDowell from a brilliant career as church news reporter on The Herald from 1908 to 1920. Her ears burned a little, though, on her first big church story in Manhattan. It was a red-hot sermon by the Rev. (later Bishop) Manning in Trinity Church in answer to insinuations that some of the church's extensive real estate holdings were being used as bawdy houses. "Bad houses," the Lady Bishop still calls them, though the Rev. Dr. Manning, she confesses, "called a spade a spade that morning."

Miss McDowell's distrust of men sometimes paid off in news beats. The late Mayor Gaynor, one day, was to address the New York City Federation of Churches. He assured reporters they would not have to take notes because his stenographer was to be there, and would distribute typed copies of his remarks after the meeting. Miss McDowell took notes, just the same, the only reporter who did. The Mayor's stenographer went off on an alcoholic toot after the session, and Miss McDowell's story on the meeting came out a clean beat. "The speech was a sizzler, too," she recalls happily.

She wept the day that Frank Munsey bought The Herald, while the rest of The Herald staff mounted desks, scattered copy paper, and let off steam in language not fit for a Lady Bishop. In the midst of all this confusion, a call came through from the late Carr Van Anda, managing editor of The Times. He wanted to see Miss McDowell. At first she thought it was some office merry-andrew taking advantage of her misery, but when she was convinced the call was genuine, she dried her tears, took from the locker a rather fancy hat which she had never dared wear home to Newark, and went to The Times. The Herald had paid her $48 a week. Mr. Van Anda took her on at $50 as a guarantee and "space" privileges—and The Times had struck a rich bargain.

From that time on, every other religious news reporter in Manhattan blanched at the Lady Bishop's tigerish ferocity when she went after a church story. She haunted churches and cathedrals, presbytery meetings and Bible conferences. She snatched exclusives from under other reporters' eyes. She detested then, and to the day of her retirement, the idea of pack reporting. She worked alone. She neither gave, nor asked, for quarter. There was not a clergyman, from the hierarchy down, that she did not know. When Bishop Manning called a press conference one day to announce a $10,000,000 campaign for the Cathedral of St. John the Divine, he held up his statement until she got there—50 minutes late. "Miss McDowell," he told her in hurtful reproach, "we have been waiting for you for 50 minutes." A tall young man at one side of the room answered before Miss McDowell had quite caught her breath. "Your Reverence," he said quietly, "Miss McDowell—and The Times—are worth waiting 50 minutes for." Her defender, head of the Bishop's New York campaign committee, was Franklin D. Roosevelt.

Though high churchmen respected the Lady Bishop, they feared her, too. One night at a meeting of the Men's Bible Class in Riverside Baptist Church, where John D. Rockefeller Jr. used to officiate, some speaker told what she calls a "smoking room story." Miss McDowell left the room in purple dudgeon and neither the pastor nor Mr. Rockefeller could ever persuade her to come to another meeting there. Her single-handed war against profanity created newspaper legend. She would stop cussers in the streets and dress them down. Her Pure Language League, founded to reform co-workers on The Herald, she continued on The Times. She would stop dead in her tracks in Times corridors to pin back the ears of office boys, or even executives, who swore or blasphemed.

Her ecclesiastical beats were innumerable. She scooped the town on the Bishop Manning—Dr. Percy Stickney Grant row. She broke the story of Bishop Manning's attempt to prevent the New York Churchmen's Association from hearing Judge Ben Lindsey of Denver, advocate of companionate marriage. She got an exclusive on the late Cardinal Farley's ban on the wicked tango. When a group of Sinn Feiners left a mass at St. Patrick's Cathedral to stone the windows of the Union League Club, where a British flag was flown, the Lady Bishop marched with them, and got the only eyewitness account. She climbed a stone fence to get a better look at this shindig, and was bombarded by indignant Irish ladies who thought she was on The London Times, instead of The New York Times.

When Princess Anastasia died abroad, her body was brought home for secret burial in her family's vault in Woodlawn. Only the Lady Bishop managed to ferret out when and where the burial was to take place. She got past the guards in the cemetery, saw the funeral, and when the mourners left, went into the tomb to get the names on the other caskets. Absorbed in her work, she never heard the tomb door close. When she tried to get out, she found the tomb locked. She called, but no one heard her. She kneeled to pray, and had given herself into Divine keeping when the door swung back. She isn't sure, to this day, if it wasn't all the trick of some puckish sexton. "Anyway," she says triumphantly, "I got a beat on that one."

No co-worker ever called the Lady Bishop "Rachel" to her face. "If they had," she says, breathing hard through her aristocratic nose, "I'd have given them you know what." In the next breath she tells you that only bishops and cardinals had that right.

Her unworldly approach led to frequent amusing incidents, most of which were never brought to her attention. Her messages to the desk sometimes had painfully worldly meanings, though she never realized it. One day, for example, a message from Atlantic City, where the Lady Bishop was covering a Methodist Convention, brought to the telegraph desk the startling information: "Copy a little late. Have been on the Boardwalk all day. Am hustling."

Miss McDowell's interviews with the late Pope Pius XI in 1935 and in 1937 were great spiritual experiences in her career. Perhaps her greatest thrill was the moment whe she kneeled in the Holy Sepulchre in Jerusalem in 1937 and toured places where the Lord had walked—Nazareth, the Mount of Olives and Gethsemane. The walls of her 10th floor office are decorated with autographed photographs of great prelates she has known. "My sky pilots," she calls them reverently. Her devotion to The Times publisher, Authur Hays Sulzberger, almost always expressed itself in high emotionalism, and tears.

When The Times ran the story of her retirement she was flooded with letters and telegrams from churchmen, great and humble, and from famous laymen—from Bishop Manning, Cardinal Spellman, John D. Rockefeller Jr., Rabbi David De Sola Pool, Dr. Ella A. Boole of the W.C.T.U., Bishop Charles K. Gilbert, among others. All these moved her to fresh weeping. The men and women who worked with her in the ink-stained vineyard in 43d Street know that her reluctant retirement marks the close of an era in religious newsgathering, and the passing of a newspaper legend. They hoped, as Mr. Rockefeller expressed it in his letter, "that the days that lie ahead will bring . . . life's richest blessing."

Meyer Berger

From *The 42nd Parallel*

FIGHTING BOB

La Follette was born in the town limits of Primrose; he worked on a farm in Dane County, Wisconsin, until he was nineteen.

At the University of Wisconsin he worked his way through. He wanted to be an actor, studied elocution and Robert Ingersoll and Shakespeare and Burke;

(who will ever explain the influence of Shakespeare in the last century, Marc Antony over Caesar's bier, Othello to the Venetian Senate, and Polonius, everywhere Polonius?)

riding home in a buggy after commencement he was Booth and Wilkes writing the Junius papers and Daniel Webster and Ingersoll defying God and the togaed great grave and incorruptible as statues magnificently spouting through the capitoline centuries;

he was the star debater in his class,
and won an interstate debate with an oration on the character of Iago.

He went to work in a law office and ran for district attorney. His schoolfriends canvassed the county riding round evenings. He bucked the machine and won the election.

It was the revolt of the young man against the state republican machine and Boss Keyes the postmaster in Madison who ran the county was so surprised he about fell out of his chair.

That gave LaFollette a salary to marry on. He was twentyfive years old.

Four years later he ran for Congress; the university was with him again; he was the youngsters' candidate. When he was elected he was the youngest representative in the house

He was introduced round Washington by Philetus Sawyer the Wisconsin lumber king who was used to stacking and selling politicians the way he stacked and sold cordwood.

He was a Republican and he'd bucked the machine. Now they thought they had him. No man could stay honest in Washington.

Booth played Shakespeare in Baltimore that winter. Booth never would go to Washington on account of the bitter memory of his brother. Bob LaFollette and his wife went to every performance.

In the parlor of the Plankinton Hotel in Milwaukee during the state fair, Boss Sawyer the lumber king tried to bribe him to influence his brother-in-law who was presiding judge over the prosecution of the Republican state treasurer;

Bob LaFollette walked out of the hotel in a white rage. From that time it was war without quarter with the Republican machine in Wisconsin until he was elected governor and wrecked the Republican machine;

this was the tenyears war that left Wisconsin the model state where the voters, orderloving Germans and Finns, Scandinavians fond of their own opinion, learned to use the new leverage, direct primaries, referendum and recall.

LaFollette taxed the railroads

John C. Payne said to a group of politicians in the lobby of the Ebbitt House in Washington "LaFollette's a damn fool if he thinks he can buck a railroad with five thousand miles of continuous track, he'll find he's mistaken . . . We'll take care of him when the time comes."

But when the time came the farmers of Wisconsin and the young lawyers and doctors and businessmen just out of school

took care of him

and elected him governor three times

and then to the United States Senate,

where he worked all his life making long speeches full of statistics, struggling to save democratic government, to make a farmers' and small businessmen's commonwealth, lonely with his back to the wall, fighting corruption and big business and high finance and trusts and combinations of combinations and the miasmic lethargy of Washington.

He was one of "the little group of willful men expressing no opinion but their own"

who stood out against Woodrow Wilson's armed ship bill that made war with Germany certain; they called it a filibuster, but it was six men with nerve straining to hold back a crazy steamroller with their bare hands;

the press pumped hatred into its readers against LaFollette,

the traitor;

they burned him in effigy in Illinois;

in Wheeling they refused to let him speak.

In nineteen-twentyfour LaFollette ran for President and without money or political machine rolled up four and a half million votes

but he was a sick man, incessant work and the breathed out air of committee rooms and legislative chambers choked him

and the dirty smell of politicians,

and he died,

an orator haranguing from the capitol of a lost republic;

but we will remember

how he sat firm in March nineteen-seventeen while Woodrow Wilson was being inaugurated for the second time, and for three days held the vast machine at deadlock. They wouldn't let him speak; the galleries glared hatred at him; the Senate was a lynching party,

a stumpy man with a lined face, one leg stuck out in the aisle and his
arms folded and a chewed cigar in the corner of his mouth
   and an undelivered speech on his desk,
   a willful man expressing no opinion but his own.

John Dos Passos

7 | Exposition

The art of expressing oneself in a logical manner we call exposition, but logical is not used here in any precise scientific sense. Indeed, we might say that exposition is the art of expressing oneself clearly, logic being implied in the structure of the sentences employed.

Herbert Read

If you wanted to analyze the causes of the Civil War, explain the uses of a jigsaw, or define the word "radical," you would write exposition. The term comes from the Latin verb *exponere*, which means literally "to set forth," and refers to writing that appeals mainly to the understanding, writing that answers the questions "What?" and "How?" Exposition can be found in pure form in dictionaries and atlases and cookbooks (see pages 24 and 40) but most of the time it is combined with description, narration, personal reflection, in short, with the kinds of writing you have been doing throughout the course.

What then distinguishes exposition from these other kinds of writing? Primarily focus and intention. Until now your observations and experiences have been the basis for most of your writing. You have been mapping your world, starting with sense impressions and moving gradually outwards toward events, people, and ideas. In exposition, however, self-expression and self-exploration become subordinate to information and explanation; subjective experience must be presented in terms that most readers can understand and evaluate. Consequently, logic, coherence, unity, development, the so-called formal and objective elements in writing, are of first importance.

But this difference in emphasis needn't produce dry, impersonal prose. Generalizations demand particulars, theories supporting evidence. A definition of "radical" calls for specific examples, some of which might be autobiographical. An essay on *Hamlet* must begin with your responses to a scene or character. It must also go beyond them, of course, yet unless your voice and your perceptions control the essay you are likely to write bombast.

197

And remember that the first cousin of bombast is propaganda. Good expository writing, therefore, combines logic and imagination, ideas and feelings, generalizations and concrete particulars. Coming to terms with *Hamlet*, or with any subject, means coming to terms with your own responses to it and then generalizing from them. Thus the expository essay should be considered a sophisticated variation of the personal essay, not a separate species.

No writer achieves complete clarity. But the nearer he comes to seeing clearly, the more his gifts prevail.

Sidney Cox

SECTION 1   Finding A Focus

The term *focus* has come up so often in this book (see Chapters 4 and 5, for example) that it may seem redundant to mention it again. Unfortunately the problem of knowing where to begin an essay persists like a summer cold and tends to become particularly severe whenever one tries to write on a large general topic like disarmament or Shakespeare. The wise student, confronted with such an impossible task, usually schedules a conference with his instructor:

I: Just Shakespeare! Isn't there something more specific you could write about? Do you have a favorite play?

S: I like all the comedies but I suppose my favorite is *A Midsummer Night's Dream*.

I: What's so appealing to you about that play?

S: The mood. It's so light and carefree. But I also like the way the characters are constantly getting confused about what's real and what's a dream. Like Bottom getting turned into an ass and not understanding what's happened or why people are acting strangely toward him.

I: The relationships between fact and imagination is certainly a prominent theme in the play. Could you explore it further with reference to one or maybe two characters?

S: Come to think of it, the passage I remember most in the whole play is Theseus's comment about how the lunatic, the lover, and the poet are all alike when it comes to seeing things that aren't there. That's pretty perceptive comment if you ask me.

I: When you say it's perceptive do you mean that it's generally true, or that it seems true for you?

S: Well, I think most people who're in love are a bit cracked as far as knowing what's actually going on is concerned. For example, I'd been dating this girl Allison for nearly a year and then one night she drops by to tell me that she's pinned to some fraternity guy. Imagine how I felt . . .

Of course it remains to be seen whether or not the student's relationship with Allison has anything to do with *A Midsummer Night's Dream* but at least he is headed in the right direction. First, he has *narrowed* his topic from Shakespeare, which would only have trapped him into clichés and glib generalizations, to a specific passage about which he might have something to say. And though his essay will have to go beyond the one passage, he has a place to begin. Furthermore, he has chosen a passage that interests *him* instead of parroting some generally approved line of thought. Focusing is, first of all, the art of discovering what you *want* to say about a topic and also what you *can* say about it. Remember that you can never cover a topic, you can only redefine it to match your interests and abilities.

But an essay is five hundred or a thousand words and all you have is an idea. How can you turn this idea into an extended piece of writing that someone will read? You can start by doing some freewriting as outlined in Appendix 2. Freewriting enables you to unearth a large amount of material in a short space of time. Much of it will be dross but mixed in may be a few nuggets of insight that you didn't know you had and that you can probably use later. At this point, however, you needn't worry about the final form your essay will take. You are simply playing with possibilities. Don't shorten this fumbling stage just to get on with your essay. Let your ideas simmer for a while.

When you have accumulated a considerable amount of information about your topic, perhaps after two or three freewritings, you can start to rough out your essay. Many texts recommend a formal outline—topic sentences, lists of examples, Roman numerals I, II, III and so on—but there are good reasons for not committing yourself to such a formal structure. Once made, a formal outline is difficult to discard and may in fact force your thinking in directions you'd do better to avoid. More importantly, it often blurs the distinction between substance and structure. It is easy to assume that because your essay has a definite beginning, middle, and end, or because it resembles a cone, inverted triangle or other geometric shape, it will necessarily be coherent and convincing. Chances are it won't unless you have also worked out some of the subtler and less conspicuous relationships among your ideas. For this you need freedom to experiment with different combinations of facts and concepts, different ways of coming at your topic. All you may need for an outline, therefore, is a few general headings and a series of statements about your topic that you can shuffle around.

The last step in the focusing process is also the first step in the development process, namely formulating one or more thesis statements. Now a thesis statement is not a capsule summary of your essay or a vague declaration of intention; it is an *assertion* meant to bring your disorganized thoughts to attention. This is not a thesis statement: "In this essay I plan to discuss the increasingly important role of the Consumer Protection Agency." Neither is this: "The Consumer Protection Agency is helping all buyers become more aware of corporation deceptions." The first is an anemic statement of purpose, the second only an announcement of the obvious. But this statement is more promising: "During the last five years the Consumer Protection Agency has done more to expose abuses of the public trust by corporations than any agency in history.'' Although still quite general, this statement nevertheless forces a writer to stick his neck out, at least temporarily. He must define his terms, find his supporting evidence, develop his comparisons. Even if this statement is later discarded, as often happens, it is bold enough to generate others that will carry the essay forward. A good thesis statement supplies momentum.

SUMMARY

Focusing is the art of distinguishing between essential and incidental information; it is also discovering what *you* can say about a topic as opposed to what might be said about it. The focusing process involves four basic steps: narrowing a topic to manageable proportions, exploring it by means of freewriting exercises; developing some type of an outline, preferably one with a series of general headings and informal classifications that allows for experimentation and revision; and, finally, formulating one or more thesis statements. These are not topic sentences or capsule summaries of an entire essay but merely assertions that force you to take a stand on some aspect of your subject. They may be rewritten a dozen times before your essay is finished but without them it may never get started.

EXERCISES

1. Select a passage of scientific or technical information from one of your textbooks and, in a single sentence, summarize its basic meaning. How would you summarize the central idea of this passage?

> The other principal reason why the flash flood is almost exclusively a feature of the desert is that nearly all the water that falls in a torrential rain runs off. Vegetation ground cover is sparse or nonexistent. The surface of the ground is often baked to an almost bricklike consistency. Very little water is absorbed. Most of it runs off into the dry riverbeds cut by previous floods. These gullies are among the most characteristic features of arid lands and are called by a variety of names—dry wash or draw in Arizona, arroyo in California, wadi in the Near East. Some of the floodwaters that periodically rage through an arroyo sink into its usually sandy or rocky bottom. A few feet below the surface, the soil may be damp, while that of the surrounding desert floor is completely dry. The difference in moisture creates a special environment for plant life. Near the borders of the dry wash there may be cottonwoods that cannot survive the desert and a special species of palo verde trees which needs just a bit more water than the easily distinguishable species that grows in more arid situations.

> Joseph Wood Krutch, *Lightning Water*

2. (a) Choose a very broad subject—pollution, women's liberation, the energy crisis, radical politics—and, following the focusing procedures outlined in this section, formulate three thesis statements that could be the basis for a five-hundred word essay. Be sure that you work through each step in the process—narrowing the subject, freewriting, outlining.

   (b) Write down half a dozen cliché generalizations ("What's good for business is good for the country," "When the going gets tough, the tough get going") and then develop at least one of them into a more substantial argument by adding supporting evidence.

3. Capsule book and film reviews make excellent focusing exercises because they restrict a writer to essential details. A good review should do three things: (1) tell what the book/film/play is about, (2) convey the reviewer's impressions of it, and (3) explain its relationship to other works in the same style or genre, or by the same artist. After studying the following example, write your own capsule review (250 words) of a current book, film, or play.

Warner Brothers is honoring itself for the release of its fifteen-hundredth motion picture (who's going to count?) with a picture fittingly entitled *Skin Game*. It turns out, however, to be charming—utterly unimportant, but another movie that almost everybody can enjoy. The director, Paul Bogart (a TV veteran) makes no distinctive contribution except for his unlabored, loose approach, but the movie is well-written, the whole thing has a good fluky spirit, and the color is sometimes lovely. It's a casual series of jokes about three bunco artists in the Old (pre-Civil War) South—reminiscent of the *Scalphunters* but not as lively (It lacks those two dynamos Burt Lancaster and Ossie Davis). The casting is a bit lacklustre. Lou Gossett is pretty good as the Northern city-slicker negro outwitting the Southern Whites, but James Garner carries a TV actor's lassitude into his screen roles; he isn't bad but his mild pleasantness just isn't enough to command one's full attention. I guess Susan Clark is better than usual (she has some comedy sense) but her attraction—if indeed, anybody besides movie moguls considers her attractive—eludes me. This example of tall-story American, with its punning title, is not much more than an entertaining time killer, but you get a good feeling when you're in an audience that simultaneously breaks into applause for outrageously silly jokes.

Pauline Kael, *Deeper Into Movies*

4. Scan a daily newspaper and take notes on any articles, headlines, or photographs that capture your interest. Next, organize these notes into a paragraph that has a single theme, thesis, or controlling impression, but in which the details speak for themselves as much as possible. What is the theme of this student piece?

The front page of the *Los Angeles Times* had a picture of a Cambodian family huddled in a foxhole. A scar ran down the cheek of the youngest child cradled in his mother's arms. At the bottom of the page was a picture of a jubilant Muhammed Ali, arms raised in victory after his conquest of Chuck Wepner. The legislature has been fighting over passage of a new tax bill. "Three people killed by a tornado in Atlanta." In Section II, just beneath a recipe for improving the taste of left-over meatloaf, Dear Abby and Ann Landers were giving advice to people who had probably made up problems to ask. The following pages were filled with ads for the most exciting and erotic experiences ever put on film. Walt Disney also has a new movie out. The sports page had more information about the Ali-Wepner fight along with the basketball and hockey scores. A football player for the University of Southern California died of a heart attack during spring drills. Snuffy Smith got drunk again. Dagwood Bumpstead was hit in the head by Blondie's rolling pin after he came home late from the office. Snoopy was in his doghouse and Beetle Bailey still had not gone to war. A seven-year old girl committed suicide, leaving no living relatives.

Tom Maurer

Style consists in the order and the movement which we introduce into our thought.

Buffon

SECTION 2   **Strategies for Development**

Let's make a few basic distinctions between development and padding, since the two are often confused. One adds muscle, the other fat; one concerns essentials, the other accidentals; one clarifies and extends meaning, the other obscures and deadens it. Supplying five illustrations when one would do, or appending a summary and a postscript to a discussion that is already self-explanatory is padding, not development. Development is organic, expansion from within instead of from without. It means inserting a metaphor, example, anecdote, or definition because your subject requires it, not because you have to come up with another fifty words or because you've been told that every essay must have a metaphor, example, anecdote, and definition.

In the preceding section we discussed ways of focusing a topic and of distinguishing true topics from false ones. Here we are concerned with techniques for developing that topic into a coherent, readable essay. Rhetoric handbooks usually list five major methods of development: definition, illustration, comparison and contrast, classification, analysis. You have met several of them already in different contexts, which points up once again the underlying connections between exposition and other modes of discourse. Despite differences in focus and purpose, exposition depends on the same rhetorical and stylistic devices as these other modes.

Definition

The definitions you wrote in Chapter 1 ("Frustration is the last letter in a crossword puzzle," "Spaced out is a mouth full of novacaine") made abstract words and phrases concrete by restricting their meaning to a particular object or situation. Formal definitions also restrict meaning but in a more rigorous, systematic manner. First an item is placed in a class and then excluded from the other members of the class by the addition of one or more specific differences. To cite the most famous example, "Man is a rational animal" places the thing to be defined, *Man,* in a class, *animal,* and then distinguishes it from the other members of the class by a specific difference, *rational.* Most *lexical* (dictionary) definitions are of this type. But in exposition we often have to go beyond a single statement in order to establish the boundaries of our discussion. Thornton Wilder begins his essay on playwriting by carefully distinguishing drama from the other arts:

Four fundamental conditions of the drama separate it from other arts. Each of these conditions has its advantages and disadvantages, each requires a particular aptitude from the dramatist, and from each there are a number of instructive consequences to be derived. These conditions are:

1. The theatre is an art which reposes upon the work of many collaborators;
2. It is addressed to the group mind;
3. It is based upon a pretense and its very nature calls out a multiplication of pretenses;
4. Its action takes place in a perpetual present time.

Some Thoughts on Playwriting

Actually, this is a very sophisticated version of the familiar "According to Webster" gambit. But it is also a definition made up entirely of firm assertions. Most extended definitions consist of assertions supported by examples, analogies and statistics.

A sign is anything that announces the existence or the imminence of some event, the presence of a thing, or a person, or a change in a state of affairs. There are signs of the weather, signs of danger, signs of future good or evil, signs of what the past has been. In every case a sign is closely bound up with something to be noted or expected in experience. It is always a part of the situation to which it refers, though the reference may be remote in space and time. Insofar as we are led to note or expect the signified event we are making correct use of a sign. This is the essence of rational behavior, which animals show in varying degrees . . . . If man had kept to the straight and narrow path of sign using, he would be like the other animals, though perhaps a little brighter. He would not talk, but grunt and gesticulate and point. He would make his wishes known, give warnings, perhaps develop a system like that of bees and ants, with such a wonderful efficiency of communal enterprises that all men would have plenty to eat, warm apartments—all exactly alike and perfectly convenient—to live in, and everybody could and would sit in the sun or by the fire, as the climate demanded, not talking but just basking, with every want satisfied, most of his life.

Susan K. Langer, *The Prince of Creation*

So far we've examined only "positive" definitions, that is, ones that tell us what the subject *is*. But one can also proceed by telling what a subject *is not*, which is known as definition by negation or exclusion. Mrs. Langer goes on to define "symbol" by explaining why it is not a sign:

A symbol differs from a sign in that it does not announce the presence of the object, the being, condition, or whatnot, which is its meaning, but merely *brings this thing to mind*. It is not a mere "substitute sign" to which we react as though it were the object itself.

Harold Taylor tells us what a student is not as preparation for telling us what he is:

> A student is not a professional athlete, although many universities and a large segment of the watching public act as if he were. He is not a little politician or junior senator looking for angles, getting a good record, getting contacts, and starting his business career in his sophomore year. He is not an amateur promoter, a glad-hander, embryo Rotarian, cafe-society leader, quiz kid, or man-about-town. He may be some of these or all these for a little while before he grows up, but none of it defines him as a student.
>
> *What Is a Student?*

Illustration

Illustration is another name for explanation by example. There are many kinds of examples—metaphors, statistics, anecdotes, quotations—and they serve many different functions. In description and narration they give writing color and texture by appealing to the senses. They can also be used to clarify a vague or difficult term:

> Almost all discussions of methods explicitly use the term "variable" or imply the concept of variables. A variable refers to a specific aspect of events or things. It differs according to the particular event being considered, and no single event or thing can have more than one value of the same variable at a given time. The concept can best be understood through examples. The weight of a person is a variable: different people weigh different amounts and the same person weighs only one amount at any given time. The number of times you blink in an hour is also a variable; in any given hour you will blink a certain number of times and this number may differ from hour to hour.
>
> Variables are not necessarily personal. The color of cars, the make of cars, the number of cylinders in a car, how far the car goes on a gallon of gasoline, how much the car cost—all are variables. The concept represented by the term "variable" is a very pervasive one. Whenever an entity or an event is described, every dimension in which it is being described can be considered a variable, including its location and the conditions under which it occurs.
>
> McCain and Segal, *The Games of Science*

or to support an assertion:

> Lord Salisbury was both the epitome of his class and uncharacteristic of it—except insofar as the freedom to be different was a class characteristic. He was six feet four inches tall, and as a young man had been thin, ungainly, stooping, and shortsighted, with hair unusually black for an Englishman. Now sixty-five, his youthful lankiness had turned to bulk, his shoulders had grown massive

and more stooped than ever, and his heavy bald head with full curly gray beard rested on them as if weighted down. Melancholy, intensely intellectual, subject to sleepwalking and fits of depression which he called "nerve storms," caustic, tactless, absent-minded, bored by society and fond of solitude, with a penetrating, skeptical, questioning mind, he had been called the Hamlet of English politics. He was above the conventions and refused to live in Downing Street. His devotion was to religion, his interest in science. In his own home he attended private chapel every morning before breakfast, and had fitted up a chemical laboratory where he conducted solitary experiments. He harnessed the river at Hatfield for an electric power plant on his estate and had strung up along the old beams of his home one of England's first electric light systems, at which his family threw cushions when the wires sparked and sputtered while they went on talking and arguing, a customary occupation of the Cecils.

Barbara Tuchman, *The Guns of August*

or to summarize a feeling:

I can't talk about Hollywood. It was a horror to me when I was there and it's a horror to look back on. I can't imagine how I did it. When I got away from it I couldn't even refer to the place by name. "Out there" I called it. You want to know what "out there" means to me? Once I was coming down a street in Beverly Hills and I saw a Cadillac about a block long, and out of the side window was a wonderfully slinky mink and an arm, and at the end of the arm a hand in a white suede glove wrinkled around the wrist, and in the hand was a bagel with a bite out of it.

Dorothy Parker, *Writers at Work*

Comparison and Contrast

Metaphors and similes are figurative (non-literal) comparisons that unite things not ordinarily thought of as similar. They make writing vivid by appealing to the senses, while also serving to interpret whatever is being described. Expanded, they become analogies. Analogies can also make writing vivid, but their main function, particularly in exposition, is to explain one thing in terms of another, usually something complex or abstract in terms of something simple and familiar. For example, D. H. Lawrence defines "Love" by drawing an analogy to a tree:

Love is a relationship between things that live, holding them together in a sort of unison. There are other vital relationships. But love is this special one.
In every living thing there is the desire, for love, or for the relationship of unison with the rest of things. That a tree should desire to develop itself between the power of the sun, and the opposite pull of the earth's centre, and to balance itself between the four winds of heaven, and to unfold itself between the rain and

the shine, to have roots and feelers in blue heaven and innermost earth, both, this is a manifestation of love: a knitting together of the diverse cosmos into a oneness, a tree.

At the same time, the tree must most powerfully exert itself and defend itself, to maintain its own integrity against the rest of things.

So that love, as a desire, is balanced against the opposite desire, to maintain the integrity of the individual self.

Love Was Once a Little Boy

In comparing and contrasting automobiles, brands of beer, rock groups, political parties, literary styles, which we do constantly in exposition, we tend to proceed more literally and straightforwardly. Instead of searching for imaginative connections, we discriminate and evaluate by enumerating specific similarities and differences:

The great leading distinction between writing and speaking is, that more time is allowed for the one than the other, and hence different faculties are required for, and different objects attained by each. He is properly the best speaker who can collect together the greatest number of apposite ideas at a moment's warning; he is properly the best writer who can give utterance to the greatest quantity of valuable knowledge in the course of his whole life. The chief requisite for the one, then, appears to be quickness and facility of perception—for the other patience of soul and a power increasing with the difficulties it has to master. He cannot be denied to be an expert speaker, a lively companion, who is never at a loss for something to say on every occasion or subject that offers. He, by the same rule, will make a respectable writer who, by dint of study, can find out anything good to say upon any one point that has not been touched upon before, or who by asking for time, can give the most complete and comprehensive view of any question. The one must be done offhand, at a single blow; the other can only be done by a repetition of blows, by having time to think and do better.

William Hazlett, *Differences Between Writing and Speaking*

You will notice that Hazlett compares one aspect of speaking with one aspect of writing, then a second aspect of speaking with a second aspect of writing and so on. This is known as the "point by point" method and is particularly useful for dealing with a great many details. He might also have discussed all the major characteristics of speaking, then all of the major characteristics of writing, referring throughout to significant similarities and differences. This is known as the "unit" method and most useful for comparing large general topics. Of course it's also possible to combine the two methods, perhaps by beginning with a "point by point" comparison, switching to a "unit" comparison in the body of the essay, and then returning to a "point by point" comparison in the final paragraph. Whichever method enables you to cover the major similarities and differences most clearly and succinctly is the one to use.

Classification and Division

Politicians classify voters according to party affiliation; zoologists classify animals according to phylum, genus, and species; literary critics classify novels by subject matter, period, and structure. Classification is the division of a whole into parts according to some consistent but also arbitrary principle. Voters, for example, might also be classified by income or religious preference or ethnic background depending on the intention of the classifier. The principle reflects his purpose, not some immutable law of the materials themselves. We must often classify a large body of information or a complex subject before we can write about it, and sometimes we insert capsule classifications, which are really miniature outlines, into the body of the essay to remind our readers of what we are and are not going to talk about. That is what these writers have done.

> We all listen to music according to our separate capacities. But for the sake of analysis, the whole listening process may become clearer if we break it up into its component parts, so to speak. In a certain sense we all listen to music on three separate planes. For lack of a better terminology, one might name these: (1) the sensuous plane, (2) the expressive plane, (3) the sheerly musical plane. The only advantage to be gained from mechanically splitting up the listening process into these hypothetical planes is the clearer view to be had of the way in which we listen.
>
> Aaron Copland, *How We Listen to Music*

> We have attempted to classify three general types of consciousness. These three types predominate in America today. One was formed in the nineteenth century, the second in the first half of this century, the third is just emerging. Consciousness I is the traditional outlook of the American farmer, small businessman, and worker who is trying to get ahead. Consciousness II represents the values of an organizational society. Consciousness III is the new generation. The three categories are, of course, highly impressionistic and arbitrary; they make no pretense to be scientific. And, since each type of consciousness is a construct, we would not expect any real individual to exhibit in symmetrical perfection all the characteristics of one type of consciousness.
>
> Charles Reich, *The Greening of America*

Remember that a principle of classification must be: (1) clear, (2) appropriate to the subject—you wouldn't classify novels by their bindings or congressmen by the color of their hair—and (3) consistent, at least within an individual paragraph or section of an essay.

Analysis

Like classification, analysis is a technique for dividing a whole into its component parts, except that the parts must be integrally rather than arbitrarily related. Items in a class have no necessary connection with one another except that they fall under a particular heading; if one or more of them disappeared the class would remain. But analysis deals with structures in which the parts are interdependent; if one is missing the entire structure, or process, or argument, is impaired. To explain how a camera works, for example, you would have to analyze the relationships between light and film and shutter speed. To explain the concept *history* you would have to identify its principal characteristics:

> The four characteristics of history which I enumerated in the Introduction were (a) that it is scientific, or begins by asking questions, whereas the writer of legends begins by knowing something and tells what he knows; (b) that it is humanistic, or asks questions about things done by men at determinate times in the past; (c) that it is rational, or bases the answers which it gives to its questions on grounds, namely appeal to evidence; (d) that it is self-revelatory, or exists in order to tell man what man is by telling him what man has done.
>
> R. G. Collingwood, *What Is History*

As these examples show, the basic patterns of development often overlap. Definitions contain illustrations, illustrations often involve comparisons, classification can merge with analysis. Memorizing the individual patterns won't make you a writer any more than memorizing the part of an engine will make you a mechanic. But knowing about them will help you to give your raw material form and direction.

SUMMARY

Development means supplying an example, quotation, or definition because your topic demands one, not because you need an additional hundred words. It is expansion from within rather than from without. Outlines and thesis statements are preliminary steps in developing a topic, definition, illustration, comparison and contrast, classification, and analysis the principal techniques for fleshing it out into a complete essay. Few essays employ all five techniques but most use two or three in combination. Not only do they give structure to individual paragraphs, they generate new ideas.

EXERCISES

1. (a) Expand at least one definition from Chapter 1 ("Happiness is . . .") into a paragraph using some of the techniques for development discussed in this section.

   (b) Write a negative definition of another general or abstract term. "Friendship is not . . . ," "Success is not. . . "

   (c) Explain why a particular word, place, event is important by describing what the world would be like without it. What would we do without the word "freedom," for example, or The Fourth of July?

2. Make a list of primary subjects (marriage, truth, cities, universities) and then a list of secondary subjects (chess, hiking, ice hockey, Hershey bars) and try to explain one in terms of the other. Avoid trite analogies such as love is like war, universities are like jails. Look for relationships that are fresh and offbeat.

3. Compare and contrast two different methods or strategies for doing the same job or achieving the same goal. Two ways to pitch a tent, make beef stroganoff, paint ceilings, get your own way.

4. Classify several of the following subjects according to at least two different principles (e.g., function, attitude, appearance, structure): news magazines, movie actresses, English teachers, beds, bookcases, franchise food shops, stereos.

5. As an an exercise in analysis, explain to someone how to do some simple physical or mechanical task such as changing a flat tire or swimming the breaststroke. Remember that in analysis you cannot simply list the steps in a process; you must indicate how they are connected as well. See *Methods of Sprouting* (page 49).

The writer should write so that his readers not only may but must understand.

Quintillian

SECTION 3   Unity and Coherence

Unity might be defined as singleness of purpose within a paragraph or an essay, *coherence* as the connectedness among the individual parts. Reading an essay without unity is like hiking in a strange forest without a map; first we follow this path, then that, expending a great deal of energy getting nowhere. In an essay without coherence, on the other hand, we can't see how point A connects to point B and to point C. It's as though we've been given a jigsaw puzzle in which some of the pieces don't fit.

Unity and coherence are ultimately reflections of a writer's insight and sensitivity, matters of thought more than technique. Nevertheless, they can be reinforced by specific stylistic and structural devices.

Transitions

These are the small connecting links within and between sentences and paragraphs that clarify the relationships among statements and give writing overall continuity. We have already listed the main transitional words and phrases (page 52); their practical function in expository prose is demonstrated in the following passage:

> The sense of doom in us today is not a fear of science; it is a fear of war. And the causes of war were not created by science; they do not differ in kind from the known causes of the War of Jenkins' Ear or the Wars of the Roses, which were carried on with only the most modest scientific aids. No, science has not invented war; but it has turned it into a very different thing. The people who distrust it are not wrong. The man in the pub who says, "It'll wipe out the world," the woman in the queue who says "It isn't natural"—they do not express themselves very well; but what they are trying to say does make sense. Science has enlarged the mechanism of war, and it has distorted it. It has done this in at least two ways.
>
> First, science has obviously multiplied the power of the warmakers. The weapons of the moment can kill more people more secretly and more unpleasantly than those of the past. This progress, as for want of another word I must call it—this progress has been going on for some time; and for some time it has been said, of each new weapon, that it is so destructive or so horrible that it will frighten people into their wits, and force the nations to give up war for lack of cannon fodder. This hope has never been fulfilled, and I know no one who takes

refuge in it today. The acts of men and women are not dictated by such simple compulsions; and they themselves do not stand in any simple relation to the decisions of the nations which they compose. Grapeshot and TNT and gas have not helped to outlaw war; and I see no sign that the hydrogen bomb or a whiff of bacteria will be more successful in making men wise by compulsion.

Secondly, science at the same time has given the nations quite new occasions for falling out. I do not mean such simple objectives as someone else's uranium mine, or a Pacific Island which happens to be knee-deep in organic fertilizer. I do not even mean merely another nation's factories and her skilled population. These are all parts of the surplus above our simple needs which they themselves help to create and which gives our civilization its character. And war in our world battens on this surplus. This is the object of the greed of nations, and this also gives them the leisure to train and the means to arm for war. At bottom, we have remained individually too greedy to distribute our surplus, and collectively too stupid to pile it up in any more useful form than the traditional mountains of arms. Science can claim to have created the surplus in our societies, and we know from the working day and the working diet how greatly it has increased it in the last two hundred years. Science has created the surplus. Now put this year's budget beside the budget of 1750, anywhere in the world, and you will see what we are doing with it.

Jacob Bronowski, *Science, the Destroyer or Creator?*

Bronowski uses a number of basic transitional devices to keep his ideas in line: (1) demonstrative pronouns ("*The progress*," "*These parts*"), (2) simple enumeration (*first, second*), (3) coordinating conjunctions (*and, but, or*). Each device helps to tie the strands of his thought together and make his overall argument coherent. He also uses repetition very skillfully. We discussed repetition in Chapter 1 mainly in terms of rhythm and emphasis. It has these functions here as well (examine the opening sentences of paragraph two, for example) but it is primarily a device for coherence. Note how often the words *war, science, progress,* and *surplus* appear, and how, by repeating key statements ("The causes of war were not created by science"; "No, science has not invented war"; "Science has created the surplus") Bronowski draws attention to his major ideas. Such skillful use of transitions comes from practice, not genius. The more consciously you use them the more conspicuous they will become in your writing.

Parallelism

Parallelism is repetition at the level of structure. Either similar ideas are expressed in similar grammatical constructions or the same parts of speech perform the same functions in successive clauses and sentences. The Shaw passage quoted in Chapter 1 is an example of antithetical parallelism: "They are not religious: they are only pewrenters. They are not moral: they are only conventional. They are not virtuous: they are only cowardly. They are not even vicious: they are only 'frail.' " Each clause begins with the verb phrase "they are" and is completed by a predicate adjective preceded by either "not" or "only" Each contains a like number of words and may be read or spoken in the same amount of time. By playing word against word, construction against construction, rhythm against rhythm, Shaw underscores the equivalence of each part of the paragraph.

Here are some other kinds of parallelism:

Wine, women, and song.
The world, the flesh, and the devil. } Nouns

To err is human, to forgive divine. (Pope) } Infinitive
To strive, to seek, to find, and not to yield. (Tennyson) } Phrases

Often the writer he [the editor] wants is a busy man who must } Verbs
be cajoled, flattered, harassed, nagged. (Norman Podhoretz)

The horses ran rhythmically, gracefully, effortlessly around } Adverbs
the track. (Mark Twain)

He who enters the sphere of faith enters the sanctuary of life.} Clauses
(Paul Tillich)

Repeating the same parts of speech in the same grammatical constructions generates a rhythm within a sentence that carries thought along, like a locomotive getting up speed. You can often play with this rhythm to make a particular idea or impression stand out. "Professor Jackson lectured slowly, cautiously, methodically—dully." The parallelism of the first three adverbs makes the twist in the fourth more striking. Churchill switched from "we shall fight" to "we shall never surrender" in the final sentence, and this slight departure from parallel structure made his statement more emphatic.

In a paragraph, parallelism keeps related ideas in touch with one another and thereby makes writing tighter and more economical.

> The difference between a slave and a citizen is that a slave is subject to his master and a citizen to the laws. It may happen that the master is very gentle and the laws are very harsh; that changes nothing. Everything lies in the difference between caprice and rule.
>
> Simon Weil

Reading maketh a full man; conference a ready man; and writing an exact man. And therefore, if a man write little, he had need have a great memory; if he confer little, he had need have a present wit; and if he read little, he had need have much cunning to seem to know that he doth not. Histories make men wise; poets, witty; the mathematics, subtle; natural philosophy, deep; moral, grave; logic and rhetoric, able to contend.

Francis Bacon, *Of Studies*

Weil's style is much less elliptical than Bacon's, but both passages show how parallel structure makes for crisp, lean prose. Ideas talk to one another directly without a lot of distracting static.

Order and Arrangement

Most physical descriptions are organized spatially (on my left, on my right), most narratives chronologically (first, later, finally). These patterns are often found in exposition, too, because they are basic and also because, as we have seen, exposition usually contains a good deal of description and narration for clarity and ballast. There are several other ordering patterns that are especially important in expository writing.

The first is *climactic* or *emphatic* order, in which items are arranged according to rank or importance. The Churchill passage quoted in Chapter 1 combines repetition with climactic arrangement in that the most dramatic and forceful statement, "We shall never surrender," comes last. The following paragraph, written by another World War II hero, Dwight Eisenhower, is also organized climactically:

If none of these three days should prove satisfactory from the standpoint of weather, consequences would ensue that were almost terrifying to contemplate. Secrecy would be lost. Assault troops would be unloaded and crowded back into assembly areas enclosed in barbed wire, where their original places would already have been taken by those to follow in subsequent waves. Complicated movement tables would be scrapped. Morale would drop. A wait of at least fourteen days, possibly twenty-eight, would be necessary—a sort of suspended animation involving more than 2,000,000 men! The good weather period available for major campaigning would become still shorter and the enemy's defenses would become still stronger! The whole of the United Kingdom would become quickly aware that something had gone wrong and national discouragement there and in America could lead to unforseen results. Finally, always lurking in the background was the knowledge that the enemy was developing new, and presumably effective, secret weapons on the French coast. What the effect of these would be on our crowded harbors, especially at Plymouth and Portsmouth, we could not even guess.

Crusade in Europe

Cause-effect is another common expository pattern, particularly when a writer is trying to analyze a subject that has many simultaneous and interrelated events or processes. He may ask himself "What caused this?" and work back from effect to cause, or he may ask, "Given this fact/event, what consequences will follow?" and proceed from cause to effect. The first creates a climactic effect, like beginning a series with the least important item and ending with the most important, the second creates an anti-climactic effect. Here is a straightforward example of the first type:

> With the collapse of the medieval structure, and the beginning of the modern mode of production, the meaning and function of work changed fundamentally, especially in the Protestant countries. Man, being afraid of his newly won freedom, was obsessed by the need to subdue his doubts and fears by developing a feverish activity. The outcome of this activity, success or failure, decided his salvation, indicating whether he was among the saved or the lost souls. *Work, instead of being an activity satisfying in itself and pleasurable, became a duty and an obsession.* The more it was possible to gain riches by work, the more it became a pure means to the aim of wealth and success. Work became, in Max Weber's terms, the chief factor in a system of "inner-worldly asceticism," an answer to man's sense of aloneness and isolation.

> Erich Fromm, *The Sane Society*

Question and Answer

Questions have a number of strategic functions in expository prose: (1) they provide a stylistic change of pace in paragraphs of straight declarative statements and thereby make specific ideas and details stand out more sharply in a reader's mind; (2) they can be used to shift the focus of a discussion, to make it pivot smoothly from one direction to another; (3) since questions usually call for answers, or at least for responses, they draw a reader into a discussion. In other words, when a writer trains his rhetorical guns on us directly, as Thoreau does in the following passage, it is difficult to remain detached. We are provoked to reflection:

> Men think that it is essential that the Nation have commerce and export ice, and talk through a telegraph, and ride thirty miles an hour, without a doubt, whether *they* do or not; but whether we should live like baboons or like men, is a little uncertain. If we do not get our sleepers, and forge rails, and devote days and nights to the work, but go on tinkering upon our *lives* to improve *them*, who will build the railroads? And if railroads are not built, how shall we get to heaven in season? But if we stay at home and mind our business, who will want railroads? We do not ride on the railroad; it rides upon us. Did you ever think what those sleepers are that underlie the railroad? Each one is a man, and Irishman or a Yan-

kee man. The rails are laid on them, and they are covered with sand, and the cars run smoothly over them. They are sound sleepers, I assure you. And every few years a new lot is laid down and run over; so that, if some have the pleasure of riding on a rail, others have the misfortune to be ridden upon.

Walden

Often the title of an essay will be a provocative question—"Are Men Tired of Masculinity?" "Who Killed King Kong?"—and the body an extended answer. Or else a writer will pose a series of questions in the opening paragraphs in order to mark the boundaries of the discussion to follow. The questions thus serve as an outline.

It strikes me as odd that in all the noise and furor now surrounding the uniquely American institution of campus beauty contests, what may be the most important question in the debate has yet to be raised. Quite simply, the issue is not: Why shouldn't we have beauty contests in our colleges? It is rather: Why should we indeed?

The first phrasing of the question suggests, of course, that homecoming queen competitions and other sexually discriminatory practices in the fun and games category are of little consequence or can do no harm to students or anyone else involved. Just a bit of frivolity, endowed with the cloak of tradition—so why not?

But beauty contests, like other institutions, have an underlying purpose, perform specific functions in the overall social scheme. When they take place within an educational setting, we must be allowed to assume that they somehow relate to the goals and philosophy of the educational establishment. To discover how, we must go beyond reflecting on the insignificance of the institution involved. To look at the question with open eyes, to truly comprehend the issue at hand, we must focus on what it is that beauty contests do on campuses and elsewhere. How do they affect the learning opportunities and life chances of the students here? What purpose do they serve, really?

Kirsten Amundsen, *The Silenced Majority:*
Women and American Democracy.

General to Particular—Particular to General

General to Particular (Deduction) and *Particular to General* (Induction) are the most familiar patterns of organization in expository prose. The term "general" usually refers to a thesis or a conclusion, the term "particular" to the examples used to explain and support it. In the selection from *The Guns of August* on page 206 a generalization about Lord Salisbury is followed by a throng of specific illustrations. The passage below has a similar structure: first the general statement, then the supporting evidence:

Ireland is not the place it used to be. The sweet, slow, sorrowful land of cheerful indolence and doleful memory is being overtaken by something called progress. Ireland is changing. It is changing today more profoundly than at any time since the Great Hunger of more than a century ago.

In the wild west of Ireland, where they say the next parish is Boston, old people sitting by turf fires in primitive cottages watch television and shake their heads at the sight of young people arguing with a priest. At Shannon Airport, where a new industrial town of Scandinavian modernity has risen beyond the runways, made-in-Ireland Dutch pianos and South African industrial diamonds fly out to customers in Europe and America. In the Bay of Bantry, undisturbed by modern times until only a few years ago, the world's largest ships deliver oil to a huge new depot on Whiddy Island. In Dublin, as rush-hour traffic jams form in the shadow of stately Georgian townhouses, dignitaries as well as plain Irishmen in search of a free drink converge at a reception for the Bolshoi Ballet. Bookshops openly display copies of *Ulysses* and some of the more shocking American paperbacks. A physician reports on TV that the use of the birth-control pill is widespread in Ireland despite the ban on contraceptives. Indeed, the new women's liberation movement is campaigning aggressively to legalize and popularize birth control in Ireland. Irish farmers, who used to count themselves lucky to own a horse, protest against national agricultural policy by blocking country roads with battalions of farm machinery. City people complain about the shortage of maids. A headline announces: PROTESTANT PRESIDES AT CATHOLIC CEREMONY. Advertisements promote sauna baths and Mediterranean holidays. . . .

Donald S. Connery, *The Irish*

Here is a *Particular to General* or inductive paragraph:

Other dangers of the massive use of synthetic pesticides are well known to biologists. Careful studies have been made on the effects of DDT, the best known and most widely used chlorinated hydrocarbon insecticide. Virtually all populations of animals throughout the world are contaminated with it. Concentrations of DDT in the fat bodies of Americans average 11 parts per million, and Israelis have been found to have as much DDT as 19.2 parts per million. More significant in some ways has been the discovery of DDT residues in such unlikely places as the fat bodies of Eskimos, antarctic penguins, and antarctic seals. Pesticide pollution is truly a worldwide problem.

Paul R. Ehrlich, *Population and Environment*

SUMMARY

Unity is singleness of purpose within a paragraph or essay, coherence is the "connectedness" among the individual elements. Although both are ultimately reflections of an author's insight and sensitivity, they can be reinforced by specific stylistic and structural devices: repetition and parallelism for emphasis, transitional words and expressions for continuity, sequence (climactic, chronological, cause-effect) for overall development. These devices are essential to all forms of discourse, not exposition alone, and are commonly used in combination with one another.

EXERCISES

1. (a) Write a series of sentences in which you use each of the kinds of parallel structure mentioned in this section.

   (b) Reread some of your daily writing and correct any faulty parallelism you find. Do the same with the following sentences:

   Purse the lips tightly before you blow into the mouthpiece.

   Annie needed quiet, reassurance, and to be loved by others.

   As a family we enjoyed boats, camping, and learning how to rock climb.

   Marilyn is tall, slender, and a German.

   Ted is not progressing as well in Physics as in his papers for English 1.

   He gave three reasons for his failing grades: having to work twenty hours a week; the university puts too much pressure on first year students; the fact that his father was a Phi Beta Kappa.

2. Write a completely associative paragraph that, in spite of transitions, repetition, and parallel structure, is incoherent and conceptually empty.

   Here is an excellent example from a student essay:

   > My favorite city in the entire country is Washington D.C., the nation's capital. As a matter of fact, I've been interested in government ever since my sophomore year in high school when we spent an entire semester studying the electoral process. But even then I was conscious of a gap between what was theoretically true and what was actually true. Take campaign financing, for example. Why should the public have to pay for scandals like Watergate out of its own pocket?

Writing Workshops

Time is the villain in every writing course. You need a lot of it to master basic skills and your instructor needs even more to observe and comment on your progress. Somehow three years' work must be crammed into fifteen weeks, and in the mathematics of composition three into fifteen won't go. Conventional solutions range from focusing on a few selected topics and exercises in hopes of doing more with less to padding the syllabus with novels and short stories, which relieves the pressure only by shifting the focus of the course from writing to literature.

A more creative solution is to set up a writing workshop, either as part of the regular class schedule or as an informal addition to it. The major benefit of a workshop is that it allows you to share your writing directly with your peers and in turn to receive immediate and abundant feedback. Not only does a workshop create a real dialogue between writer and reader, it clarifies relationships between style and audience that are always talked about but seldom seen. You no longer have to guess how your words struck your readers; they show you by their smiles and scowls and questions. Think how our writing might improve if everytime we used a word like "essentiality" or "objectification" someone hissed or held his nose. And just as a workshop frees you from total dependence on an instructor's criticisms, which often come too late to be useful anyway, the instructor is relieved of the responsibility of commenting on every piece of writing done during the semester. With a class of thirty that's a lot of relief. In a workshop everyone becomes a teacher.

Another advantage of a workshop is that it is devoted almost exclusively to *student writing in progress.* Theoretically, our writing skills and our critical skills, by which we generally mean our reading skills, complement and reinforce one another. The better we read the better we write and vice versa. Yet because writing is mainly generative and criticism mainly analytical the two tend to go their separate ways unless circumstances couple them. When you examine only the polished works of professionals criticism is largely academic, since no matter what you say you can't change the text in front of you. Principles are discussed without reference to their practical application, which is about as sensible as trying to learn to ride a bicycle by studying the theory of balance. You will become a good critic when you can see what good criticism can do for a piece of writing, which means that you need to work with texts that can still be revised. Watching one essay develop and improve over several weeks will teach you more about the process of writing than studying a dozen completed pieces.

The governing assumption behind a workshop is that we all learn through dialogue with one another and that the more dialogue we have about our writing the faster it improves. But a workshop is not committed to a particular theory of rhetoric or to a single set of critical principles. Rather it is meant to be a forum for discussing many kinds of writing—letters, poems, journals, critical essays, reviews, term papers—and many kinds of style. Growth and mutual encouragement are its goals, not judgment and competition. By humanizing the task of trying to write, a workshop can transform a classroom of strangers into a community of learners.

For a workshop to function effectively, however, there must be a few guidelines about format and procedure. Those below are meant to stimulate the exchange of ideas and responses and to reduce pointless bickering.

1. Ideally, there should be 6-8 people in each workshop, which would mean 3-4 workshops in an average writing class. With more than eight it becomes difficult for everyone to participate, and a workshop with several non-participants is like an automobile engine with several dead cylinders. With only two or three people in a group the range of responses to each piece of writing is too restricted.

2. A workshop should meet once a week at whatever place seems most congenial for discussion (e.g., classroom, dormitory, study lounge). It should also meet at the same time and for the same length of time whenever possible. The key is to make the atmosphere relaxed, but not the scheduling.

3. Individual groups should stay together long enough for people to get to know one another's writing habits. This usually takes about four meetings, after which you can switch groups.

4. Everyone contributes a piece of writing to each session including the instructor when he is present. No silent auditors allowed. All kinds of writing are acceptable but for purposes of discussion it is advisable to have several common assignments during the semester. One meeting might be devoted to autobiographical writing, for example, and another to critical essays or factual reports. It is also profitable for the individual groups to share their best pieces of writing.

5. Each person reads his work aloud, even when copies have been distributed beforehand. Reading aloud generates energy and excitement in the group that silent reading does not and also highlights problems in tone and structure that might be overlooked on the printed page.

6. Each person is responsible for reviewing his personal writing goals and for informing the group about specific problems he is having. In this way a writer gets the help he really needs.

Honesty and clarity are the pillars of a successful workshop. Honesty comes with mutual trust and therefore takes time, but clarity comes with practice. Here are a few suggestions for discussing writing in a group.

1. Always refer to specific passages and details, never to general theories about style and composition. Focus on what is said, in other words, instead of what you think ought to be said. Talk about *this* comparison, *this* construction, *this* transition and avoid vague impressionistic terms like "interesting," "fantastic," and "terrible" unless you can clarify them with particular examples. Even then there are more helpful terms.

2. Support whoever is reading by (1) listening carefully to the entire piece before expressing an opinion, (2) expressing positive reactions before negative ones, (3) avoiding tactless comments like "That's a silly topic to write about" or "What's so special about that experience?" In a workshop you are striving for dialogue, not debate. Question, clarify, suggest, but don't argue. Arguments make people defensive, close down discussion, and do nothing to improve writing.

3. Express your emotional as well as your intellectual reactions to each piece of writing. Identify them ("I felt sad when I read that passage," "This image makes my head swim"), describe them figuratively ("That description is as ordinary as dishwater "), dramatize them by laughing, clapping your hands, sighing. Silence is an enemy in a workshop. Let a writer know what his words do to you.

4. Concentrate on the major strengths and weaknesses in a piece of writing, not on minor grammatical and stylistic faults. Remember that a person can absorb only so much criticism before his brain throws the overload switch. Be selective in order to be helpful.

5. Never attempt to rewrite another person's work. It's up to the author to decide what use, if any, he wishes to make of the workshop's suggestions. Otherwise we have composition by committee, a form of group-think.

6. Have one person summarize, either orally or in writing, the group's comments on each piece that is read so that the author will have a clear idea of what worked and what might be improved. These summaries are also a review of the group's performance.

APPENDIX 2

A Note on Freewriting

Freewriting is another name for spontaneous, nonstop writing. It is a strategy for priming the pump during dry spells and for sustaining the habit of writing when you're pressed for time or simply not in the mood. It is also an effective technique for focusing a topic.

The basic procedure is simple. Set aside 15 minutes in which you jot down anything that comes to mind without worrying about grammar, style, or coherence. Open the gates and let the words pour across the page. You will undoubtedly produce a lot of gibberish but in freewriting the process is more important than the quality of the product. You can always edit and revise but your first job, as William Faulkner observed, is to "get it down. Take chances. It may be bad but it's the only way you can do anything really good." Freewriting puts words on paper, not immortal words, not words you'd want for an epitaph, but ordinary, serviceable words that may generate others that are more exciting.

After 15 minutes look over what you have written and if you come across an idea or an image that interests you, try to develop it. If not, toss the pages into the wastebasket. No one is going to grade your freewriting exercises or insist that you "do something" with each one. They are simply a form of verbal calisthenics.

The procedure for focusing a topic is similar. Set a time limit, jot down whatever thoughts occur to you about the topic, group those that appear related. Then, using one of these groups as a starting point, do a second and perhaps a third freewriting exercise until you have a tentative thesis or sequence of ideas that might be developed further. Remember, however, that even at this stage you are only mapping your topic, learning its boundaries and configurations. Be willing to move in unexpected directions and try not to become so frustrated by working with fragments that you *force* your ideas into a pattern. Better to brainstorm for an hour or two than to spend days staring at a blank sheet of paper waiting for that perfect opening sentence to pop into your head. Your muse may be asleep or on vacation and that perfect opening might not appear until after you've written several drafts of the essay. The advantages of freewriting are that it gets you started and enables you to uncover a great deal of raw material in a short space of time. Besides being enjoyable it is economical.

Index

1 2 3 4 5 6 7 8 9